PINOT
GIRL

Los Gatos, California 1967

A FAMILY. A REGION.
AN INDUSTRY.

PINOT
GIRL

A MEMOIR

ANNA MARIA PONZI

BRISTOL
PRESS

Published by Bristol Press

Edited and designed by Girl Friday Productions
www.girlfridayproductions.com

Cover and interior design: Rachel Marek
Editorial: Alexander Rigby, Amara Holstein,
Michelle Horn, Ben Grossblatt
Image credits: cover © Paolo Tralli/Shutterstock,
p. xii © jenesesimre/Adobe Stock and © suwi19/Adobe Stock,
p. 1 and p. 313 © Ирина Колесниченко/Adobe Stock

ISBN: 978-1-7345788-0-5

For Mom and Pop.

Thanks for sharing your big adventure.
I love you.

CONTENTS

INTRODUCTION

A child's view often varies from a parent's intention. Similarly, public perception often conflicts with reality. At first glance, a young girl born into the wine business may seem like she has a charmed life. While the romance has slowly evolved, it was far from that in my early years.

I am an avid observer, far from an academic. My preferred tack for gathering information has been to ask a friend, colleague, cab driver, or stranger. I've found I discover as much as, or more than, intended this way. Personal experiences fascinate me. I've always been drawn to real people and real lives, as everyone has a story.

This is mine.

I have had the great fortune of growing up with fiercely independent parents who had an audacious dream. It was *their* dream that became *my* story. This is an intimate tale of what it was like growing up alongside driven individuals who helped to establish Oregon's wine industry. It draws almost entirely from childhood memories, keen eavesdropping, and lengthy tableside conversations.

Nearly twenty years ago, inspired by our journey, I requested interviews with a handful of the original Oregon wine pioneers. I discovered their family histories intertwined with ours. I realized we shared similar struggles and achievements, and these stories sparked my desire to write this book.

I was convinced this story needed to be told, perhaps most importantly from an insider's perspective. The result is my personal account of the founding of the state's wine business. The early days were driven by curiosity and ingenuity and were much less about glamour, ego, or financial gain.

It is with immense respect and admiration that I share my story with the early trailblazers, women and men, who respectfully collaborated to establish their shared vision from which so many now benefit. I am equally grateful to those who believed in us and supported the young industry.

There are many memories of the early days. This is only one. While the original interviews inspired me and the following research kept me focused, most of this story draws from my own recollections, which is what makes it uniquely mine. Like a child's view, it is intimate, honest, and pure.

"At Nonno and Nanna's house, we find rainbows."

—Lauren Fogelstrom, age three

PART ONE

CALIFORNIA ROOTS

A twisted eucalyptus branch stabilized the stout elderly man as he moved slowly but purposefully across his property. With his rough hand gripping the top of the well-worn cane, Mr. Galbo was able to enjoy the simple pleasures of his modest grounds. The Italian immigrant wore his many years of working outdoors on his weather-beaten, wrinkled face, which contrasted with the gentle demeanor revealed through his soft voice, easy smile, and twinkling eyes.

When I was just two years old, my mother often took my brother and me on the long walk to Mr. Galbo's home. We would turn right after our driveway and head along the stream that followed Wood Acres Road, reaching a dead end. The pavement ended here, and we were left to follow a narrow gravel road that wound up and around the lush, green hillside. We'd climb an enchanting route through dense trees until the sun began to flicker on our faces, becoming brighter as we came out from under the canopy and caught sight of brilliant yellow lemons hanging from the trees lining his drive. The powerful sounds of a symphony playing Verdi's *Aida* fused with the warm air as we approached the humble home built into the side of the hill. We often found the quiet old man sitting alone in his dark basement, as his wife preferred to live separately upstairs in the home. The basement, originally built as a cellar, had large wooden doors that faced the outdoors. California's warm, sunny days encouraged him to often leave them open, allowing dappled light to enter the space. He had a water glass of homemade wine in one hand and twirled his pasta on a fork with the other as the opera filled the hidden room. The old man looked up and smiled at our little family peering around the old framed door.

"Vieni, vieni!" He motioned for us to come sit with him on his wooden bench. He poured Mom a glass of wine and turned the music down. My brother, Michel, and I patiently sat for a few minutes before racing to the rustic swing tied to the tallest branch of an ancient eucalyptus tree situated on the very highest point of the mountain. This splendid perch allowed us to swing out and over what felt like the entire Santa Clara valley. The immense view of the fields below and the warm air hitting my face as I flew up into the sky and sank back down into the intoxicating, minty cloud of eucalyptus was stimulating. I was entertained for hours there. I loved the place.

Always happy to see us, Mr. Galbo enthusiastically gave us a tour around his well-tended grounds, which consisted of a vegetable garden featuring a large variety of tomatoes, a fig orchard, and an olive grove. Prickly pear cactus intermingled with his old lemon and apple trees. He took pride in growing almost everything he ate. Galbo respected the slow growing process and valued the finished product just as much. An apple was not savagely bitten into, but rather slowly stripped of its outer layer with a sharp knife, then cut into tender slices and thoughtfully enjoyed bite by bite. He indulged in the exotic flavors of each object, thoroughly appreciating each one. After walking, talking, and exploring new treasures in his garden, Galbo and Mom would sit quietly and share a small bottle of his homemade wine on a weather-beaten picnic table while Michel and I continued to explore the mountaintop.

For me, a curious toddler, Galbo's place was simply magical. For my father, Galbo was a reminder of his Italian family's tradition of respecting homegrown food and wine. For my mother, Galbo represented authenticity. He represented her ideal—one who honored and enjoyed the gifts of the earth and was grounded in simplicity. The only critique I ever heard about Galbo was in reference to his wine. My parents would drink it, then later complain about its terrible taste, leaving me to assume that Galbo's endearing company and peaceful residence was what they enjoyed so profoundly.

My parents, Dick and Nancy Ponzi, had moved to our quiet home tucked away in the foothills of Northern California's Santa Cruz Mountains following their brief wedding at the Santa Monica courthouse on May 11, 1962. They had instantly fallen in love less than a year earlier at a Halloween party in Orange County and decided to move north. My father left his good-paying job at North American Aviation in Southern California for an engineering position at United Technologies in what is now known as Silicon Valley.

My pop grew up in Michigan, the youngest son of an Italian immigrant family. Like the rest of his family, he struggled with an untraditional life. At home he spoke Italian with his parents, but outside the home he spoke English and learned how to be an American. His home was filled with the kitchen's aromas of garlic and olive oil that often permeated out to the street. Occasionally shots would be heard through the low-income neighborhood when their father hunted pigeons in their small backyard from his bedroom window on weekends.

My father was determined to work hard, and as a young boy he delivered newspapers on a route before school. As a teenager he worked various jobs, including one at Ford Motor Company, which allowed him to cover his tuition at the University of Michigan. After receiving his diploma in mechanical engineering there, he immediately left the cold winters of the Midwest for the warmth of Southern California.

In contrast to the iconic California scene of sunny blue skies, palm trees, and beaches, the place my parents chose to live was damp and dark. Nestled among tall pines, eucalyptus trees, and thick vegetation, the wood-shingled house was protected by two large concrete cats proudly mounted in front of the short driveway. They symbolized the township of Los Gatos, Spanish for "the cats."

I was born on Easter Sunday in 1965. I always thought that was quite special. Enamored with Italian culture and perhaps hopeful I'd became a glamorous opera singer someday, my parents named me Anna Maria. My grandmother referred to me as Anne Marie, so I ended up as simply Maria. According to my mother, I was an unattractive, bald infant, and she often hid me from the public with a blanket. A blonde, blue-eyed baby girl with an innate desire to be active, I shared most of my early years with my brother. Born in June of 1963, Michel was two years older, and in contrast to me had dark-brown hair and green eyes and was timid and self-controlled. Despite our differences, we spent hours together, and I grew up admiring his courage and focus.

* * *

After I was born, my father left his corporate position at the aerospace engineering firm to start a tile factory with his good friend Jim Marino. The Marino family lived on the outskirts of Los Gatos, and their home provided another place for childhood adventure. The authentic adobe house was made entirely by hand, brick by brick, by a group of tough women in the 1940s. The windowpanes were constructed from recycled old car windows they had scavenged from local junkyards, and the house was built directly into the earth, resulting in varying heights and floor levels. Adults would often hit their heads walking down a hall, but for smaller people like me, the place was enchanting.

The surrounding property provided Michel and me outdoor exploration while Mom and Wendy discussed the latest chapter of *How You Can Live on Nothing*. The grounds were lush, with creamy-orange persimmons, bright-red pomegranate, and vibrant yellow and orange citrus trees. The color popped against the textured backdrop of sage grass, aloe vera, and varied green cactus. The Marinos also had a large garden where they grew their produce. Like Mr. Galbo's, the place was abundant with life. It excited me.

I believe these visits to Mr. Galbo's and the Marinos' had a significant impact on shaping our family's life. They introduced us to the concept of growing food, working with the land, respecting the earth, and practicing self-reliance. As I was growing up, I often overheard the adults speak about the virtues of wine during unusually long conversations at a meal while I would play in another room with Michel. They would discuss how most American wines were produced in California and were recognized as Hearty Burgundy or Chablis. Names like Blue Nun, Lambrusco, and Mateus were called out as uninteresting wines, drunk without food or much consideration for flavor. They would go on to note how quality wines were hard to find, with only a few Napa Valley producers beginning to research how to improve winemaking techniques. Other names like Martin Ray and Robert Mondavi were mentioned as having a shared desire to offer American wine drinkers a broader perspective of better wines that could vie with those from Europe. But it sounded like very few, if any, had found their way into the market.

Jim and Pop sought out these rare wines, but mainly focused on those imported from France or Italy. Although these bottles were more expensive, my folks and the Marinos felt they were more interesting and pleasing to the palate than local wines. Conversations moved beyond how to live a life of simplicity to the attributes of one wine over another. The more my parents experienced these European wines, the more they developed an affection for them.

The late 1960s was a time of social unrest in the country, and my parents felt like it was a good time to head out on an adventure to reevaluate their path. They decided to take our family on a drive across the country to New York. At the time, Mom was several months pregnant with my sister, but she managed the long journey with Pop and the two of us sleeping in tents and preparing food over campfires in campgrounds along the way. Once the four of us arrived in New York, we stored the car in the city and boarded a plane at JFK airport.

ICELAND

Our final destination was a faraway island situated in the middle of the North Atlantic Ocean. In 1967, Iceland was relatively unknown, considered exotic and alien. But relatives on my father's side lived there. Both my grandfather, Atillio Ponzi, and my grandmother, Josephina Lerzi, were immigrants originally from Campotosto, of Italy's Abruzzo region. Attilio was thirty-one and Josephina just eighteen when they married. They settled in New Castle, Pennsylvania, and had three sons: Frank, David, and Richard (Richie), my father.

After struggling with employment that included some bootlegging post-Prohibition, the couple moved their young family to a low-income neighborhood outside of Detroit, Michigan, where Attilio found a stable job working at the Ford Motor Company. Their neighborhood, much like the one in New Castle, was home to other Italians who had sought a new life in America. They stayed in an area with the same ethnic group to help relieve the daily hardships of living in a new country, with a new culture and a new language.

Like many immigrants, my grandfather was challenged by the constant stress of his new life and eventually left his family as a result. This left my father to seek guidance from others, and he found it in his eldest brother, Frank, who quickly became his mentor. He saw Frank as ambitious, confident, intelligent, and creative. His other brother, David, was charming, handsome, and athletic—the one the girls swooned over. And although my father claimed to admire David for his popularity, he was more attracted to Frank's interests as he introduced Pop to the arts, music, math, and science.

My father often shared with me how my nonna (Josephina) used to taunt him in the evenings as he studied for hours with his books while working on his degree at the University of Michigan.

"Thosa booksa," she would tell him, "they justa gonna makeya crazy. The morya readah, the lessaya gonna know."

I found this especially humorous because my father had earned a college diploma, and my uncle Frank had managed to become an Oxford scholar and art historian despite their mother's lack of support for higher education. Frank moved to New York and went on to become an eccentric painter, author, and musician. There, he met Duna Thomasdottir, an accomplished opera soprano from Iceland. They fell in love and moved to her home country, where they embraced its Scandinavian culture and raised two children. And this is how we found ourselves in Iceland.

Upon arrival at Reykjavik Airport, we were met by my rugged uncle in his well-used 1944 Land Rover. I remember peering outside the windows of the noisy rig, the place having a huge impression on me. Despite my very young age on this trip and a following visit, I was struck with the beauty of the landscape. Like the hundreds of sheep, spirited horses wandered the hills freely, their thick, wild manes blowing violently in the cold wind. Without fences these beauties were free to roam, and that sense of freedom played vividly in my head. There were no trees over three feet tall, and vegetation was limited to carpets of chartreuse-green moss and pink and purple wildflowers that popped from the otherwise empty hillsides.

Once off the country's solitary highway, we rattled down a dirt road to a small piece of property referred to as Brennholt. This was basically a patch of weather-beaten land surrounded by barren landscape. The shamble of a home was built directly into a sloping hillside. Its wooden exterior showed signs of being battered by the regular strong winds and heavy snowstorms, but inside it was warm and cozy.

Duna played the most beautiful classical music on her piano, and it filled the tiny house with life. Paintings in an assortment of sizes, styles, and frames cluttered the walls, and hundreds more were stacked upon each other against the base of the walls. Piles of sketch pads, canvases, and paints completely covered rustic tabletops, and shelves were jam-packed with books that reached from the floor to the ceiling. Everything about the place was interesting, odd, and fascinating. The amount of clutter and crowded spaces was overwhelming. Although my uncle was rather distant, Duna was kind and often asked me to join her in her simple kitchen to bake banana bread. Like Mr. Galbo, she was a strong person with a gentle heart, who made sure we felt comfortable in what was otherwise an unusual setting.

The natural spring that sat above their tiny home allowed my relatives to instantly tap into either extremely cold or extremely hot water directly from their faucets. This is something we had to consider when washing our faces in the mornings. Mom would take the time to carefully mix the two water temperatures so we could avoid burning ourselves. Frank had built a small aboveground pool in front of the home that he would fill with the hot sulfur water. I remember its terrible stench and clenching my face and pinching my nose as long as I could stand it.

Like most Italian immigrants, Frank had watched his father make wine at home as a child; therefore, it seemed natural he'd attempt to make it as an adult. But instead of producing it in the fertile agricultural lands of California or France, he did it in Iceland. Finding the proper ingredients for winemaking was tough. There were no vineyards on the island. There were no grapes to purchase. But Frank cherished his greenhouse, which housed an abundant supply of tomatoes and basil and an aggressive celery crop. That healthy crop became Frank's answer to making wine—good wine.

While I sat on the worn rug of the living room floor one afternoon, sucking my thumb and rubbing my forehead, I listened to the murmur of my uncle and father in the next room. Although it was difficult to make out the conversation, I was later told it went something like this:

"You see," Frank professed to Pop as he puffed on his pipe, the smoke hitting the ceiling with a sweet scent that flooded his intimate studio and entered my space, "it's quite simple. Any fruit or vegetable can naturally ferment itself into alcohol. You may only need to add raisins or sugar to create enough acid or alcohol, but it's possible. Even with celery."

Pop barely nodded, seeming doubtful. He reached for one of the small wineglasses and sniffed the contents and then slowly sipped his brother's wine. He allowed the drink to coat his mouth, then swallowed it.

He was clearly surprised by the sensation. "It's so aromatic, so clean—like a well-made German Riesling." He took another sip and nodded, seeming startled that he actually enjoyed the unusual wine. "It's good, Frank. This celery wine is actually pretty good. How can something so plain be so delightful?"

"Not bad, huh? You just have to be gentle with the raw ingredients to retain their subtle flavors."

Further conversation revealed it was much more than that. Frank had done his research. He had read a book—an important book—a manual on how to make good wine. It was called *Guidelines to Practical Winemaking*. The small paperback by Julius Fessler, among other things, explained one key difference between making quality wine and bad wine. It had to do with oxygen.

Together, Pop and Frank remembered aloud the wines their father made in the basement of their childhood home in Michigan. There was never any discussion of his winemaking, but as they reflected, they realized he had never protected the grape juice from oxygen. Because of this single missed step, what may have become good wine instead turned to vinegar within days. The men agreed: in order for any fruit's initial flavors to be retained, it was essential for wine to be protected from air. This conversation and the delicious celery wine sparked something in my father that night. He left the island inspired.

THE IDEA

Back home in Los Gatos, Pop began to make trips to the local library to check out any book he could find on grape growing and winemaking. However, it seemed *Guidelines to Practical Winemaking* became his Bible, as I found it was a permanent fixture on his bedside table. It was often open and flipped onto its pages next to several other large hardbound books marked with bits of torn pieces of paper between the pages.

"Nancy, I called the brothers at the Novitiate Winery. They said we can pick grapes this weekend," Pop announced one morning.

"Oh great!" Mom exclaimed, despite being in her final trimester of pregnancy. Nothing stopped her from an adventure.

"Let's plan to pick on Saturday and crush on Sunday."

Cared for by the gentle hands of the Jesuits, the Novitiate Winery had grapes they referred to as Burgundy. All I knew was that they were red, and it was fun trying to find them among the vines that towered over my small frame. Our young family picked the ripe clusters into small buckets and lugged them home in our family wagon. Once home, we readied ourselves for what my parents called the "crush." Pop had constructed wooden frames tightly strung across with chicken wire, providing a tool to remove the berries from the stems. Michel and I used our small hands to rub the grapes across the mesh, breaking the berries and allowing the juice to run into a clean metal bucket placed underneath the frames. With extra baby weight pulling on her back, Mom sat on an overturned wooden box and handpicked the fruit off the stems, dropping whole berries into the bucket.

After we removed all the grapes from the clusters, the bucket of broken berries and juice was emptied into a small cider press Pop had rented from a nearby orchard. The juice ran slowly into the basin below, then was funneled down to a small oak cask he had picked up at a home winemaking shop in St. Helena. He left the grape skins in the press and sealed the single barrel of juice with a bung and carefully moved it to a back corner of the garage.

Two months later, on November 30, 1967, while the precious barrel of wine aged, my mom gave birth to my little sister, Luisa. This would be her third child. My mother was barely twenty-six years old at the time and later confessed to me she was overwhelmed with responsibilities.

My mother, Nancy Berry, grew up as if she were an only child despite having two siblings. They were seven and eight years older than her. My maternal grandfather, Charlie Berry, worked in the oil fields, and for a period of time, his job required the family to move to Venezuela. There, my grandma Alice was concerned about the level of education her youngest daughter would receive. She decided to send Nancy on a ship back to America, where she would live with her eldest daughter's family in Orange County, California. In the States, she could attend a proper American high school and receive a conventional education. Mom shared with me how at just fourteen years old, she spent several lonely, frightening nights on the ocean, taking her farther away from the safety of her parents and closer to an unfamiliar world with people she barely knew and a place completely unknown.

During her high school years, my mother was short and slightly chubby with pale skin and freckles. Despite her beautiful, high Cherokee cheekbones, she struggled to fit in with the tanned, blonde Southern California girls and as a result was rebellious and sought an alternative lifestyle.

After graduating from Fullerton High School, she moved to Mexico City and took classes at the University of Mexico. It only lasted a year before she returned to California and attended a junior college, where she enjoyed literature, poetry, and philosophy and continued her education in Spanish. Although she loved learning, she never completed her formal education. Instead, she met a quiet Italian American engineer at a party on October 31, 1961. He was seven years her senior. She fell in love with his enthusiasm for life and his brilliant intellect. He, in turn, fell in love with her beauty and boundless curiosity.

Dick and Nancy married less than a year later at the Chapel of the Chimes in Santa Monica with my aunt Barbara as the sole witness. My father was unable to take any days off from work, so a weekend camping trip in the Santa Cruz mountains served as their honeymoon. Five years later, they embarked on an adventure that would change the lives of many.

THE QUEST

By January of 1968, it seemed as though Mom and Pop had developed a plan for their future. They kept talking about wanting to plant wine grapes, which apparently meant getting out of Los Gatos. The plan was accelerated when they received an offer on our home on Wood Acres Road almost immediately after putting it on the market. Pop took a job as a design engineer for Disneyland to pay the bills while Mom searched for a rental, knowing it would be a temporary move. My mother quickly learned that landlords weren't interested in renting to a family with three young children, a dog, and a cat. Because of the quick sale, we were forced to purchase a small tract home in the middle of a housing development in nearby Campbell. I'd often hear Mom complain about her disdain for suburban life, but she endured it knowing it was only for the short term. The following year was all about research and exploration.

Michel, Luisa, and I entertained ourselves with tricycles and a large box of paints we found in the garage as our parents were constantly distracted, mulling over stacks of guides, brochures, magazines, and books. Mom spent her days reading about wine varieties while Pop scoured maps of the West

Coast after work. I would snuggle up to him and lean into all the colored maps, smoothing out the creases of the folds so he could see them better. I was intrigued by the graphs and lines and wondered what he found so interesting. Mom researched how different varieties grew in different regions around the world and how the wines tasted different according to their location. Pop sought out cool areas along the coast that might be suitable for growing grapes, particularly Pinot Noir, which had become his favorite. For my parents, this wine was the most exciting.

When there was time on the weekends, we'd often take long drives to visit the nearby wine areas of Mendocino County and its Alexander and Russian River valleys. While the three of us restlessly sat in the back seat, we tried to avoid listening to our parents declare their love for this grape. Apparently they'd fallen for this wine called Pinot Noir while sharing bottles of it with their friends and sipping it during dinners at home. They'd noticed a difference in the local Pinot Noir versus those made in France. They talked about how the French Pinot Noirs were elegant and graceful, and the most memorable ones seemed to linger on the palate, enhancing a meal. They described Pinot Noir as a thoughtful wine, saying something about how it didn't call attention to itself—instead it quietly seduced the drinker with its hints of black cherry, mild cigar, and cedar. They would go on and on about how one sip invited complex flavors into the mouth and how hints of earth, mushroom, plum, meat, and truffles could be detected. It all sounded pretty weird to us. We just giggled and made faces when they described how wine tasted like food.

Our parents' hunt took us as far as the Okanagan Valley in British Columbia as they searched for the ideal site for growing this grape. They claimed the best Pinot Noir had a natural balance of acid and fruit with little alcohol. My parents were convinced that in order to replicate this wine in America, it would be essential to find a place similar to that of Burgundy, France. Despite their limited knowledge, they knew the place must have fertile soil and moderate temperatures year round. Although some of these areas appeared to have some of the agricultural qualities they were seeking, we also heard Mom and Pop speak about how good schools and a progressive spirit were also important criteria. We didn't really understand what any of this was all about and like most kids found ways of entertaining ourselves. As they continued to obsess over their big plan, we'd slip away to the garage and cover our naked bodies with green and purple paint.

For further education, my parents decided it would be invaluable for them to visit the vineyards in Europe. It was difficult for Pop to take time off from his work at Disney, but he managed to set aside a week for the trip. The plan was to drop us kids in Iceland, this time with young Luisa too. All three of us spent our days in the land of natural hot springs, brisk air, enormous glaciers, and those beautiful horses. Duna served us steaming bowls of fish soup and dried cod.

When Mom and Pop returned to Brennholt, we heard how they spent their days touring the regions of Luxembourg, Mosel, and Burgundy. I was relieved we had been spared the lengthy wine-focused visits. They camped the entire week, choosing to spend their limited funds on food and wine. It seemed after just one week of visiting the vineyards, tasting hundreds of wines, and meeting many friendly vintners, they were more interested in wine and its rich lifestyle than ever before. From that point on my parents were off, seriously plotting their future—and ultimately, ours.

OREGON

That summer, we visited Grandma and Grandpa Berry's home in the Willamette Valley. Since all I knew about my grandparents was they had lived in the faraway land of Venezuela, I found it odd when I learned they had decided to retire to rural Oregon.

Charlie and Alice were married in Compton, California, on Charlie's birthday in 1931. The family's first home was small, surrounded by orange trees, a chicken yard, and a large garden. My grandpa was born in 1907, a twin of ten births, and grew up in the Ozarks of Arkansas at a time in America when many were poor. Grandpa simply claimed that they "were the poorest." As in most large families, the young twin boys were raised by their older sisters. Soon after high school graduation, I learned that Grandpa and his brother, Fred, managed to save enough money to head across the country, like some kind of scene from *The Grapes of Wrath*. Eventually they both found jobs working as ditch diggers for the Union Oil Company in California. And this is where he met my grandmother, Alice Morton.

My grandma Alice also came from a dirt-poor family, living in Goodland, Kansas, and was in search of a better life in California. Born in 1911, Alice was the third of five sisters. Her father died at a young age in the flu epidemic, leaving my great-grandmother a widow and solely responsible for the entire family and farm without any financial support. Through hard work and perseverance, she managed to keep the family's wheat farm together and the girls educated. It's no wonder my grandma Alice was considered a tomboy and had a reputation for being wicked-smart, independent, stubborn, and opinionated.

Nestled in the rolling hills of Forest Grove, half of their forty-acre property was home to old-growth fir trees, while the rest spread to open pasture, a big red barn, and a small farmhouse. My hardworking grandma had a glorious garden, bursting with pungently sweet-smelling roses in the spring and juicy red and golden raspberries in the summer. My kind grandpa kept the estate tidy with his golf-course manicured lawn, perfectly stacked wood, and a healthy stock of cattle, whose main purpose was to keep the fields well groomed.

One afternoon, as we were enjoying an outdoor lunch on the lawn overlooking the valley view below, my grandmother mentioned she had heard about a neighbor who was making wine.

"I heard from one of the farmers down the road that he's just arrived from California," Grandma announced at one of our frequent picnics. I felt the warm sunshine on my cheeks and reached for more potato salad as she continued. "Apparently he's over there on David Hill and wants to make wine here."

"How interesting!" Mom replied, looking surprised by the news.

"We should definitely go over and meet him," Pop said. David Hill was just ten minutes from Grandma and Grandpa's farm. We finished our fried chicken and made plans to take the drive. Of course, I wanted to join in the field trip.

I sat in the back seat, staring out the window while Mom and Pop drove up a twisting, dusty gravel road to the top of a clearing where an old farmhouse stood. It was built in 1883 and needed attention, but I was more distracted by the surrounding 140 acres. The property was magnificent. Ancient oaks dotted the perimeter, adding to the grandeur of the site. Hopping out of the car, we walked up to the front door of the old house, where we were met by a very distinctive individual.

There stood Charles Coury. He was a sturdy, tall man with a bushy, black mustache and dark-rimmed glasses. When Pop introduced himself as also interested in the Pinot Noir grape, he stepped outside, and the two began a hearty conversation. Coury, or Chuck as they later called him, was a true scholar and visionary. We learned that day how Coury received his degree from UC Davis, and his master's thesis was entitled "Wine Grape Adaptation in the Napa Valley." It discussed the importance of site selection to the wine varietal in order to achieve the highest fruit quality in wine grapes. His thesis emphasized that it was much more than heat summation, as his professors dictated in the classroom. He showed how soil, rainfall, water balance, and day length played equally important roles.

After graduation, Coury continued to study cool climate viticulture in Alsace in 1964 before finding this ideal site at the old David Hill farm in the summer of 1965. He moved his wife, Shirley, and their two young boys up from California to plant his vineyard that February. My parents were struck by his intense focus on quality winemaking and his adamant belief that the Willamette Valley was the ideal place to grow the world's most difficult grape: Pinot Noir. As a young girl, I was more struck by his heavy mustache, which contrasted with his balding head.

It was after that meeting in Forest Grove when everything seemed to fall into place for my parents. They had found what they'd been searching for: fertile farmland and an idyllic climate inhabited by Portland's forward-thinking citizens. They were swept away by the valley's beauty, its serenity, and the nearby city's open-minded culture. We could sense Mom and Pop's excitement and knew this would become our new home.

After we returned to our builder home outside of San Jose, things began to accelerate. Over the following months, Pop was gone most weekends, visiting with realtors in the Willamette Valley in search of finding the right place for our family to live. I'd overhear them at night talking about their desire to be near Portland as neither of them had lived in the country. They wanted to be close to the small city's amenities and a part of its community. Simultaneously, they discussed the importance of finding land with healthy soil, good drainage, and wind flow. It all seemed very complicated to me.

One weekend that fall, my father brought home more grapes from the Jesuit Novitiate, and the three of us got ready for another suburban crush. However, Pop decided to use a different technique this time: he told us this was called "manual punch down." We watched as he poured full buckets of red grapes into a large tote that sat on the floor of the garage. Mom secured plastic sandwich baggies onto our bare feet with rubber bands and told us to climb into the tote. Luisa, not quite a year old and in her diapers, couldn't wait to jump into the bath of berries. At three years old, I was intrigued, but waited for guidance from my five-year-old brother. He was also apprehensive, but curious. The warm liquid swished between our plastic-covered toes as we climbed in. It felt strange at first, but we quickly enjoyed the sensation. The slippery skins made us lose our balance, making us laugh. We didn't mind that and anxiously looked for a bunch of grapes swimming in the bath to squash with our tiny feet. Luisa spent most of her time bending down to taste the fresh juice, while Michel and I treaded on the big clusters. After we had been playing in the tote, swishing around in the "red grapes" for about an hour, Mom pulled us out. Pop used pots from the kitchen to move the slush into a small press he had painstakingly made himself. Michel was instructed to pull hard on the crank that tightly pressed the juice as it drained into two oak barrels. The treasured juice, now secured in the barrel, was stored in the back of the garage. The resulting wine would age for another year, or maybe even two, before it was ready to drink.

My father's visits to Oregon in search of the ideal site proved unsuccessful. Then one night, Grandma Alice called to say she'd found the perfect place near the small farming community of Scholls. Apparently, Grandma's good friend Erma Cron had heard about it, as she lived nearby. This small township was just minutes outside of Beaverton, a Portland suburb. The property was home to twelve acres of strawberries, five acres of forest, a creek, a barn, a large garage, and a very, very small house. It was listed at $40,000. Were we interested? Mom hung up with Grandma, discussed it with Pop for about ten minutes, then called her back.

"We'll take it!" she shrieked.

"What's happening, Mom?" I asked, looking up from the shag carpet where I had been cramming red and green rods into wooden Tinkertoy spools.

"It looks like we're moving!" She rushed over and kissed Pop's face.

We figured it must be a good thing, so we picked ourselves off the floor and gave our parents each a hug. We knew whatever our parents were scheming would be fun. Their excitement filled the room. Adventure was ahead.

NEW FRONTIER

All three of us kids were crammed into the back seat of our 1966 Town and Country Chrysler, along with our cat, Kitty, and the dog, Tzena. It was the first week of November 1968. Pop trailed behind the family wagon in his recently purchased propane-powered truck. This stored the piano, a few basic pieces of furniture, and our two barrels of California Pinot Noir.

At least it started that way. We must have gotten caught up in our private thoughts, watching the world go by outside the car windows, when Mom realized we'd lost Pop. We were about four hours into the journey. We'd been flying along north Interstate 5, listening to Joan Baez on the radio, when my mother had her first panic attack. She realized she didn't have the address of where we were going, and the maps were with her husband.

Without the safety of cellphones, Mom did the next best thing she could and pulled into the nearest rest area. Luisa and I took Tzena for a walk, visited the dark, cold restrooms, and got back into the wagon. Michel held Kitty in his lap as he flipped through one of his Superman comic books. And then we waited. After nearly two hours, we caught sight of the vehicle pulling into the parking lot.

Mom jumped out of the car. "Oh dear! Where were you?"

Pop calmly climbed down from the truck. "This fuel-efficient vehicle takes a little longer on those inclines. And it didn't help running out of fuel about fifty miles back. It's not easy finding propane out here!"

This made me wonder why Pop decided on this vehicle instead of a normal one, but I didn't ask questions.

"So, let's try to stick together from here on up. Okay? And, hey, here's the address in case we get separated again." He handed Mom a piece of paper with a grin.

She nodded, took the directions, and gave him a hug. My father tugged at the straps on the canoe on the roof rack before climbing back into his truck. He smiled at us. Once the animals were settled, we were off again.

My mother turned up "Hey Jude" on the radio.

After hours on the freeway, I awoke as the car slowed, my neck sore from resting against the door. It was raining as I peered out of the foggy window. Kids walking their dogs and apartment buildings slid past my view. The divided highway eventually turned into a two-lane road, and suddenly, there were no more cars on the road. Sidewalks and streetlights disappeared, as did street signs and people. Instead stretches of brown and yellow fields came into view. The land darkened as we entered a low-hanging cloud, and the rain seemed to soak the earth's surface. We passed a red barn and two chestnut-colored horses who were sheltering themselves from the wet sky under a large oak tree. It was quiet, except for the sound of the heavy rain pelting down on the car's metal roof.

We turned left onto a muddy dirt lane called Vandermost Road. Mom followed Pop's truck up an incline, and a mile later, I felt the car slow again as we neared the end of the stretch of gravel and turned down an even smaller drive. In front of us was a scrappy field. I leaned forward over the front passenger seat, trying to get a better look as the rain continued to fall.

"Well, I think this is it!" Mom exclaimed.

"What?" Michel sat up. "Where are we?"

"Are we here?" Luisa managed as she pulled her sleepy head off my lap. Our black cat jumped onto the front seat.

I was silent, scanning the view. I rubbed my eyes. To my right was a wretched patch of land covered in mixed grasses and weeds. Dark clouds encroached on the flat land. Beyond it, I saw two dilapidated buildings tucked under towering firs. The whole scene was dreary and damp. It looked especially cold peering out from inside our cozy car. The rain continued to pour, and I watched as the water fell onto the dirt road, creating brown pools of water.

The tall woods reminded me of our home in Los Gatos, but the sky was absent the sunshine that would filter through the canopy there. There were no nearby houses. It was as if we were alone inside a huge, gray, wet cloud, hidden beneath massive trees. Mom parked the car in front of a shack next to Pop's stinky truck. My body ached from being stuck in the car for so long, but I stayed inside, peering around at the new surroundings.

It was clear we were not in California anymore.

SETTLING IN

The battered, single-story, seven-hundred-square-foot shack had a glass front door that stuck when you tried to slide it. It was especially difficult for those of us under the age of six to open. The space was small, with low ceilings prohibiting the already limited light to filter in from outside. We moved our things inside. The dinner table was set a few feet in front of the sliding door, and just next to it was a worn-out sleeper sofa, a green bucket chair, and a hand-carved Chinese chest. This stored Mom and Pop's large record collection. Our turntable sat on top of a long, narrow wooden bookshelf crammed with hundreds of books on art, poetry, and architecture. Our twenty-inch black-and-white television was nestled on top of a couple of stacked wooden wine crates a couple feet from the table. All my parents' limited possessions were crammed into the tiny space. We didn't have much either. Our toys were limited to Hot Wheels, Tinkertoys, and our cherished Little People. Once we got settled, the home felt cozy, especially as we found ourselves surrounded by the moist outdoors.

The only hall in the house also served as the kitchen. The stove and oven sat on one side, the sink on the other. A refrigerator was stuck in at the end of the hall with two doors situated on either side of it. One of the hollow-core doors opened into a narrow space originally built as a sun porch but had been enclosed by walls. It was now full of unpacked items. The other door opened to a small room without windows. This was the only bedroom, and we were told all three of us would share it.

My parents furnished the room with a bunk bed, one twin bed, and a chest of drawers. Each of us was assigned two small drawers to store our limited wardrobe, and we shared the only closet. Michel, being the oldest, was assigned the top bunk, and Luisa, the youngest, took the bottom. Being the lucky middle child, I got the twin bed. Each night, after Mom and Pop had tucked us in, they'd quietly pull out the full-sized sleeper sofa in the front room and return it to its original couch position each morning before we awoke.

For me, the place was pretty dismal. The permanent low clouds and constant drizzle made it all the drearier against the shabby structures of our new home. We were isolated. Forest and fields surrounded us in every direction. Since the home's size was restrictive, it forced us to get out and explore.

We often went roaming outdoors, and on one of the first days I remember, the three of us discovered a weather-beaten barn down the hill. The shelter's interior had a now-familiar moist sensation, with enormous spider webs hanging in every corner and a heavy film of dust on every surface. The vacant stalls appeared eerie. I was sure it was haunted and would quickly panic and run after Michel whenever he'd suddenly leave my side.

Just outside the barn's back door was a well-worn deer path, and one day we followed it into a hidden forest down a steep hill. Ancient firs with their massive trunks and old bark towered overhead, making us feel like little gnomes. Their moss-covered branches dripped water onto our heads as we moved deeper into the green. Our fingers quickly became cold and wet from touching their dewy bases. We passed ferns and exotic mushrooms, and as we went farther, we went into the low, lush vegetation. The foul smell of skunk cabbage got stronger and stronger the deeper we traveled.

Moving too quickly, I tripped over a dead log and when I looked up spied a rare white trillium that delighted me with its dash of color.

"Look!" Luisa pointed at another one. This one was deep purple.

"It's so beautiful, but don't pick it!" I warned. My mother had told me these flowers were rare.

We continued to race through the magical place. Following the muddy path, we eventually reached a narrow creek. This shallow stream allowed us to view crawdads, frogs, and water skippers in the cold water. Luisa immediately stopped and bent down to get a closer look. She was attracted to creatures, the creepier the better. She never hesitated to pick up a slug, snail, or earthworm and bring it to her face for closer observation.

"Come on, Luey," I called to her. It made me squirm just thinking of all those bugs in the water. I was unable to relate to her earnest curiosity. She lingered at the creek, trying to snatch tadpoles and pull out crawdads from the slow-moving water. I shook my head and started hunting for tiny yellow and purple Johnny-jump-ups scattered among the moist forest floor. For me, the dark, cool woods were a mystical place where my imagination soared, but I never ventured down there alone.

For the first few weeks following our move, our time was usually spent outdoors exploring the property since our home was so small. We soon realized we had to ignore the rain because it felt like the sun would never come. Only occasionally would Oregon's dismal weather turn so bad we'd be forced to explore indoor places. The garage, just a few feet from our home, became a regular haunt for the three of us, specifically its attic.

"Come on!" Michel called to me as Luisa and I slowly pulled on our clothes one morning. "Let's go to the attic today."

Reluctant about this adventure, but having nothing else to do, I followed my big brother's lead. Once inside the garage, I peered around a corner and looked up the tight, spooky wooden staircase. Michel went ahead first, timidly climbing up the narrow steps. I heard each stair creak as he put his weight onto it. I followed closely behind, afraid of what was behind me as much as what was ahead. He stopped at the small landing, and we found ourselves under a very low ceiling in a musty, old room. A single light bulb dangled from the end of an electrical cord in the open space.

We learned the previous owners, in their final stages of a bad divorce, had left a fair amount of unwanted belongings in their rush to get away from each other. Here is where we found many of those treasures, including a turntable, hundreds of vinyl records, a huge collection of porcelain figurines, odd clothing, and decorative hats. We thought it was a gold mine.

Michel managed to get the record player running and found a 45 record of "Windy." We played that and "Daydream Believer" by the Monkees over and over again as we unpacked dusty boxes full of more surprises. Luisa and I dressed up in the dank old costumes and fancy hats and played with the glass and porcelain figurines. We were kept amused for hours in the dark, tight space.

The barn, attic, our claustrophobic bedroom, and the woods were all part of our daily playground. For most kids at the time, television was the main attraction, but for us, that was only used to receive the daily news either before or after dinner. Each evening, Walter Cronkite's voice would echo through our little home with reports of the day, emphasizing the Vietnam War. Bloody, violent scenes flashed on the black-and-white screen as I'd try to quickly pass, shielding my eyes and ears to avoid hearing the daily count of dead bodies. I was horrified by the images of war and the constant news of death. It was difficult to imagine that kind of violence was possible beyond our peaceful surroundings.

Pop needed to find work. It would be tough to replace his former steady corporate job at Disney in the small city of Portland. He needed something that would cover the household bills, but that could also allow him time to focus on his new ambition: becoming a winemaker. Fortunately, Grandma's friend and our new neighbor, Erma, invited us to a New Year's Eve party, where we met other young families in the area. Derek Down and his wife, Heather, were charming folks, with their elegant English accents. They had recently moved their four children from a conventional English life in the UK for a less formal one in rural Oregon. Derek was a math professor at Portland Community College (PCC) while his wife attended to their children and small farm. They lived just across the highway from Vandermost Road. The Down kids were much older than we, so we didn't consider them playmates, but it felt nice knowing my parents had friends in this new place.

Although Portland was an open-minded city, the surrounding rural areas remained relatively conservative. Those who lived here enjoyed the freedom and privacy of their large acreages, and, when they weren't farming, most enjoyed hunting ducks or deer or watching college football. The Downs were one of the few progressive families in the Scholls farming community. Mom and Pop were thrilled to find another couple who enjoyed listening to a symphony or discussing European travels—both uncommon activities at the time.

Thanks to Derek's passing his résumé along, Pop landed a teaching job at PCC. That winter, he started his new career as an instructor of mechanical engineering. The position was well-suited to Pop, who loved discussing ideas with young people and problem-solving. It was also the ideal profession for him as it would leave his summers free.

It had been weeks after settling into his teaching role when Pop came home late one evening. My mother seemed worried as he was almost two hours behind his usual schedule when we saw him finally arrive at the front door.

"Hi! Where have you been?" Mom asked as she placed a steaming bowl of lentil soup onto the kitchen table.

"I just had the most interesting meeting," my father said as he placed his briefcase near the sofa and sat down with us, giving Luisa a kiss on the cheek.

"What happened?" she asked.

"I was just wrapping things up when I heard a knock on my office door," Pop began as he ladled the hot soup into his bowl, and we began to sip ours. "The door opens, and this slight man with bright-blue eyes and a tweed jacket walks in. He was very friendly and introduced himself as David Lett."

Luisa and I both grabbed another warm frite. The only thing good about lentil soup dinner was the fresh bread and cheese Mom served with it. I hated any dish that involved beans. We continued to listen to Pop's story.

"He said he heard I was looking for some grape plants. Apparently he got word from Chuck Coury about us as he and Coury were classmates at Davis and graduated together in 1964."

"Oh my!" Mom exclaimed. "How ironic! What was he doing at PCC?"

"He's selling textbooks! When he heard from Coury we were getting ready to plant, he wanted to stop by and introduce himself. Sounds like he's got a nursery in McMinnville."

"Ha. How interesting!"

"Yes, we ended up talking for over an hour, which is why I am so late. It turns out we have a lot in common. I ended up buying about ninety Pinot Noir plants from him, but no textbooks."

We laughed, and then Pop continued to explain how Lett was previously practicing to be a dentist when he fell in love with the idea of making wine, most specifically Pinot Noir. Like Pop and Coury, he was intrigued with the grape's delicacy, its complexity, and overall elegance. My father went on and on about how both Coury and Lett were influenced by French Ampelographer Victor Pulliat of the 1800s, whose work, entitled Mille Variétés de Vignes, emphasized the principles of ripening dates to select vinifera (the main source of European grapes).

Pop explained how in the fall of 1964, Coury remained in Alsace while Lett returned to the United States and began gathering cuttings from UCD and other sources and brought them with him to the Willamette Valley. In 1965, Lett planted the valley's first nursery in McMinnville with multiple varieties including Pinot Noir, Chardonnay, Pinot Meunier, and Riesling, among others. Coury returned to California just a few months after, sending up additional cuttings for him to plant. David and his wife, Diana, and their two young sons transplanted their young plantings that same year in the Red Hills of Dundee. Other young adventurers.

ON WITH
THE DREAM

I noticed Pop sitting at our small wooden kitchen table, flipping through the pages of the local newspaper. It was February of 1970. Mom pulled a batch of hot granola from the oven as I walked into the tight space. I hadn't bothered to brush my hair or my teeth, anxious for my first meal of the day.

"Good morning, honey." Mom flashed me her warm smile as I walked behind her. I leaned in, hoping for a hug as I looked to my father.

"Morning. What are you doing, Pop?"

Still reading the paper, he replied, "Looking for a well-used tractor."

"A tractor? For what?"

He looked up and smiled. "Well, we've got a lot work to do, hon." Then he turned back to the classifieds with pen in hand.

A few weeks later, Pop came home with one of his most important finds. He had found a tractor, but it was miserable. Both headlights were missing and the metal had been badly beaten, resulting in a discombobulated mix of orange and brown painted steel. Pop bought it at one of the farm auctions he sometimes went to with Grandpa Charlie, a favorite place to find farming gear. With his trusty welder and lots of time spent tinkering, my engineering father managed to bring the machine back to life. It didn't take long to realize this would become Pop's new activity: fixing broken-down equipment and creating whatever was needed at the moment to get the job done.

A lot of junk had been acquired since our move to Oregon. In addition to the cheap old tractor, a bright-yellow farm truck was now parked in front of our little shack: a 1966 Ford. Surely Pop got a deal on it as I couldn't imagine anyone actually wanting anything painted that vibrant color. We later referred to the embarrassing vehicle as "the banana."

We also managed to collect some enormous metal machinery that started to accumulate around the property. We found the strange equipment great to play on with our Little People, which were small wooden characters that entertained us throughout our childhood. Mom and Pop called some of the equipment "implements." We were told it was what farmers dragged along the back of their tractors to work the soil. Of course, we'd never seen any of this stuff before, and I doubted Mom or Pop had either. The collection had items that seemed similar in style: rusty, beat up, broken, or barely working. I never saw anything shiny or new.

The inside of our little shack was about as chaotic as the outside, but instead of busted-up equipment there were books. Lots of books. Whenever my parents weren't working, they were reading. Mom devoured the *Farmers' Almanac* and the *Whole Earth Catalog*, and it seemed the many hardbacks on wine written by Hugh Johnson and André Tchelistcheff were always open. But nearest the pullout couch, I'd usually find her latest favorite Agatha Christie mystery. For Pop, it was that same small paperback with a cartoon of a happy winemaker on its cover, *Guidelines to Practical Winemaking*, that seemed to get the most wear.

I often asked Mom if I could run errands with her. Mainly because it meant I could get off the property and see people. One afternoon, as we were heading to the grocery store, we passed the usual acres of crops as we did whenever we headed to town. But on this day, Mom noted the soil was being tilled in one of the fields.

"It looks like they're getting ready to plant seed," my mother said as we watched the farmer pull his trawl behind his tractor. "It must be time to start planting. Spring is coming. I need to tell Dick."

At night they'd exchange observations of what they'd seen the neighbors doing in their fields. Then they'd pull out another how-to book. Instead of taking classes to learn this stuff, they'd just pick up another book and read.

Many of these same farmers my parents silently took lessons from were "nonbelievers." We'd often run into them at the general store when we were buying feed for our pets. It was then we were reminded that we didn't belong. Once while checking out at the front register at Petrich's General Store, an old farmer who lived across the highway from us leaned in as Mom paid for a bag of dog food.

"So, I heard you're planning to plant grapes. How's that going for ya?" he said with a little smirk.

"Yes, hoping to plant this spring. Getting close," my mother replied with a sincere smile.

"Well, good luck with that." He chuckled as Mom grabbed the twenty-pound bag off the counter. I watched as he grinned at Tom, the shop owner, while we walked out. We didn't often hear the whispered words when we'd attend a community gathering, but we felt the stares of disapproval. We didn't fit in here. It was understood our parents were "crazy hippies from California" who had this strange idea to grow wine grapes in the cool valley. We heard the rumors from our grandparents and Erma. It was general knowledge that nobody grew grapes here. It was too cold. It rained too much. It won't work. "Go back to California," they'd whisper between their quiet chuckles.

I was embarrassed by their comments and often hid behind Mom to avoid the glares. I struggled with their judgment and rude behavior. But as much as their remarks made me uncomfortable, they didn't seem to affect my folks one bit. In fact, I wondered if the negative opinions actually fueled my parents' determination because the next thing I knew, we were planting grapes.

DIRT

It was the beginning of March, and for the past several weeks, Mom and Pop had been getting up early on the weekends to clear some of the land in front of our house. Just beyond our patch of weedy grass and a scraggly spider tree was an old strawberry field—or so we were told. We had never seen any berries there; it was just a huge piece of land covered with weeds.

Pop had managed to get the ratty tractor to work. After several trips to the junkyard and Petrich's, the engine sputtered to a start. The tractor still didn't have headlights and could only operate with two gears, but I guess it ran well enough. With Grandpa's help, Pop collected several other pieces of equipment from the local farm auction in Forest Grove. Grandpa loved those auctions as much as Pop did. When Pop found another plow, Grandpa picked up another couple of calves to add to his growing herd of cattle.

My father was clearly beginning to feel more like a farmer now, with his tractor in tolerable working order and his very own "implement." It didn't bother him that the plow was significantly oversized for the tractor and a couple of the discs were bent out of shape. He went straight to work, banging away at them until they resembled the others, at least well enough for them to rotate correctly along the frame.

As a favor, a neighboring farmer had knocked down the highest grasses with a large mower, leaving the rest to us. Pop backed the tractor up to the single metal plow as Mom held up the fifty-pound object until the rear of the tractor anchored the two parts together. On his first pass down the open field, Pop dropped the sharp, curved blade into the earth. As he moved slowly down the field, the fork dove deep under the surface, cutting the weeds' roots at their base. The swath it created was nearly two feet wide, and it flipped the soil, folding the weeds underneath and away from the sun. Mimicking the work of adjacent farmers, Pop made pass after pass along the flat ground, causing earthworms and other little creatures to scramble from the loud noise.

The smell of fresh soil began to permeate our property. With the changes on our land came a strange sense of newness. Even at my very young age, I could tell something exciting was happening. I watched from the edge of the field as my father bounced through the open space on the noisy old tractor. He moved along slowly, until about two acres were prepped. From the sidelines, I breathed in the smell of newly tilled soil—a scent I'd come to associate with my childhood.

The next day, Pop switched out the plow for the disc. This piece had four axles that stretched out several feet on either side, housing eight round metal blades on each arm. Like all the rest, it had been parked near the field for weeks, and we'd gotten used to playing around it. We would spin our Hot Wheels cars in and around the metal, imagining they were the walls of a big city. But that day, our city had been taken away from us and put into motion. That's how it usually went. All three of us kids were under the age of six and curious, which meant we always found these interesting objects to play with outside. We'd consider them permanently ours until Pop found a use for them, at which point they'd be whisked away and we'd have to find another playground. It seemed another activity was always waiting to be discovered.

After hooking up the disc to the back of the tractor, my father returned to the patch of land he had tilled the day before. As he pulled the disc, he watched to ensure the speed and depth of the blades were just right. This would break up the large layers of soil and grind up the leftover weeds, readying the land for planting. Again, his day was spent moving back and forth through the dirt, over and over until it was groomed fine enough to handle with smaller tools. It seemed like it took forever.

TWIGS

With the soil finally prepared, it was now time to plant the twigs. At least they looked like twigs to me. The sticks were brown and dried up and had been covered with a blue tarp and lying in a heap on the edge of the field for weeks. Mom and Pop couldn't stop talking about them, referring to them as "the cuttings."

"Come on, Luisa! Let's go!" I shouted as soon as I saw the cover had been removed that morning. My two-year-old sister followed behind me, out the front sliding glass door that I had to tug hard at to unstick, as always. Once I flung it open, we raced across the yard through tangles of dandelions until we reached the tarp.

My father had added to the original ninety plants from Lett. Now the collection of twigs had grown to nearly five thousand, a sizable purchase for my parents. We had no idea that most of these precious cuttings had been carefully selected and shipped to us from California. We later learned the white varieties, including Chardonnay, came from the famous Napa Valley wineries of Mirrasou and Wente. The others all had strange names, like Müller-Thurgau, Sauvignon

Blanc, Silvaner, and Gewürztraminer. But the nastiest ones were called *pee-no new-wore*. These sounded so ugly to me. We later learned most of those came from Coury and another guy named Dick Erath, who apparently had been farming a vineyard near Lett in Dundee. He and Coury had established a little nursery together as there was nowhere else to buy wine grapes in the valley. Mom and Pop thought these varieties would have the best chance in the valley, from what they had learned from the winegrowers they met previously in France and from all their reading.

With the tarp off, we started our giant game of Pick Up Sticks. Jumping in, Luisa and I began moving the 18-inch canes onto the ground, using them to mark an imaginary roadway and stacking them to build towers and tepees.

"This is going to be the coolest town ever!" Luisa shrieked.

"Hey, girls, what are you doing?" Pop called to us from the front door. "Those are grape plants! Please don't shuffle them around. It's very important."

Alarmed, I jumped back. I was surprised to see him looking so serious.

Full of apologies, Luisa and I quickly started putting them back the way we thought they were before we moved them. The fact was, dried brown sticks all look the same. And what was the fuss all about anyway?

"Come on, let's load them up," Pop said, pushing his worn-out wheelbarrow up to us. He was no longer upset, instead seeming happy to see us so curious about the pile. We immediately fed off Pop's energy. Luisa and I now gently picked up the grape cuttings one by one, mimicking our father, and laid them carefully onto the bed of the rusty yellow wheelbarrow, trying to avoid the hole at the bottom. Once we filled the wheelbarrow, he pushed it out into the field.

"Hey, Pop"—I tried to keep up with his fast pace—"what are we doing with these things anyway?"

He stopped pushing the wheelbarrow and turned to us. "Well, honey, we're going to plant a nursery row right here in front of the house. It will take some time before they establish themselves, but this is the first step." Pop always made time for us. Even though we were young, he was patient and showed us respect. He spoke thoughtfully so we could understand what we were doing and why it mattered.

I later learned the nursery row was only the first step. This is where the cuttings would begin to grow their roots. In a year, they would be ready to replant in the larger field, and we would set them into rows to create a real vineyard. But for now, we dug into the long, narrow mound of just-tilled earth my father had prepared. We stuck the canes into the soil, leaving about half of each one sticking up. We used our bare hands to push dirt up against them, ensuring they were well covered. Then we pushed away a little bit of soil around each stick, creating a trough to collect water. Once all the sticks were embedded, we returned with five-gallon buckets of water and soaked each plant. As the water drained off, it moved down into the base of the cutting. Finally they were left to themselves, in hopes that their root systems would grow over the following months, and we would have sparked healthy, new life.

THE FARM

After completing the nursery row, Mom and Pop turned to their many other interests and needs, most importantly growing our food. Summer was coming, and it was time to plant the garden. My mother had found a sunny spot behind the house.

Grandma Alice brought over her trusted rototiller to prepare the ground. It reminded me of what Pop had done out in the field, but on a much smaller scale. After the soil was ready, Mom spent hours planting seeds for zucchini, tomatoes, cucumbers, watermelons, and a few rare artichokes just to keep things interesting.

I tried to stay away from that part of the property in fear of being asked to help. The last thing I wanted to do was more work in the dirt—planting those twigs was enough for me. Little Luisa, on the other hand, loved to help Mom grow things. We called her "Shrimp" because she was the smallest of all of us. Later, she developed the pet name "Slug" because she left a trail wherever she went. Shrimp didn't mind getting dirty. She was constantly sniffling, rubbing her nose with her hand and then wiping it on her worn pants. I found it disgusting. I also found it gross watching her hunt for earthworms, digging for them with her bare hands. If she found a slug, she would pet it; if she found a tree frog, she'd capture it and cup it in her small hands until she could surprise me with it.

I preferred wandering into the fields, picking wildflowers and bringing back fresh bouquets of cream-colored Queen Anne's lace, blue bachelor button, and yellow daisies. I felt they brightened our otherwise simple home.

When the first signs of the garden began to appear, so did the farm animals. Chickens were first, as they were relatively easy to raise and most practical. But things didn't stop there. In fact, it got out of hand quickly. Mom and Pop had this grand idea of living off the land, which meant having livestock as well as a large garden.

To me, the cows they chose were intimidating. They were nothing like the friendly ones I saw when we drove through Tillamook on one of our rare trips to the beach. Those were Jersey cows. They had polished coats that shone in the sun, big brown noses, and soft brown eyes that looked ever so gentle. I didn't understand why my parents hadn't selected those for our farm.

Instead, they had found these huge hairy beasts called Scottish Highlanders. From my four-year-old view, they were giant, daunting beasts with tangled red hair. They had large ivory horns with pointed ends, huge heads, and big, black wet noses. I couldn't tell if they were nice or not since their long bangs covered their eyes. I figured they must be mean because they were so enormous.

But Mom and Pop informed us these were the most gentle of all cows. Their unusual look made them often misunderstood, they explained. My parents were convinced they were the loveliest and smartest of all cows and that they provided healthier meat than any other breed.

My mother had researched other necessary farm animals and determined the very best milk came from Nubian goats. Not only did they produce the healthiest milk, but they too were apparently the smartest and friendliest of all goats, according to Mom. Our quiet, spooky barn was soon home to three of these lively pets. Two were brown, and the other one was black with white spots, but all of them had long, floppy ears that would dance when they ran and jumped—which they did whenever they saw us.

"Aren't they cute?" Mom said proudly, looking over her herd. "Two of them are already ready for milking, and the other one will be later this year."

"We're going to milk them?" Michel asked with a questioning sneer.

"Yes, it's the best milk you can get!"

We named the goats Daisy, Dahlia, and Daphne. I liked them. They were a good addition to our family.

With the new projects of gardening and animal care, we all found ourselves with less time to play. It seemed like all at once we were given chores around the farm. Michel and I were to feed the cows hay and grain twice a day. I hated this job mainly because I feared the cows so much. I discovered if I climbed up to the highest rail and watched Michel toss the hay over the fence, I could be helpful by holding the grain for him until he could toss that over as well. This way I was still involved, but also staying clear of any danger. Luisa fed the chickens scratch and brought any leftover kitchen food to them each morning. Mom never missed milking the goats once in the morning and again in the late afternoon. The three of us kids took turns collecting the fresh eggs each day. Weekends were reserved for hoeing the weeds in the garden and watering the plants on hot summer days. Just before dinner each evening, my mother would ask one of us to harvest some lettuce, basil, tomatoes, or whatever else was ripe in the garden.

We ate what we grew and lived off the garden and our farm most of the year.

THE BEES

Caring for our little farm wasn't enough for my parents. The books had gotten to them. When my mother wasn't researching a strange mushroom she'd found on the forest floor, she was reading about bees. She'd discovered the many benefits of pure honey. Naturally, my father had to experience the science of beekeeping for himself.

I walked into the kitchen one morning to see him zipping up a white canvas jumpsuit over his jeans and T-shirt near the front door.

"Where you going, Pop?"

"I've got to go check the hives. You want to join me?"

"Sure!" I said. Trips with Pop were always exciting. I rushed back to the bedroom, pulled on my work clothes, splashed my face with cold water, pulled back my hair, and met Pop outside.

My father placed his special bee hat on the seat between us inside the cab of the banana truck, and we headed down the gravel road. The clover fields were plentiful in Scholls. I found them especially beautiful when the morning sun cast a glow on the red canvas against the blue sky. Bumping along the road, I scanned the world outside the windshield, trying to spy the white boxes. Then, suddenly there they were. The bright wooden crates shone in the distance against a carpet of crimson and chartreuse green. The hives were stacked in fours on top of each other. Pop pulled the pickup to a slow stop and turned off the engine.

He grabbed the funny-looking hat next to me and a glass gallon jar on the floor. "Okay, sweetie. Now you stay here until I get back. You should be comfortable here in the cab. I shouldn't be too long."

"All right." I looked up at my brave father and nodded. I had no interest in getting stung by a bunch of bees and thought it odd that he did.

His hat was tied securely around his face, its black net completely covering his open collar and beard. Slamming the door, he reached for the smoker. I later learned this was an essential part of beekeeping, but to me it looked like some kind of accordion. He grabbed it from the back of the truck and walked over to the hives.

I noticed the truck key was still in the ignition and reached over, turning right just one notch as Pop had shown me. I powered on the radio and scrolled through the stations. With the sun shining into the cab of the truck, and the Archies softly playing "Sugar, Sugar," I was content. I watched Pop use the smoker as he walked, pumping air into the contraption. This created smoke, relaxing the bees and making them drowsy enough that he could approach their hives without disturbing them.

I watched as he worked, skillfully pulling one rack at a time out of the hive. One by one, he gently scraped the fresh honey from each screen into the big gallon jar, then carefully replaced them inside the box. With every screen, the bees came out and swarmed him. It didn't take long before he was covered. His white jumpsuit was now dotted black, but he paid no notice.

Instead, he took his jar of honey, tucked the smoker under his arm and headed back to the pickup. The bees buzzed around his head. Before opening the cab, he calmly pulled off his mask and set it in the bed of the truck. Then, with his hands still covered with thick gloves, he gently brushed the anxious bees away from his body while speaking softly to them.

"All right, guys, time to go now." Pop's whispering and slow movements seemed to have encouraged the bees to find their way off his jumpsuit, and he was able to slip it off. He checked himself again to be sure every bee was gone before reaching down for the jar. Opening the heavy car door, he handed the jar to me, climbed onto the seat, and slammed the door behind him.

"Look at that beautiful honey. Let's taste some." He reached over and pulled out a chunk of fresh honeycomb sitting above the granulated liquid. As he handed it to me a bee flew out of his thick hair and landed on the windshield.

"Oops, looks like I missed one." He laughed. "Don't worry. It won't hurt you. Bees can sense our thoughts. If you seem anxious, they'll be anxious. If you're relaxed, they're relaxed."

I trusted Pop, but I still cringed away from the windshield as I bit into the juicy honeycomb. It immediately filled my mouth with fresh, natural sugar.

"Yum." The luscious syrup coated my mouth. "It's soo good. Thanks, Pop!"

As I continued to chew, the sweetness dulled and soon turned to bland wax. I spit it into my hand and tossed it out the open window. I clenched onto the precious jar of honey as we bounced along the road back home. I breathed in the summer scent of freshly cut grass and smiled. *As strange as that all was, this is going to make Mom so happy.*

CULTURE

Weeks later, I felt the air shift, signifying the end of summer. The warm, gentle breezes began to cool, and the mornings brought a chill with them. Soon it would be time for Pop to go back to his PCC classroom, and Michel and I would head to a local Montessori school. Back in California, while Pop cared for us at home, Mom had earned her certificate in Montessori education after attending evening classes in Palo Alto. My mother firmly believed that learning in this unconventional manner would allow us to explore our individual talents and nurture creativity. She believed it would build self-confidence and drive. Mom sought out one of the few accredited schools in the Portland area, a thirty-minute drive from our little farm. She offset some of the tuition by teaching Spanish there. The Montessori method and its philosophy of building self-awareness through self-guided activities and a strong belief in collaboration fit in beautifully with our family's lifestyle and values.

We may have moved to the country, but Mom was determined to remain a cultured, sophisticated, current woman of the 1970s. As often as she could, she drove us to downtown

Portland and parked in front of the main library. We would head up the big staircase, welcomed by the marble walls and floors, then take a sharp right down a dimly lit, narrow hall into the art area. It was like a hidden vault. It was always empty, which made me wonder how my mother even knew about it.

The space held reprints of thousands of famous paintings for visitors to browse. They were displayed on racks and large canvases stretched across metal frames. With Luisa cradled on her hip, Mom slowly flipped through the heavy panels of work, scanning for favorites.

"Oh, wow," she whispered. "Look, it's a Picasso!" I looked up to see a frightening image of a distorted man's face, one black eye larger than the other. Disturbed by the image, I stepped back while my mother leaned forward. I watched in disbelief as she put Luisa down and pulled the print off the rack.

Michel and I tried to keep an eye on Luisa as Mom continued to view more pieces. I smiled when I saw a pastel landscapes by Charles Monet, but Mom seemed less excited about those. She was more attracted to modern, abstract designs by Joan Miro, Alexander Calder, Piet Mondrian, and Marc Chagall.

She would usually choose three or four new prints, passing them to Michel, who struggled to carry the large frames back up the stairs to the checkout counter. I'd grab Luisa's hand and follow closely behind, afraid we might lose our mother in this grand building in the center of the big city.

"I'm so excited!" Mom would often remark as we walked back outside. "Dick is going to love that Calder." I just rolled my eyes, wondering how anyone could get that excited about someone else's simple line drawing.

My mother immersed herself in art. On the largest wall in our little home hung the rented pieces while music from our record player filled the space with sounds of Bob Dylan, Duke

Ellington, Cat Stevens, Bob Seeger, Chopin, or some Italian opera. Among all the vinyls, Luisa and I favored one the most: a Jewish folk song, "Hava Nagila." We played it over and over, dancing and singing in our tiny, crowded front room.

ALL ABOUT
THE FOOD

Mom was almost as fixated with eating well as she was about her art, music, and books. In her opinion, the healthiest food was grown in one's own garden and on the farm, but if that wasn't possible, people should at least know its origin and how it was produced. Luckily she met another woman who shared similar thoughts. Her name was Jere Grimm, and she lived with her large family in northwest Portland. Together, the two helped form an organization called the Educated Consumer Food Council (ECFC) with a goal of educating consumers about the content of their food. They were passionate about passing an "ingredient labeling" law that would require manufacturers to list all ingredients on the label of their products.

Most of the women involved with the ECFC were other mothers who firmly believed they should know what they were feeding their families. I was often surrounded by the flock of opinionated women wearing embroidered tops and clogs when Mom took us to loud cooperative markets every couple of weeks. The markets were organized by the ECFC and moved from one private residence to another. They were full of strong, progressive women with lofty ideals.

Market days began by cramming empty produce boxes into the back of our station wagon. Earlier in the week, we would scrounge the used cardboard from local grocery stores specifically for this purpose. D'Angelo's Market in Progress and Corno and Sons on Garden Home Road were frequent destinations. Once we were well loaded with Chiquita banana boxes, we drove the thirty minutes into Portland. Because these peculiar markets were held all over the city, it was always interesting to see where we would end up. I enjoyed the drives into Portland, always curious about what other people did when they didn't live in the country.

One afternoon, we found ourselves at one of the largest homes in East Portland, near Reed College. I'd never seen a home so majestic and thought it strange its owners would be involved in this hippie gathering. We parked the car and hauled the empty boxes across the street. I knew we must be in the right place based on the number of people rushing into the home with their multiuse containers, dressed in bell-bottom denim and wearing bandannas. Once inside the crowded living room, we found hundred-pound burlap bags set around its perimeter. Each one contained some type of grain: black-eyed beans or split peas, lentils, cornmeal, or rice. In the kitchen, crates burst with fresh organic produce. It got chaotic as more people moved into the space, grabbing their favorite food items and packing them into their personal containers.

"Hey, Nancy!" someone shouted across the room. "So good to see you! Have you checked out the blue lentils? They're gorgeous!"

Mom recognized the friend and shared her excitement with a big smile as she waved.

"I know! They're amazing!"

I tried desperately to find something normal to do while my mother fixated over whole-kernel barley. I tried to understand what I was told: that buying in bulk saved us money and was healthier. I had an ongoing wish to just once buy a bunch of Concord grapes or maybe a can of fruit salad I had seen in the regular markets. I often wondered what those canned fruits must taste like, coated in their sugary syrup. Instead, I was staring at a bucket of dried apricots and hoping we'd be out of the craziness soon. I was ready to head home.

THE GRIMMS

Jere and Mom became close friends. She and her husband, Ray, were both artists, and Mom and Pop, of course, thought that was fantastic. There were six kids, but it was hard to keep track of them because people were often coming and going out of their city house. I was often confused trying to understand who lived there and who was just passing through, a much different dynamic than that of our secluded life in Scholls.

It was a long drive to get to the Grimms' house. I knew we were close when the main freeway led us through a tunnel that framed the stunning Mount Hood in the distance. This was my clue we had entered the city. We traveled through one of Portland's oldest neighborhoods into the West Hills. The homes here were grand and stately, many of them built into the hillside with views back to the north and east. Climbing one of the steepest hills, we'd finally arrive at their bungalow situated at the very top.

Handmade clay and glass fixtures covered their yard and urban garden. Wind chimes gently sang on the front porch, and balls of whimsical ceramic hung from the eaves of the porch. It was a playful home, funky and cheerful. On this day like so many others, Jasper, their friendly retriever, greeted us at the door as Jere opened it, with her fiery-red hair, bright-blue eyes, and brilliant smile.

"Hello, everyone! So glad you made it!" She invited us into the bustling life inside. One of her daughters rushed up the staircase, another one was on the phone, and her youngest son grabbed a skateboard and headed past us. "Come in!"

We sat at their rustic table as she brought us glasses of water served in hand-blown goblets. Each one had been made into a different shape and colored by her husband. Like my parents, the Grimms enjoyed making things, figuring out problems, and exploring new techniques and processes.

"What's happening up here?" A short older man walked up to us, his round face smiling behind wire-rimmed glasses and a scraggly gray beard.

"Hi, Ray!" Pop stepped toward him. "What are you working on?"

"Oh boy, lots of things." He grinned, pulling a chair up next to Pop.

The next three hours were spent listening to adults talk about politics, healthy food, glassblowing, and whatever else happened to come to mind. Luisa, Michel, and I were relatively bored with their never-ending conversation and moved into an adjacent room. Luisa and I found some paper and colored pencils and began to draw, while Michel sat down at their piano and played a Scott Joplin tune. As usual, we found ways to occupy our time as our parents focused on nurturing their new friendship based on mutual curiosity. I often felt out of place here as the family's creative energy and progressive thought were in abundance.

LAND
DEVELOPMENT

Once Luisa, Michel, and I had gotten our routines down with farm chores, the three of us would find new dirt to play in, trees to climb, or flowers to pick. It was March of 1970, just over a year since our move, and we felt the weather change as another spring approached. On rare sunny afternoons, I took walks behind the house, searching for the season's first bright-yellow daffodils. Mounds of them grew wild in our field near the barn. I couldn't resist their simple beauty and brought back several bouquets to decorate the house. Bristol, the shaggy Old English sheepdog who replaced Tzena, kept me company on those treks through the lush, tall green grass. He was my constant companion. I'd frequently get lost in thought while walking with Bristol, unconcerned with the daily chores and my parents' big projects. With my big, sweet dog by my side, our silence brought me joy.

Fearless Luisa, nearly three years old with her always-messy brown hair, found her entertainment with the cows. She'd walk directly up to the fence and push her small hands through the rails in hopes of touching one of their wet noses. She'd giggle in delight, completely unafraid of their massive size.

Springtime also meant it was time for Mom and Pop's big project to continue. A year had passed since we planted the nursery row in front of the house. The young vines had remained healthy through the year, and their roots had grown deep into the soil. They were ready to be transplanted into the larger field.

It was big news the day my parents scored thousands of poles and wire. The valley's bean farmers had switched out labor-intensive pole beans for machine-harvested bush beans. They were selling off the used material at rock-bottom prices. For just two cents, we could acquire either cedar end posts or tall beanpoles, and they'd throw in plenty of wire for free. It was a gold rush for the early winegrowers. Pop headed to Salem and loaded his truck bed as high as he could with the material.

The next day, my mother prepared two drums of creosote. This thick oil contained phenolic compounds distilled from tar that would prohibit creatures, like termites, from destroying the wood. She filled the hundred-pound drums three-quarters full with the tacky black liquid. Over the next several weeks, six or seven posts at a time would soak in the open containers for two days, then Mom would rotate the ends and soak the other side for another two days. It was a long, sticky project, and the stench of the toxic product seemed to linger forever.

Following several days of preparation, it was time for the old tractor to perform again. After multiple runs to Pop's favorite junkyard, he had finally found everything needed to get his machine up and working after sitting idle for almost a year. It took him weeks to prepare the twelve acres. He would come home from teaching around five at night and work in the field until the sun dropped. Then I'd run out and call for him to come in for dinner. On the weekends, I'd watch from the house as the dust spun above the tractor as it moved back and forth, making another pass with the plow, my father constantly glancing back to be sure the implement was digging into the earth evenly. The smell of fresh soil became familiar again, as did the dust that left a light coating wherever the wind blew it.

At last the ground was loose and smooth, exposing the ladybugs and earthworms once again to the elements. No longer home to common weeds, red clover, and blue bachelor's buttons, the acreage was now granulated and a deep, rich brown. It was ready to lay out something called the vineyard.

To start, my father created an access road through the center of the field, defining a north and south block. Then, perpendicular to this, he marked the rows every eight feet with a small stake. The distance would allow our tractor to pass with equipment in tow. On the weekends, he borrowed a surveyor's transit compass from PCC's Engineering department to verify the direction of the rows.

Pop knew work went faster with help and one day recruited his nearly seven-year-old son for the job, feeling that Michel was old enough to be trusted with the important job of marking the second stake at the opposite end of each row. It seemed pretty simple: walk to the end of the field and place a stake where our father directed.

They started the process. Pop tied a roll of string around a small stake and pounded it into the earth, then handed one end to Michel along with a bucket of stakes, a pocketknife, and a hammer. My brother walked down the first row to the opposite end of the land, allowing the string to drag along the ground as he shuffled his feet through the dry earth. The call of a falcon overhead distracted him, and as he gazed up at the sky, he wandered a bit off center, then tried to correct himself before he made it to the other side. He turned to face Pop, who was now two hundred yards away. Michel dropped the bucket and hammer to the ground.

"There!" Pop shouted. He raised his right arm, waving a little to the right. He took a look through the transit, then back at his young son and yelled, "Okay, just a bit more. Good. That's it." He gestured. I sat on the dirt next to my father, sitting cross-legged and pulling leaves from a daisy while I watched the process begin. Even from my five-year-old view, it seemed this was going to take a while.

My brother stood in the open field, waiting as patiently as he could as my father took several minutes adjusting the equipment to be sure the transit was set perfectly. I watched as Michel dodged a large monarch butterfly passing by his face or pushed a grasshopper off his pants. It was sometimes difficult for Michel to stay focused, but I know he tried his best since he knew it was an important job. It was pretty obvious that the two of them were struggling to hear each other, but occasionally Michel bent down and pounded one of the small stakes into the ground. He wrapped the string around it, tied it off, and cut it from the roll with his pocketknife. I was pretty sure it wasn't the exact spot Pop intended, but it was probably close enough.

My big brother kept tying string around stakes as my father yelled down the row with directions. The boys worked together, moving farther down the property throughout the day. Pop continued to check his work, using his measuring tape and the transit for accuracy to ensure each row was of equal distance from the other. It was just a question of what Michel was doing on his end.

Years later, when running tractors through this vineyard, we realized the practice of having a young child stake rows was not a precise technique. The amateurish approach resulted in rows that would significantly narrow as one moved from one end to the other. Due to the inconsistent nature of the widths, farming this particular vineyard required close attention and a strong knowledge of each block.

With the rows now marked, it was time to dig holes for the end posts. I jumped aboard the tractor and hung on as Pop and I bounded down the dusty vineyard lane. Mom followed on foot. We'd stop at each end of a row, and I'd watch as the steel blade of the auger would spin, cutting deep into the soil and forming a hole about three feet deep. The used auger had been purchased through the classified ads and adapted by Pop for this task. It took my parents several days to complete this work as they dug a hole at both ends of each row.

The next step was to install those awful end posts, now sealed in creosote. As usual, Pop tried to make the work efficient. This meant creating something new from something old. This time he pulled out his welding machine and hauled some heavy strips of metal from his largest junk pile. For hours every weekend, I heard him banging on the metal, bending it, pounding some more, and shaping it. Bright-orange and yellow sparks danced in front of his face, which was shielded by a gray metal mask, but as he had with the bees that swarmed his face in the clover, he seemed indifferent to the hot scraps of metal and fire flying about his body. He worked for hours, welding pieces together until he had formed two large U-shaped arms. These would be attached to either side of the tractor to create a cradle to hold the creosote posts.

Gloves were required to handle the foul posts. Luisa and I tried to pick one up to load onto the carrier, but they were so long and heavy our efforts didn't last long.

"Pop, these posts are soo stinky! I'm getting a headache from the chemicals," I whined.

"Yeah, and they're way too heavy!" Luisa chimed in.

My father looked over at us with a smile. "I know. Don't worry about it. Michel and your mom will help."

Relieved, we stepped back and sat on the ground. I snuggled up to Bristol and watched as the rest of my family continued to stack the heavy logs onto the tractor's cradles. They spent the rest of the afternoon in the field, setting each post into the prepared holes. Next, they secured the posts by shoving dirt around their bases with a shovel, and then they compacted the earth by stepping around each one. The work was monotonous and methodical, but with each end post they installed, an outline began to form around our field. I eventually learned how important these were to establishing our vineyard as they created the framework for everything to grow within. I sensed progress was being made. At least those stinky posts were farther away from the house.

Once the end posts were in place, our focus turned to the ratty beanpoles that had been mounded in front of our home for months. They'd been there so long without the protection of a tarp that grass had grown over the heap, as if it were a fresh grave. I was relieved to hear that another one of our piles would begin to vanish from the familiar landscape. I liked when it seemed as though we were finishing a project, neatening things up. However, this was rarely the case.

THE TRACTOR

"Good morning!" Mom poked her head into our windowless bedroom. "Time to get up. We need your help today." It was Saturday. I turned my body away from her voice to face the wall.

Minutes later, Mom's anticipated "Let's go, guys!" echoed from the hall. I gathered my strength, took a deep breath, and pulled myself out of the warm sheets, pushing my body into wrinkled work clothes as I walked the short steps to the kitchen. Luisa and Michel followed several minutes later. A bowl of oatmeal with raw honey and goat's milk sat waiting at the table. The cream was so thick, it stayed on top of the mush, seeping along its sides. It looked like I felt. Tired and uninspired. It was going to be another long day.

Today we were to load all those beanpoles onto the tractor cradles and stage them in the field. I found my worn garden gloves in a basket next to the front door and pulled on my dirty hiking boots. I met Pop in front of the house near the heap. He had geared up the tractor and was starting to load it.

"Hey, good morning, Maria!" He cheerfully reached out his arms and greeted me with a warm hug. "How are you this morning?" It seemed as though my father was always stationed outside and my mother always inside, both preparing to get us to work. It was like an unspoken, well-planned system they'd figured out. No way to escape. *And why were they both so happy about all this work?*

Pop and I started working while we waited for Luisa and Michel to join us. Even though the wood was much lighter and less toxic than the heavy, treated posts, there were hundreds of them to haul onto the tractor. We spent the morning moving them all. Even little Luisa got involved when she wasn't wiping her nose. I would slow down to help her lift one end. I enjoyed being by her side, as she would often point things out I didn't notice. I tended to be more focused on the task, while she would easily get distracted. For example, I'd make sure the posts were in alignment as she'd observe how an ant was carrying its food. By lunchtime we had a fully loaded tractor.

"Nice job, everyone. Now, I'll need someone to drive the tractor. Maria, do you want to try?" Pop asked as we finished our tuna fish sandwiches and tall glasses of water. "What do you think?"

I was thrilled he thought of me, but anxious. Could I really do it?

Back at the tractor, I jumped onto the rusty, ripped driver's seat, its yellow foam exposed from its many years of use. Pop was at my side. As I sat down, I realized my feet barely touched the pedals. I panicked.

"Now, let's practice first," my father said in his usual calm manner. With the engine off, he walked me through the lesson.

I stepped up and pushed down hard on my left foot to engage the clutch. With my right hand, I reached down to the steel gearshift. I moved it from side to side to ensure the tractor was still in neutral. It took most of my body weight to get the pedal to the ground, and I realized I had to stand to see over the hood of the tractor. Michel intimidated me as he watched from the ground. He always got to drive, so this was a big deal. I needed to show him that I could do this, even though my heart was racing.

"Go ahead," Pop encouraged me. "Start it up." I looked over at him with nervous eyes, then refocused. I stood up and pushed down hard onto the clutch with my left foot, checked my gear was still in neutral, and then turned the key to the right. The engine started to rumble. I looked over to Pop for guidance. He nodded.

"Okay, now put it into first gear," he said as he held on to the open cage of the vehicle. "You're fine. Now, give it some gas with your right foot."

My left foot was trembling, but I was determined. I pushed down on the pedal and again reached for the cold gearshift. With some effort, I moved it up into first position.

"Good. Now let's go."

I swallowed hard. "Stay here, okay?"

He nodded in support, offering me a little smile. I switched pedals, my left foot shaking, and the tractor started to move forward. The stiff steering wheel was tight and slow to react. Like the heavy pedals, it took a lot of strength and concentration to maneuver. I sensed Luisa and Michel following behind, kicking their feet in the dirt below, disappointed they weren't at the helm and instead were forced to catch dust in their faces. I kept the tractor in first gear and settled down on the lopsided seat, as Pop and I bounced the tractor down the main lane into the field.

"Right here!" Pop shouted. I slid off the seat and stood up again, letting up on the gas, cranking hard to the right and using most of my upper-body strength to make sure not to hit the end post.

"Good job. Now slowly straighten it out and give it a bit more gas." He reached over my left arm and pulled the steering wheel hard toward his body, ensuring we were lined up correctly. I pulled down the row about fifty yards, pushing down hard on that left pedal, and moved the gear back into neutral. The tractor stopped.

"Nice work, Maria." Pop patted my head and smiled as he hopped off the tractor. I wiped the sweat from my brow, shook my hands out, and sighed with relief.

"Okay, guys. Let's pull and drop as Maria moves down the row." Michel looked less than enthused. Luisa pulled her oversized gloves up over her small hands. They didn't make working gloves for three-year-olds. She reached up and tugged on a pole. It was more than half her weight, but she was determined. Eventually one came loose, and she walked it down the row, dragging one end along the ground.

Pop shouted, "That's good, Luisa. Right there." She dropped the stake on the ground and headed back to the tractor, where Michel was stationed to wrestle them from the pile. I proudly waited in the driver's seat, my tractor engine rumbling.

After plenty of stakes had been dropped on either side of the row, I was told to move the tractor forward. At the time, I didn't consider being five years old was young to be driving a tractor. We were farmers now, and Mom and Pop expected us to help. It was that simple. So, I gathered up some courage and got the machine moving again. Luisa and Michel continued to pull and position the stakes within the rows. Even though all three of us were under the age of seven, we were completely focused on the important work. The more we did, the more confidence we gained.

The sun was beginning to set when Pop decided to call it a day. We shuffled back to our little house and sat on the rough, hard lawn. Luisa showed me the calluses on her palms while

Michel quietly pulled tiny splinters from his hands. I felt small blisters forming on my knuckles from clinging to the steering wheel, and the muscles in my left leg were aching from pushing down on the clutch.

"Dinner is ready!" Mom called to us. I kicked off my boots at the front door and gave Bristol a hug before walking inside. The familiar aroma of my mother's luscious tomato sauce simmering on the stove and the voices of National Public Radio filled the intimate space. I was suddenly encompassed by a deep sense of comfort. I sank down into the sofa, realizing how tired and hungry I was from the day's labor.

The project didn't end until Sunday. We loaded and dropped the rest of the poles all weekend. Michel took over driving since Pop realized I was more valuable working on the ground. Although only two years older than me, my brother was taller and stronger and therefore more capable of handling the tractor. Now, working behind the equipment, I complained about the constant dust in my eyes, but nobody seemed to care. At least my gloves fit so I didn't have as many calluses as Luisa. *But, oh, this dirt!*

The following weekend meant more work. Pop removed the cradles from the tractor, replacing them with a new contraption that required working on something called hydraulics. It was designed to pound all those poles into the ground. Mom walked behind the tractor as Pop stopped every five feet, waiting for her to insert a chunk of two-by-four on top of each pole, then into the mechanism. Pop activated the tool, which would pound the wood deep into the ground. It would hit once, then again and again. The hammering echoed back to the house all day long— for weeks. I watched my parents work side by side, relieved to not be needed, but also with a slight tinge of guilt. The two of them methodically worked through the entire twelve acres until the field was complete. The interior structure of the vineyard had taken shape. Something was happening.

TIME FOR PLANTS

Once the poles had been placed across the property, we were ready to plant grapes. It felt as if Mom and Pop invited every person they had met since we moved to Oregon for this major occasion. Dick Wysong, a math instructor from PCC, and his family; the Grimms; the Downs; and even the Taylors, who lived at the end of our road, came to help. It was time to break into the cuttings from the nursery row and establish their new home along the rows.

I put on my work clothes again. Mom had assigned us two drawers within the single dresser we shared. One was labeled "work clothes" and the other "school clothes." I hated that my school clothes only filled half the drawer while my "work clothes" were always crammed to the top of the drawer. I imagined one day I would have one large chest of drawers all to myself, and it would be filled with only "nice clothes." Even more, I dreamed of having outfits that matched and nothing from the Goodwill. How dreamy it would be to have no "work clothes" at all!

That morning, Pop stood near the nursery row, organizing everyone.

"So, first we're going to loosen the soil around each plant." He crouched down, digging his rough hands into the nursery row, carefully carving the soil away from one of the plants. "Then you'll want to gently rock the plant at its base, very carefully, as you pull it from the dirt. It's very important not to rip it out. All the tender roots must stay intact." My father's blue eyes sparkled as he looked up at his enthusiastic crew.

"Like this?" Luisa had already gotten to work, pulling a brown stick out of the mound.

"Yes. That's the right idea." He nodded.

We began pulling plants from the pile. There were thousands of them. We carefully placed each one in our rusty wheelbarrow. Pop observed each young shoot as it was collected, ensuring it was in stable condition. He used a pair of hand shears to clip the roots if they were too long.

The work party was on, adults and kids all chattering, laughing, and walking back and forth from the wheelbarrow. Family dogs ran across the field in excitement. I couldn't help but think it would have been much more productive if it were just the five of us, but Mom and Pop were having a ball and had insisted "the more the merrier" for today.

Mom took over trimming the plants as Pop left to fetch the tractor. He loaded up a pallet stacked with thousands of colored cardboard sheets. These were flattened milk cartons Mom purchased from Alpenrose, a local dairy down the street from our Montessori school. Pop heard these cartons would help protect the young starts from direct sunlight and prevent weeds from competing with their growth.

Mom followed Pop down the vineyard road with the wheelbarrow now overflowing with the freshly uprooted plants. The cheerful crowd of kids, adults, dogs, and cats paraded behind.

I chose to take up the rear. The procession suddenly stopped at the far end of the field, as the tractor pulled into the last row. The boisterous mob rejoined him as he turned off the rattling engine and hopped onto the ground.

"Okay, what's next, Dick?" A smile flashed across Mom's sun-kissed face. Her long brown hair was often styled in a tidy, soft bun on the back of her head. She always managed to maintain her poise, no matter the situation. I always thought she resembled Jackie Kennedy.

My father shifted into teacher mode again, explaining the steps for proper grape planting. As he stroked his trimmed beard, he instructed us to take one cutting at a time and place it on the ground every three feet. He divided up the group. Some would be in charge of placing the plants, while another group would follow with milk cartons.

And so we began. Pop started down another row with Mom pushing the wheelbarrow through the heavy soil behind him. Luisa and three other kids grabbed a few Pinot Noir cuttings and marched ahead, counting out three large steps. They placed a plant on top of the soil as directed. Three other kids and I followed behind with a handful of the flattened cartons. We laid one next to each plant, the waxed carton sliding easily out of our hands. Our outdoor assembly line moved back and forth through the rows, distributing plants and large cards along the dirt until noon. During our break, Mom brought out sandwiches and slices of juicy oranges to reward us as we sat on our dandelion lawn.

The next day, the five of us got up early. We anticipated a long workday. Hand trowels and hoes were necessary. My parents worked ahead of us, digging deep holes into the ground for each plant. Luisa and I followed, carefully taking each one and dropping it into the hole, ensuring all the roots were tucked under the earth. As I held a plant in the opening with one hand, I used the other one to fill it with loosened soil. Then I'd pat down the dirt to secure it. Once each cutting was stable and straight, Luisa would place a milk carton over it. We'd push more soil up around the sides of the cartons, first with our hands and then with the side of our feet, stomping around the perimeter. Michel worked alone on the other side of the row. Shaggy Bristol paced circles around us, and every once in a while one of our adopted barn cats would come by, stroking our ankles with a brisk tail. Occasionally a white butterfly would fly by, or a feisty grasshopper would jump into our faces. We were silent laborers except when Mom started humming "Make it with You," by Bread. Otherwise we were each alone in our thoughts. I passed the time imagining what life must be like for kids who didn't have to work in a dusty field every weekend.

The silence suddenly broke by the familiar rumbling of the tractor coming down the lane. We heard it stop at the end of our row.

"Hey, girls!" Pop shouted to us. "You're doing a great job, but we need to get these little guys some water."

My father had removed the pallet of milk cartons and replaced it with a fifty-gallon stainless steel barrel filled with water to which he'd attached a garden hose. With Michel acting as driver, my mother walked behind the noisy tractor as it made its way down the vineyard road. He kept the vehicle moving slowly enough for Mom to water each plant. She moved across the rows, kinking the hose to avoid wasting water as she strode back and forth, moistening each young plant with about an inch of water.

Out on that straggled piece of land, we cared for each one of those silly sticks. It felt like the planting and watering would never end, but just as the spring rains turned into warm, sunny days, we realized we had established the entire twelve acres. It was now home to thousands of grapes. My parents could finally claim they had a vineyard.

SCHOOL DAYS

Our summer had been consumed with the vineyard project, but we'd also found time to play with our joyful goats, explore the open meadow, and investigate the quiet creek. I tried to ignore the coolness I felt in the morning air when I stepped outside our little house one morning to throw grain at the chickens. I didn't want summer to end, especially this year, because this fall meant Michel and I would attend Groner Elementary, the local grade school, while lucky Luisa would remain under Mom's care at Montessori.

Michel and I would be forced to take the bus and mix with the locals for the first time. I would enter as a young first grader, and Michel would be a third grader. We'd passed the small school plenty of times because it sat right on the main highway. It was just five minutes from our home, but as the first day of school approached, I knew it would feel like an entirely different world. Deathly shy, I was anxious about meeting new kids, feared sitting in a conventional classroom, and worried I might get lost in the halls. But going was inevitable.

When the dreaded day at last arrived, I selected the slightly worn yellow-and-green floral sundress Mom and I had found at one of her favorite consignment shops. I spent some extra time brushing my teeth and my long, scraggly sandy-blonde hair. I thought perhaps if I spent more time getting ready, we would miss the bus, and Mom would have to drive us.

"Okay!" Mom was rushing us out the sliding glass door. "It's time! You'll be fine. Let's take a quick photo, and then you better get going!"

Michel, dressed in a green-and-purple striped T-shirt and blue corduroy pants, reluctantly shuffled out the door. I joined him in front of our spiky Monkey Puzzle tree, which stood on the edge of our messy lawn. We managed a small smile for the Kodak Brownie camera, but our fear was difficult to hide. After the snap, Mom gave us a big hug and wished us good luck.

"Now you better go so you don't miss the bus!" she warned.

We turned and began what would become our daily quarter-mile walk down our gravel driveway to the neighbor's mailbox. This was the official stop where the school bus would find us. About midway down the drive, the rain began. I watched as it hit the dirt and rocks, splashing my bright-white knee-high socks and shoes. The field of milk cartons seemed to follow us as we walked.

We were the only kids who lived down Vandermost Road, so the wait that day was long and quiet. My brother was not a great conversationalist and was probably more frightened than I was about the first day of school. The anticipation built, my heart was pounding, and I felt a pit in my stomach. I hoped the bus would get lost, or maybe it just wouldn't come. But then a yellow shape broke through the fog that had crested on the hill just ahead of us. I bent down to wipe the mud off my shoes. I felt sick.

"Good morning!" Mrs. Cole shouted down from her high seat in front of the steering wheel as she pulled the folding door open, allowing me and my brother to step up and out of the rain and wind. We entered a noisy bus full of excited kids.

"Morning," I quietly responded, with a quick glance up to her and then back down to the wet black tread. Michel didn't say a word. I quickly scanned the situation and took an open seat in the second row. I kept my head down all the way to the school, eavesdropping on the conversations and laughter behind me. It was the first time we had been in a space with so many other kids. We were usually with our parents, or alone, or within the common comfort of our Montessori classroom. Everything immediately felt foreign.

TRYING TO
FIT IN

I struggled each day with my shyness, concerned from the moment I stepped onto the bus, my eyes glued to the floor to avoid contact with anyone. The most agonizing part of my day was recess. I found it ironic since it seemed like this was everyone else's favorite time. I felt nauseated when I thought about the playground and having to find something to do out there with all those kids. I also feared lunch, which meant maneuvering through a crowded cafeteria and navigating a place to sit next to someone who was hopefully nice.

I did well in most of my classes except for math. The hands-on Montessori approach to problem-solving conflicted with the conventional math instruction. It didn't seem to matter how much I studied or how hard I tried to understand the numbers, nothing made sense. At home I struggled with the homework despite my father's patient help. My stomach in knots, I'd regularly end up crying, turning in tear-stained pages to the teacher the next day. Additionally, I struggled to embrace our family's reputation as California hippies, a joke in this well-established farming community. I wanted to be smarter and prettier, but mostly I just wanted to fit in.

Most of the Groner kids came from generational farms. These people grew hay or alfalfa, Christmas trees, strawberries, walnuts, or nursery stock. They were normal. Contrarily, we were transplants from the disliked state of California and were growing an unknown crop. At the time, radio and TV were running ads aimed at the tourists beyond Oregon's southern border: "Oregonians Don't Tan. They Rust," "Visit. But Don't Stay." Oregonians didn't want outsiders spoiling their state. The natives liked things as they were.

Each morning the school bus came to pick us up, and each afternoon it dropped us off at the weather-beaten mailbox perched atop a worn stump of timber. The daily view provided a clear path into our unusual life, an ideal vantage point for the entire load of kids to gawk and remark on our field of milk cartons.

"What are you guys doing out there? Planting a dairy?" one boy joked.

My head stayed down. I was wishing it *was* a dairy with beautiful Jersey cows. I quietly replied, "No, it's a vineyard."

"A what?"

"A vineyard. We're growing grapes."

"Grapes? That's weird."

"Yeah. My parents want to make wine." I tried to defend my family's oddity as my face began to redden. Fortunately, I had long hair that I could hide behind. I was uncomfortable trying to explain our situation, mainly because I didn't understand it myself. I just wanted to get off the bus.

The laughing and ridicule would then erupt over how my parents must be crazy drunks. It seemed the locals knew nothing about making wine. I agreed—it sounded stupid. Especially in this part of Oregon, where I learned that the two community granges and three churches prohibited alcohol from being served. As an impressionable kid, this made me feel as though what we were doing made us evil. I thought perhaps we were sinners. The fact we did not attend church didn't help. Even though we were minutes from liberal Portland, out here, it seemed like most folks disapproved of us and our lifestyle.

As the bus stopped at other kids' homes, I saw how they lived. I thought how wonderful it must be to live in a traditional American house with a manicured lawn enclosed by a sparkling-white picket fence. It was a stark contrast to our place, with its lumpy, unkempt dandelion yard surrounded by piles of damaged equipment, metal, and wood; an ancient tractor; a weedy organic garden; weird farm animals; and a field of milk cartons.

At the end of my third stressful day at Groner, I walked outside to the bus lineup. There were two parked buses: one marked A, the other, B. Michel had been picked up earlier for his Suzuki piano lesson, something he'd been doing since he was three years old. The piano was a natural extension of my brother. Nobody understood him better than this instrument. The piano was his closest friend, and he was addicted to playing it. Today it was up to me to get on the right bus. I had never done it without him. The drivers looked the same, the buses looked the same, and being too shy to ask, I took a chance and jumped on the one marked A.

After loading a full bus, the driver pulled onto the highway. I watched as the kids hopped off the bus one by one. I didn't recognize the stops or the kids. We climbed more hills and lurched down more gravel roads. An hour passed and still nothing looked familiar. As we drove, it got quieter. A pit grew in my stomach. I no longer looked out the window; I was now wondering what to do. I watched as the last student stepped off the bus. I sat quietly in the second row, looking down at the green vinyl seat. I was afraid to speak, and the bus stood still. The driver slowly turned around and faced me. "So, where do you live, honey?"

I hesitated. "I don't really know. Nothing looks right." I trembled, almost near tears.

"No problem. We'll head back to the school and figure it out."

I felt cool tears begin to roll down my red cheeks. I was embarrassed, ashamed, and scared. I didn't even know where I lived.

Back at Groner, I mustered the nerve to ask Mrs. Haack, the receptionist, to borrow the office phone. I dialed our home number: 503-628-1227. Fortunately, Mom answered. They were back from the lesson. I started to cry as I tried to explain the situation. Twenty minutes later, our white station wagon pulled up to the curb while I repeated in my head, "Bus B, stupid. Bus B." Mom walked over and gave me a big hug. "Don't worry, honey. You'll figure it all out soon enough." But I wasn't so sure.

THE CORPSE

Death arrived at our door on a particularly cold day in January. It was Derek Down's idea. Our eccentric British neighbor decided it was time to butcher one of his pigs, and my parents thought it would be interesting to see how many parts of the animal they could make into products beyond traditional cuts of meat. I figured they must have been inspired by something they read in one of their *Mother Earth News* pamphlets.

The cloaked beast arrived at the front door one gray Saturday morning. I could barely make out Derek's crooked teeth against the foggy glass when he smiled and his warm breath created puffs in the cold air. He waited for someone to relieve him of the heavy load.

"Ha! Great!" My father rushed to jerk the sliding door open wide enough to allow the man to enter with his large bundle. "Good morning! Wow. This is going to be great!" Pop's face lit up, his vibrant smile beamed within his trimmed beard. "Let's clear the table. Maria, could you grab some old newspaper?"

I didn't really understand what was happening, but, as usual, I did as I was told and found a stack of old *Hillsboro Argus* newspapers sitting next to our small woodstove. I opened up the inky paper and smoothed the layers to cover the entire surface of the table.

Our family friend stood in our tiny living space supporting the wrapped corpse on his thigh as Mom and Pop gushed over the treasure. "Fantastic!" Pop said. Mom laughed, caught up in the excitement of this adventure. I didn't want to know what was mummified under the white sheet. As Derek placed the corpse down, the dead pig's feet hung off the edge of our small kitchen table. It was horrid. I quickly dropped the newspaper on a chair and left. I couldn't bear to think what was going to happen next. Being relatively new to this idea of living off the land, I hadn't witnessed death or butchering farm animals. In fact, I was a huge animal lover, and I couldn't bear the idea of killing another living thing.

Luisa and Michel followed my lead after they got a quick peek of the scene about to unfold in our tiny kitchen. We shut the bedroom door and turned on the transistor radio, trying to block the activity from the other side of the wall. Gilbert O'Sullivan sang "Alone Again," distracting us as we played with our Hot Wheels and Little People, trying not to think about what was happening just yards away. The laughter and conversation grew louder as we heard Ray and Jere Grimm join in the morbid affair. We kept our door closed and turned up the volume.

Nearly three hours passed before we dared Michel to go see what was happening. He sheepishly opened our door and peeked out. He took about three steps into the kitchen and immediately returned. The initial chaos of the morning had died down to moderate chatter.

"I think it's okay," my brother said. We crept slowly into the narrow hall. I anticipated blood, but instead was hit with the strong smell of raw meat and fresh guts. I felt my stomach turn. It didn't help that the small space was humid and crowded.

Obviously, everyone else had gotten used to the stench, distracted with discovering what could be produced from a single pig.

While Jere was at the stove stirring something in a large pot over boiling water, Mom was at the sink washing something else.

"What are you guys doing?" I asked quietly.

"We're making soap from the pig's fat!" Jere couldn't contain her delight.

"And, look, pig's teeth!" Mom turned around to show us a handful of tiny, narrow white nuggets she was cleaning. "Jere and I are going to turn these into earrings!"

Are you kidding?

I later learned they turned those feet into "good luck charms" and deep-fried the ears. They cut up the rest of the pork into pounds of bacon and pork chops, and my father made prosciutto.

For the next several months, we were forced to clean ourselves with pig body wash. This so-called soap was more like a lard scrub. Its lava-like surface was painful when I rubbed it against my tender skin. It was completely void of any lather or scent, and I would toss the slightly used bars into the garbage can whenever I could, hoping to exhaust the supply. But each morning, another one would mysteriously appear. There was always one found in the tiny closet shower and a second one at the hand sink. Hundreds of these dreadful bars remained in our home for months.

Why can't we buy Dove like normal people? I love Dove! I want Dove!

WELCOME TO
MY WORLD

By spring of second grade, I'd made a friend. Her name was Luann, and she didn't seem to mind that my parents were hippie freaks. I invited her over one weekend afternoon after helping Mom in the vineyard. Among other things, Luann was a Brownie and got to spend her time baking cookies and learning how to sew. It was nice to have a normal friend.

I was nervous watching her car come down the gravel driveway for the first time. Fortunately, Mom greeted our guests outside so they weren't overwhelmed by the eccentricity inside our tiny house. As the moms chatted in the drive, Luann and I headed down to the creek. Luckily, the sun was out, and it had turned out to be a decent day. I thought introducing her to our place from the outside was a good plan.

Due to the light rain earlier that morning, our feet slid on the slippery bank tucked beneath the giant firs as we made our way down the slope. We grabbed on to the tree trunks, and the loose bark covered in thick dark moss came off in our hands as we slid down to the even ground below. The narrow path was bordered by densely planted ferns of all sizes and varying colors of green. We tugged at the horsetail rusk, their sections inviting us to pull them apart. We laughed as we tried to put them back together. We grabbed funky-looking fiddleheads and tried to open them too, their tight green curlicues quickly recoiling to their original state. The grasses were so tall, they hit our faces as we passed, leaving wet dew on our cheeks and eyelashes as we tried to avoid the slimy gray-green slugs sitting along the trail.

Once we got to the stream, we heard voices and giggles. It was Luisa and her friend Angie, who lived at the end of our road.

"Hi, guys!" I shouted.

"Hi!" they chorused and ran down the bank with us to search for crawdads. I was quietly relieved Luisa was there since I really didn't want to pick up any critters, but wanted to show them to Luann.

"Look how cute this one is!" Luisa handed it to me with her cold hands. "Do you want to hold it?"

"No way!" I shrieked, stepping back. Everyone laughed.

"Maybe you should put him in the water again," Luann suggested.

"No, he's fine," Luisa replied as she and Angie took a closer look. She felt its smooth body, sliding her fingers up to feel its tiny claws. Only after a thorough review of its entire anatomy did she return it to the cold creek and begin to search for others. I kept a distance, admiring her bravery. Luann and I giggled as we made up stories about how bears might get us if we stayed down in the forest too long.

"We're off, guys!" My friend and I left the little girls and their water adventures to race back up the slippery hill to the barn across from the hidden forest. The structure was barely standing and most of its panels had fallen off. I was ashamed of its weather-beaten exterior, but we heard movement and poked our heads inside.

"There you go, Daisy." I heard my mother softly speaking to our goats as we entered through the crooked doors. Mom was sitting on top of a bucket, preparing to milk our eldest doe.

"Oh! Hi, girls." She turned around. "What are you two up to?"

"Nothing," I replied. I was embarrassed my friend was witnessing the goat milking.

"Could you please grab me that jug over there, Maria." Mom gestured with a nod of her head as her hands continued to rhythmically pull down on Daisy's nipples, extracting small amounts of white liquid into a small bucket under her belly.

"Sure." I passed her the jug, turning my body to block the scene from Luann. "We gotta go!"

"Wait. What is she doing?" my friend asked as I tried to walk out of the barn.

"Nothing. Just milking."

"What do you do with it?"

"We drink it."

"What? Really?!" She giggled.

"Yeah." I blushed.

"That's so gross. Doesn't it stink?"

"Well, no, not really." I heard myself defending our strange daily beverage.

"Huh. Weird." We left the barn.

Later that afternoon we sat at the kitchen table with wine-glasses filled with the thick, creamy milk. Luann looked at me with concern as she picked up the glass and smelled it.

"It's okay. It's really not bad," I encouraged.

"Really? Okay." She reluctantly took a drink. "Do you guys always drink out of wineglasses?"

"Yeah, I guess we do," I cautiously replied.

A second later Mom came to the table with a basket of colored eggs.

"Aren't these beautiful? I just collected them." She smiled as she set her brown, green, and blue treasures in the center of the table.

My friend looked again to me for reassurance.

"We have Araucana chickens," I tried to explain. "They lay colored eggs."

"No way! That is *soo* cool."

Then the sandwiches arrived. Mom had made the bread out of whole-wheat flour combined with several different grains, various nuts, and our honey. The other signature element to her bread was how it crumbled due to the many healthy items it contained. The more we chewed, the more the seeds would stick in our teeth.

Furthermore, we did not stock creamy Skippy. Instead, Mom always made crunchy peanut butter. Instead of spreading smoothly, it pulled against the nutty slice of bread, ripping holes in the center. I promised myself that when I grew up, I would only buy Skippy or Jif because I wanted a real peanut butter and jelly sandwich like everyone else. I apologized to my friend.

Following our weird lunch, I was pretty sure Luann had had enough. I imagined the stories she'd tell her family that night.

THE BIG BUILD

We made it through another school year and welcomed another summer in Scholls. When you live in a rural community in the Willamette Valley, the year is marked by the seasons. The many ripening crops introduce summer. You can smell sweet berry juice in the air and see harvesters gather in the fields. It begins with the harvest of strawberries, followed by raspberries, then blueberries, and finally peaches and blackberries. This busy season also signifies no school and longer days, meaning more time to help with the daily chores. For us, it meant every day the animals needed to be fed, eggs needed to be collected, the garden needed watering, and the vineyard needed attention.

The small grape starts we planted as ratty sticks now showed signs of life. Their green heads poked beyond the top of the milk cartons. At least now you could see there was something more than cardboard growing in our field. The spring rains had helped the plants dig deeper into the soil, but the moisture had the same effect on all the other seeds living there. The weeds had grown just as fast and were now suffocating our little friends.

These ruthless pests were competing with the wine grapes both inside and outside the cartons' walls. Our plants wouldn't survive unless we continuously cleared around them. Since my parents didn't believe in conventional farming techniques that involved the use of chemicals, it meant we had to control the weeds by hand.

One morning, Mom anchored a worn hoe to her left shoulder and held Luisa's hand as we walked into the young green vineyard. We started with the very first plant in the very first row.

"Okay, girls. Why don't you start pulling the weeds inside the carton, and I'll work around the outside."

I reluctantly kneeled on the dirt in front of the protected plant. I knew I was doomed for most of the day with this task since there were literally thousands of plants that required the same care. Forgetting my gloves, I reached inside the carton to pull out the stubborn grasses around the plant. I couldn't help but think it was a hopeless chore. It was clear the same weeds would begin to grow almost as soon as I moved on to the neighboring plant. I feared this job could go on forever, since we were surrounded by acres of work.

My mother worked across from me on another row. She gripped the hoe's worn wooden handle, raising it up into the air and then bringing it down firmly onto the hard ground. The sharp metal edge cut into the aggressive weeds and broke the hard surface around the carton. She continued the attack, working her way around the target, the tool swinging straight up and down, over and over again. After finishing one plant, she would swiftly move to the next, row after row. Luisa and I followed behind her, trying to keep up.

When we broke for lunch, we found Pop at the table, flipping large sheets of white paper back and forth. I could see they had blue-lined drawings on them.

"What are you doing?"

"These are the house designs. I needed to check on a couple things."

"How's it going?"

"Pretty well." He closed the large document, rolled it up, and headed outside.

In between preparing and teaching his classes, planting the vineyard, constructing new and repairing old equipment, and beekeeping, Pop was also building us a new house. It seemed more like a hobby than a real focus for him, since he had to attend to all the other projects he had going on. I knew Mom was anxious to move into a larger place, but she was plenty busy with the daily demands of our busy household and farm, and she remained patient.

I was pretty sure my father had never built a house before, so I wondered how he thought he could do it alone. But, as usual, he never considered hiring any help. Like everything he did, he seemed to enjoy the process and got a thrill out of problem-solving. I imagined it was his independent character, but just as likely it could have been that we simply didn't have the money to do things any other way. I often wondered about this, as it was hard for me to keep up with all the projects he had lying around.

The pounding of his hammer and the piercing sound of the table saw echoed throughout the property one morning before we woke. The sun felt good against my face as I took the short walk to the site that had been cleared for our new home. The concrete for the basement had been poured a month ago, so he was beginning to frame the structure.

"Hey, Pop!" I watched as he nailed a couple of two-by-fours together. "What're you doing?"

"Oh! Hi, honey. Well, right now I'm working on our bedroom. Just a lot of framing. Could you give me a hand?" He pulled a tape measure from his tool belt and handed me the end.

"Grab this and take it to the other side of the floor, over there." He pointed across the space. I held the end of the tape and walked the length of the floor to the other side, pulling the tape along with me, once again doing as I was told.

"That's it. Perfect. Now what does it read?"

"Um," I looked down at the metal ruler on the floor. "I think it's twenty-two feet six inches. And a little."

"How much of a little?" He laughed at me.

"Uh. I think like a quarter of an inch," I gulped, hoping I was right. I hated numbers.

"Great. Thanks." I dropped the tape, and it recoiled, snapping back into its shell. Pop gave me a smile and used his stubby, thick carpenter pencil to write the measurement down on a piece of scrap wood. He continued to work, pulling nails out of his bag and pounding them into the long wooden boards with ease.

I stayed and watched for a while, marveling at my father's skills. How did he know how to do so much? I enjoyed being around him, but I was restless. It was hard for me to just sit and watch, so I found a broom and swept up the dust under the saw. As I cleaned up the space, I noticed some wood remnants on the floor, wooden triangles left from cutting corners off boards and lots of unusable, oddly shaped chunks of wood. Using a bottle of wood glue I found, I started sticking the varied shapes together and created funny creatures, leaving them among the other scraps. The activity kept me amused for hours and gave me more time with Pop. When the afternoons heated up, I brought him a cold thermos of water since I knew he wouldn't take time to get it himself.

While my father spent most of the summer working on the house, Mom continued to work in the vineyard. Both of them were up against these three months of warm weather. Each day they'd both put in long hours, pushing themselves until the sun began to set and the darkness would eventually force them to put down their tools and come in for the night. We rarely had dinner before nine-thirty most evenings.

WORKING
WOMAN

As the crisp air and cool breezes transitioned us into autumn, the bustle of the apple and hazelnut harvests began, rushing us into another school year. It was the fall of 1972 and time for all of us to switch back to our academic routine.

My father traded in his worn leather tool belt for his equally worn leather briefcase. Instead of checking his blueprints daily, he now reviewed his lecture notes. Luisa started first grade at Groner as my mother falsified the day of her birth to allow her to begin a year earlier than required. Mom justified it by claiming her daughter was smart enough—"she can read, after all"—but we all understood the real reason was to allow her more uninterrupted vineyard time. I entered the third grade, and Michel moved into fifth. Our motley crew of three headed up to meet the dreaded school bus early in the mornings. Our mother was left behind to attend to the domestic duties, most notably the vines and the farm.

I'd imagine her day would begin like all the others: putting away the Uncle Sam's cereal, wheat germ, raw honey, and

Nancy's organic plain yogurt. I'm pretty sure she'd leave the dirty dishes stacked in the sink as the animals took priority. She'd rinse out the steel milking bucket, lace up her sturdy leather boots, and head out into the fresh air. The clouds wouldn't have lifted, the world still dim and dripping. With Bristol and Kitty by her side, I imagined Mom would quietly walk down the worn path to the shabby barn, as she did every morning.

Her cheerful greeting would break the silence as the goats and chickens mixed inside the single pen. "Good morning, my friends!" she'd say, walking around the fenced area, pushing open the rickety doors, setting down the bucket, and opening a fifty-pound bag of chicken feed. Cobwebs would hit her face as she opened the side door, tossing the yellow kernels into the air. As they scattered onto the ground, the chickens would squawk and flutter toward their prize.

"There you go! Now be nice to each other." Returning to the barn, she'd grab an empty basket and head over to the chicken beds. Fresh eggs were nestled in the cozy straw nests, waiting to be harvested. She'd pick up the warm gifts, one at a time, carefully placing them into her basket. Then she'd scoop some grain from a bag of goat feed and dump it into the trough.

"Daisy! Daphne! Time to come inside, girls!" Her voice meant food and udder relief. They'd gallop down the slope, ears flopping, and follow her into the barn, anxious to be free of their heavy load. Mom would loosely tie both their necks to the rails with a heavy rope, allowing them to eat while she sat on top of a small wooden stool and readied the bucket. She'd gently pull down on one of the teats and with her other hand, pull down on the other. After a few firm thrusts, warm milk would begin to flow, and she'd continue the motion until both teats were cleared of the sweet liquid. A honey-like scent would fill the soggy barn. Once Daisy was finished,

Mom would move on to Daphne and began the same exercise. Rewarded with a full bucket of milk, she'd set it to the side and release her friends back to the pasture.

Walking back into the barn, she'd pull half a bale of fresh timothy hay from a high stack. She'd shake her head as stray reeds would fall into her face and onto her hair. Tripping over the flock of chickens, she'd reach the fence and toss the straw over, calling for the long-haired beasts.

"Woop! Woop! Rosemary!" This would bring three enormous animals sauntering up the hillside—horns first. Swaying back and forth, they'd march up the hill to the food.

"Good girls," she'd praise them and return to the barn for her morning bounty.

Once back inside our house, Mom would pour the raw milk into a large glass jar and set it and the eggs in the refrigerator. Over the course of the day, the cream would naturally begin to separate from the milk, leaving a thick layer at the top of the bottle.

With the housework and farm taken care of, my mother would circle her attention back to her other job: tending the vineyard. Like us kids, the vines were growing and demanded constant care and attention. They never gave her a break. She would spend the rest of the day minding the twelve acres.

While I spent my day managing to avoid a verbal pop quiz in math class, back at home, Mom would set out for another day of physical labor. She'd grab her gloves and a short apron with plastic ties stuffed in its pockets. She'd tug at the irritating front door and call to her loyal coworker.

"Come on, Bristol! There's lots of work to do."

The morning sun would begin to break through the clouds as she'd sit on the concrete step to put her leather boots back on. Lacing them up, she'd quietly hum "I Am Woman" by Helen Reddy as our black cat would rub against her knee. With her apron tied, she'd take the hoe near the front door and head out to the open field of vines. The lingering dew on the young plants made them sparkle in the early light. She'd take a deep breath, appreciating the beauty while also considering the amount of work that remained. Walking through the vineyard, she'd try to locate where she left off from the previous day.

By now, the growing vines needed support. Mom would use a plastic tie to secure the main cane at the base of each post. As she worked along, she'd use her hoe to knock away the growing weeds around the plant since the cartons had been pulled, no longer needed. She brought along her small transistor radio for the solitary work, setting it on an end post, and would sing along with "It's Too Late" by Carole King or "Song Sung Blue" by Neil Diamond. She'd work down a row until she couldn't hear the music, then walk back to collect the radio and start again. Bristol and Kitty would keep her company along the way.

By three in the afternoon, she'd spot us shuffling down the road from the bus stop. Waving from the middle of the field, she would smile and walk out of the young vineyard.

"Hi, guys. How was school?"

"It was okay. How did you do today?"

"Good. I got quite a few rows done. There's so much more to do!" She wiped her forehead with the back of her hand and grabbed her hoe. "But we're getting there." Her smile remained, but I noticed her concerned glance at the vines as we walked back to the house. I felt bad knowing she needed help.

How was she ever going to keep up?

NEW HOME

My father had committed nearly every weekend over the past several months to finishing the house. By the time school was over in June of 1973, it was done. At least, it was done enough. Like most of the other projects on the farm, the construction site had become another part of the landscape. In fact, we often forgot it was even there. Pop would disappear every Saturday morning, and we would forget about the whole thing, so it came as a bit of a surprise when he finally announced we could sleep in our new home. The first overnight was spent with all five of us in sleeping bags on the wooden floor in the main room. I remember it being an adventure, and I was thrilled to be moving into a new place. The large space felt grand after being under the low ceilings and crowded spaces of our previous little home.

The next morning, Mom started hauling over the unpacked boxes. I recognized them as the ones that had been tucked away in the enclosed sun porch for the past years. We finally had room for all our belongings. Mom was especially elated to place many of them into our brand-new kitchen. Pop designed this communal space to have one large built-in table, which immediately became the center of our lives. The open shelves allowed Mom plenty of room for her cherished bulk items: polenta, lentils, and Arborio rice. She chose to store these items in large glass jars, along with the essential wheat germ, flax, and pumpkin seeds. She beamed with pride—her raw ingredients were now on display.

The living room was surrounded by windows designed to capture the rare beams of light that made their way through the valley's heavy clouds. The southern view behind the house framed gentle rolling hills patterned by fir trees, cherry orchards, stretches of berry fields, green pastures, and a century-old farm. A small woodstove that Pop had made from some stray sheet metal sat in the middle of the large living space, creating a division between the sitting area and our dining room. Our new dining table sat in front of a large picture window with a prominent view to our young vineyard just yards from the house. The vineyard provided a gentle break from the world beyond. It became increasingly appropriate as the years passed, making it not only physically impossible to separate from the subject of grapes and wine, but also socially and culturally impossible. This was the topic of nearly every dinner conversation. It had become the focus of our lives.

At the other end of the house, past the open kitchen and down a short hall, a wooden door opened into my parents' bedroom and bathroom. Here, they splurged and installed a tiny sauna across from the shower. I learned that while building the house, Pop discovered an unused open space just large enough for such an amenity. I thought it was odd and tried to avoid imagining my parents sitting in there naked, as that's what I heard people did in those things.

My parents' full-sized bed sat directly on the floor since a bed frame was considered unnecessary. More importantly, tall bookshelves lined both walls and were instantly filled with their hundreds of books. The ones that didn't fit were stacked in disorganized piles on the floor, including Mom's favorite paperback mysteries and numerous copies of *Farmers' Almanac*. I often wondered if they actually read all those books because I couldn't understand how they ever found the time.

The best part of the new house was upstairs. In fact, to simply have an "upstairs" was pretty incredible. Here were our semiprivate bedrooms, a bathroom, and a dedicated room to watch television. We couldn't believe it at first—an entire room built for television viewing! This was progressive for the 1970s, but especially for our bohemian lifestyle. My parents had upgraded the black-and-white set to a thirty-five-inch full-color screen that sometimes broadcast up to three channels. Our TV almost made us normal, but it was still only available after dinner and only for an hour a day. There were a lot of rules surrounding the television.

The three of us kids shared a bathroom equipped with one small sink and a walk-in shower. We were supposed to be quick, allowing the next person to get in and out, but with two girls and one boy it didn't always work out that way.

Each of us had a small bedroom and closet, which we were thrilled about as this was a huge upgrade for us. But they weren't exactly private. Only Michel's room had a door. Not only did he get a door, but it had a lock. For Luisa and me, however, Pop had designed our rooms to open along a single hall. I heard he wanted to keep the area spacious. He didn't consider how girls need privacy, or perhaps he did and wanted to ensure we didn't have any. I never figured it out.

Cleverly, my father had provided each room with a built-in bunk bed, using the space underneath as the closet space for the adjacent room. He built each of us a heavy wooden ladder that leaned against a large bulletin board below the bed. This was a favorite part of my new room, as I could pin miscellaneous cards and inspiring items on it.

Getting to my room meant walking past Luisa's unkept domain. I found it nearly impossible most days as her floor was covered with dirty clothes, books, and other random items that had been pushed out into the common narrow hall. I preferred to keep things tidy, and I couldn't understand how she could live in such mess. Surprisingly, it never bothered her unless she was forced to clean up, which would take an entire day—or two.

The truth was Luisa couldn't keep up with all her interests. She loved starting a new activity and digging into it wholeheartedly. In contrast, I kept projects to a minimum and ensured they were completed before starting anything new. For her, the more going on, the better. She especially loved to read, and a book was almost always in front of her face. It was as if she couldn't hear or see anything else when she opened the pages. When we couldn't find her, she was hiding in her bunk, devouring an Archie comic or a *CRICKET Magazine*. In her teenage years, she chose to read poetry or some classic like *War and Peace*. I wouldn't have managed the first chapter without falling asleep. I envied her ability to block out everything around her and give complete focus to her curiosities. That was not me. I was an observer, sensitively aware of other people and their needs and concerned with what was happening next.

In contrast to Luisa's space, mine was a calm oasis. Just weeks after moving in, I realized the lack of privacy was going to be an issue that needed to be resolved. When I learned Pop had no plans to install doors, it was clear it would be up to me to fix the problem. Fortunately, I could sew. I begged Mom to take me to buy two queen flat sheets, one twin flat sheet, and a couple of matching pillowcases. I chose a cheerful blue vintage floral print. When we got home, I pulled out our 1956 Singer and sewed the two sheets together to create one huge panel. Mom generously bought me a large rod that when extended would span the open hall. I threaded the rod through the enlarged sheet and hung it up, instantly separating my room from the common space. It was fantastic! I cut and hemmed the twin sheet into two and glued these panels to cover my closet doors, which were previously just sheets of plywood. The finishing touch was the set of fresh pillowcases, which I switched out from the plain white ones. Everything now matched with my cherished new door. At last my room was in order, and most of all, I had real privacy. It was perfect!

Each bedroom had a large picture window facing south. I loved how the sunlight spilled into my room during the day, framing the view back to the Scholls valley. At night, I watched the traffic flow on Scholls-Sherwood Road, and I'd follow the cars' headlights until they put me to sleep. During the day, the view allowed me to daydream. From my perch on my bunk bed, I often just stared out those windows to the sky and down to the stream below, recognizing our quiet isolation and dreaming of what life was like beyond our secluded world.

My father built small desks at the end of each bed. This tucked-away place became my favorite spot. I'd go here to hide from the work outside, write in my journal, or craft letters to my pen pals and cousins. I collected all types of cards and notepads and dreamed that one day I would design a line of stationery. While Michel found his solace playing the piano and Luisa found hers reading her many books, I found mine writing at my quiet desk.

LIKE MINDS

It had been about five years since our move to Oregon and, despite people snickering and telling us we should pack up and go back to California, a few folks shared in our dream. They, like us, were assumed to be nuts, were told they had it all wrong, were called drunks and hippies, and were considered fools. They heard the same sentiments about the "too-wet, too-cold" climate and hadn't cared. My parents realized that many of these progressives shared their same spirit of adventure, respect for the earth, and living off the land.

Furthermore, I learned many of them had little at stake, like us. They were smart, young, and ambitious and weren't afraid of taking risks. It seemed they shared my parents' values that anything was possible if you worked hard and did your research. It was the early 1970s, and the country was restless. You could sense it from the daily news. Many Americans were resisting current cultural standards and seeking new paths. Some of these determined adventure seekers shared my parents' love affair with Pinot Noir and made their way to the unknown Willamette Valley. Most were completely unaware there were other like-minded folks until they arrived here.

One of my parents' closest comrades remained one of the most driven and eccentric: Chuck Coury. He was the guy we met years earlier in Forest Grove. He showed up at our place quite often, and every time he did, it was unsettling.

He walked with a swagger and always carried a lit cigarette between his lips. His loud, gruff tone voiced strong opinions that were definitive and unsympathetic. He rarely smiled, but when he did, it was accompanied by a deep chuckle. Coury was incredibly intense; nothing was light and easy. Unlike many of the others who visited, this man never seemed to notice us kids. I got the feeling he thought we didn't matter much, which was contrary to the way Mom and Pop involved us in everything they did. Without a greeting, he'd stride inside the house to discuss his singular interest: Pinot Noir. He was captivated by it. His always-present cigarette smashed between his lips as he enthusiastically spoke. I couldn't help but associate his intolerable nicotine habit to his abrasive manner. But Pop and Chuck spent a lot of time together, and my father seemed to truly admire him. I guessed his passion made up for his bad behavior.

I much preferred his short, curvy, and bubbly wife, Shirley. She was the exact opposite of her husband, always taking time to acknowledge Luisa, Michel, and me with an inviting smile and hug. She was warm and engaging and shared many interests beyond wine. Her main activity was updating the old farmhouse on their property. She was particularly involved with the interiors, which always sparked my curiosity. Her style choice was daring, and she selected brilliant blues, yellows, and oranges in varied patterns for pillows in her kitchen nook. I was enraptured by the vibrancy they brought to the otherwise gray scene outside the walls. I loved her spirit and found her creativity inspiring.

But there were others. Even without cellphones or the internet, my parents managed to meet a handful of folks in the valley who were planting vineyards and had an interest in making wine. We learned many of them had things in common with us. First, nobody had any experience farming, especially with wine grapes, and only a couple of them had winemaking experience. Secondly, everybody was completely consumed with the Pinot Noir grape and had little interest in any other variety. Thirdly, they were motivated by the sense of adventure rather than financial gain. But lastly and perhaps most audacious of all was the belief that some of the world's best wine could be made here despite the obvious shortcomings. Of course, the whole thing seemed ridiculous to me. But since I was under the age of ten, what did I know? Nobody was asking, and I really didn't care.

The initial gatherings of the "Pinot Obsessed" began in the early 1970s. One of the very first was held in our new home. The three of us kids had no idea what was going on, but were asked to go to bed early.

"Good night, my jewel," Pop whispered as he kissed my cheek one evening, tucking me into bed. He wrapped the blankets tightly around my legs and feet. "We have a meeting tonight, but it shouldn't last too long. Try to get some sleep."

"Okay. Good night, Pop," I said, watching from my bunk as he thumped down the stairs to the living room. The chimes of the grandfather clock at the foot of the staircase struck eight and echoed throughout the house. Moments later, as I lay in bed waiting to drift off, headlights began to flash across my bedroom wall. I watched as more lights bounced over my head, and I heard tires grinding on the gravel driveway as guests began to park in front of the house. Heavy car doors slammed, and chatter and laughter broke the evening's silence. Bristol barked as guests approached the front door.

"Hello, hello!" Mom opened the front door. "How are you? Come in!"

"Hi, Nancy," I overheard Lett's wife, Diana, say. I recognized her seductive Southern accent. "We brought a couple baguettes, some cheese, and a couple of our latest bottles to taste."

"I'll get some glasses. Come in!"

The Letts' bottles would not be the only wine tasted that night. Each guest came armed with at least two or three bottles for the occasion. Instead of sleeping, we heard glasses clicking, corks popping, and people talking and talking and talking. Discussions broke into laughter, followed by more chatter. Listening with irritation, I wondered how people could talk so long about one thing and why they had to be so loud about it. It was hard to make out the conversation, but once in a while there was a break in the ruckus, and I could overhear them.

"Hey, Dick, did you get that disc working? I could really use it this weekend." I recognized Myron's voice. An iconic hippie, Myron Redford was tall, skinny, and long-bearded. He won the prize for having more hair than any of the other guys. He had a level of intensity and curiosity not easily disguised and often asked the toughest questions. Unlike most of the others, Myron seemed less caught up with creating an image for himself and was instead more interested in getting things done right. He had come from Seattle and landed thirty minutes south of Dundee in a one-stop town called Amity.

His mother helped finance a seventy-acre property there that already had ten acres planted in wine grapes by its previous owner. The initial plantings began in 1970, but Myron didn't get ownership of the land until four years later, and by that time, it was so neglected, it was home to acres of well-established weeds and blackberries. Only if one looked very carefully would they find a few sad grape plants hidden among the brambles. It was a mess.

Instead of bulldozing the unkept vineyard, Myron and his partner at the time, Janice Checcia, took it upon themselves to restore it, plant by plant. Digging through the knee-high grasses and tough weeds, they would search for a stake signifying where a plant should be, and if they found one, they'd determine whether or not it was alive or had any chance of survival. If it did not, they would pull and replace it with a healthy cutting. It was a painstaking project. A year later, they realized half their vineyard died regardless of their nurturing and care, whether it was a new planting or an original one. Unshaken, the couple continued to farm their land and was determined to make wine from it.

"Yes," Pop replied. "The disc works great. You're welcome to it."

"What do you think, Chuck?" I listened as Erath started in on his observation of one of the wines. "I think this has potential." At six foot four, Dick Erath had a brawny build and commanding walk that tended to conflict with his amiable smile and easygoing character. He shared Pop's balance of intensity with a laid-back approach to life. He also shared my father's background in engineering and had been raised by immigrant parents. Erath was experimenting with Zinfandel and Cabernet at his home in Walnut Creek, California, when he enrolled for enology classes at UCD and met acclaimed vintners Louis Martini and André Tchelistcheff. This experience inspired him to dive into winemaking as a profession.

His UCD classmate Richard Sommer shared Oregon's potential for grape growing. Sommer was a quiet rebel, a small-framed man with beady eyes who always wore a beret.

After being drafted in the Korean War, Sommer returned to the States in the late 1950s, joining his mother in Ashland, Oregon, with plans of growing grapes in the fertile Umpqua Valley. In 1960, he planted the state's first Pinot Noir and Riesling on an old turkey farm west of Roseburg and released the 1967 HillCrest Vineyard's Pinot Noir a year later. This made it Oregon's first commercial post-Prohibition wine and Oregon's first Pinot Noir.

After school, Erath heard through Sommer that Coury and Lett had headed up to Oregon with dreams of making wine there. He called on Coury while in the valley to interview for a position at Tektronix. In the summer of 1967, they met up at Coury's place and discussed winemaking incessantly and drank wine until four a.m. The next morning, Erath decided to take the engineering job and plant some grapes.

By 1968, Erath moved his wife, Kina, and their two sons to a logger's cabin in Dundee and began his search for the perfect piece of land. He eventually selected fifty acres and told his work friends if they helped him clear the walnut trees, he would compensate them with wine and burgers. They agreed.

With thirty-five acres cleared, he began planting his first four acres. After surviving heavy rains, a frost, and invading twig borers from the original timbered walnut trees nearby, Erath celebrated his first harvest in 1972.

That night, Coury replied, "I agree. It has those beautiful earthy characters. I love the bright cherry notes. I think there is something very special here. I just know it."

Lett chimed in. "Yes, I think over time, this wine could really develop into something quite spectacular. Let's try it against the Cotes de Nuits-Saint-Georges."

With Mom's lavish platters of sliced homemade bread, brie, and apples on the candlelit table, the comfortable ambiance encouraged the company to stay for hours. I slowly drifted off to sleep while the enthusiastic crowd lost themselves in conversation. I envisioned all the arms stretched across the table grabbing bread, cheese, and another bottle to taste. The slurping and swirling and spitting into various vessels went until late into the night. As the fog nestled up against the large glass windows, the group of young winemakers were completely unaware of the hours passing as they huddled together, sharing a mutual love for the Pinot Noir grape and dreams of what could be. They were wine revolutionaries.

I later learned that ten or so of those passionate individuals wedged around that vibrant table were the original members of the Oregon Viticulture Development Committee. Although these were casual gatherings, a lot of important things happened whenever the group met. This small collection of dreamers was developing an understanding of the Pinot Noir varietal and how they wanted to develop the wine. It was not a competition, but rather an exploration. The discussions surrounded wine styles, flavors, and characteristics as they tasted hundreds of Burgundies. There was constant talk about the similarity between the Willamette Valley and that of Burgundy. Although they boldly voiced their opinions on the varietals, those who had already made wine—Lett, Coury, and Erath in particular—shared their initial winemaking findings. They were constantly offering their support and whatever meager resources they had: tools, books, or labor. They were more than willing to help each other on this shared journey.

I sensed at times the conversations becoming quite serious. For example, I overheard how Coury, Erath, and Lett lobbied the Oregon legislature against allowing grape vines into the state without the plants being virus free. There was great concern over the possible spread of phylloxera, which was notorious for destroying many great European vineyards at the turn of the century. The louse was causing the same destruction in

California vineyards. There were many conversations around the table about creating "clean clones" instead of taking cuttings from California grapes. Coury and Lett were so serious about this that they established a nursery where they could produce protected vinifera clones for the fledgling industry.

It was also apparent how much the wine group wanted to preserve the pristine farmland. They felt the hillsides and its fertile soil were precious resources that needed to be protected. In 1973, many of them helped support Senate Bill 100 forcing cities and counties to meet mandatory state standards and planning goals dealing with land use, development, housing, transportation, and the conservation of natural resources. They obviously had their eye on the future.

THE BIRDS

It was a sunny April day with brilliant blue skies, and I had just celebrated my ninth birthday. That made it five years since we'd started this winegrowing thing. As the three of us made our way up to the bus stop that morning, we passed the vineyard on our left, as we did each day. But that day, I looked closer and noticed a change. There was life in the field. For the first time, the tender young vines had finally stretched themselves up above the main wire and were gripping on to the wire trellis. I could see tiny, rosy-pink buds on some of the canes.

"Look!" I said to Michel as he walked ahead of me, his head down to protect his hair from the annoying drizzle.

"What?" he replied, irritated.

"Look at the little vines. Look how much they've grown and look at the cute baby buds! I wonder if we'll get grapes this year."

"Yeah, maybe." He seemed more concerned with how to avoid the rain and keep himself warm. Maybe because it was my birthday, and I was unusually spirited, I found myself slightly excited as I spotted the newborn pink-and-white flowers presenting themselves among their delicate green leaves.

For the first time, there was something colorful among the mass plantings of brown canes.

By the time school ended that June, the fresh buds had transitioned into tiny grapes. I thought the chartreuse baby clusters were adorable. Their bright-green tendrils coming from the tight bunches were so delicate, and apparently delicious, as we started to see deer move through the vineyard. It was now common for us to spot entire families feeding in the rows. I loved watching them graze in our front yard, happy they chose our safe home.

It seemed that my parents didn't share my view. That summer was our most important season, marking the final months of growth before our first harvest. It was critical we did all we could to produce fruit this year. Mom seemed particularly anxious, as she had been so dedicated to readying the plants for harvest: pruning, tying down, and training the vines all year. As soon as school was officially over, we received marching orders.

"Okay, guys. Here's the deal," Mom started as we sat around the kitchen table finishing up our last bites of boring oatmeal. I brushed my bare feet across Bristol's soft coat beneath my chair. His thick hair always warmed up my cold feet.

"Oh, Mom," we all grumbled.

"Can we just relax for a few days? It's summer! Maybe we could watch *Gilligan's Island* or *The Brady Bunch*?" I pleaded. It was my attempt to remind her what other kids got to do when school was out.

"Ha!" She laughed, quickly shrugging off my suggestion. "So, we need each of you to go and scare the robins and deer out of the vineyard this morning. As you know, we're planning to harvest this year, so it's important we protect the fruit."

"How are we supposed to do that?" asked my brother.

"With pots and pans." She pulled out her largest sauté pan and a lid from the kitchen drawer, setting them on the counter. She continued to pull other pots from the kitchen cupboard, then selected spatulas and wooden spoons of various sizes from the drawer. We stared at our mother, trying to figure out her unusual behavior.

"Okay, so once you get changed for the day, I want you to take a couple of these things and go outside and make some noise." We stared at her with our sleepy eyes.

"Now, clean up the kitchen, and I'll see you out there." She grabbed the largest pan and a wooden spoon and headed for the door. Sitting down on the concrete porch, she laced up her hiking boots and walked straight into the vineyard, shouting and clanking the steel equipment together.

"Shoo, shoo, shoo now," she called out. "Get now. Go on." Birds began to fly out of the vines, landing in the neighboring firs and poplar trees along the driveway.

"There we go," she said, satisfied, and turned back to us watching her from the front door. "See!" she shouted. "Now you guys get out here and try it." We looked at each other, rolling our eyes. Luisa and I started cleaning the dishes as Michel petted Bristol, all of us reluctant to start the day of work.

Several minutes later, we had grabbed our pot or pan of choice, a lid or large wooden spoon or spatula, and found ourselves marching up the road, shouting, "Shoo, birdies, shoo now!"

I'm so glad we don't have neighbors. Only at my house would this happen.

This technique was only a temporary solution. As soon as we went indoors, the flocks returned. Other measures were necessary. Since Pop wasn't a gun-owning type, unlike some of the other vineyardists, shooting the problem was never an option. Instead, he read about other ways that might prevent fruit damage and loss. He learned how birds of prey were often used in vineyards to frighten away smaller birds. Since most of the birds attacking our vines were migrating robins, he decided to give this method a try. So, he bought a kite. A hawk kite.

The toy became Michel's new job. For the following two weeks, he tried to keep the enormous contraption in the air despite the lack of wind. He would take off with the kite in one hand and slowly let it unravel from its spool as he raced several yards down the vineyard road. As Michel ran faster, he occasionally lifted it slightly but only for seconds before it crashed to the ground, nose-diving into the dirt. He'd retrieve it, straightening the line along the ground, and then run a few more hundred yards down the opposite direction. Unfortunately, he never found a strong flight path, and sprinting back and forth got exhausting.

My father's next big idea was to purchase a real bird of prey: a falcon. Finally, a pet of significant purpose. Pop and Michel worked together to build a large cage for the new addition to our family just outside the garage. Mom took Michel with her to pick out the bird, and when they got home, Pop helped to tie a long string from one of the bird's claws onto a glove Michel wore on his right hand. My brother carefully held on to the bird as they walked out into the vineyard. At twelve years old, he had hands that didn't fit the adult-sized glove very well.

With Michel eagerly following Pop's directions, his sights were set on becoming the hero of bird control. He stopped in the middle of the vineyard and slowly removed his grip on the falcon, stroking it while lifting his right arm into the air, inviting the bird to fly. However, as the falcon began its ascent into the air, so did the loose-fitting glove. By the time Michel realized what was happening, the glove and the bird had both slid off his hand. Away the falcon flew, high above Michel, soaring with grandeur over the vineyard. The glove dangled beneath its body. My brother just stood there with a look of complete astonishment. Another flawed plan.

Determined, Pop continued to pursue his goal of preventing birds and wildlife from stealing his first crop. In another book, he read how in cool wine regions like Alsace and Germany farmers practiced the technique of netting vineyards. Many believed covering each side of the vines with black plastic netting would prevent hungry wildlife from getting to the valuable fruit. One day, he came home with a load of this plastic mesh in the back of his truck. I had no idea how horrible it was going to be. Once parked in the front of the house, he started pulling out several dowels of the black, wiry mesh.

"Come on, help out!" he shouted. I had hoped he hadn't seen me tucked behind one of the poplar trees. Michel and Luisa hopped off their bikes.

"What's this stuff, Pop?" I slowly walked toward the truck.

"Fruit protection." He smiled. "Can you grab an end?"

I pulled one end of a heavy dowel off the bed of the truck as my father guided it on the other side. We walked a few hundred yards to the vineyard and set it down carefully. Luisa and Michel joined us. After several trips, we had created a stack of black rolls near the edge of the vineyard.

Pop went to get more help and left us staring at our new project. Michel had his hands behind his back, mine were in my pockets, and Luisa crouched down as she petted Bristol. It was quite evident none of us were too eager to assist. *What was this all about?*

A few minutes later, we heard the rumble of the tractor. Pop pulled up, hopped off the rusty machine, and left it running.

"Okay, let's load 'em up!" he barked.

After all the heavy dowels were set on the tractor forks, Pop asked his son to jump into the driver's seat and take the load to the end of the vineyard road. My father walked behind with Luisa, me, and Bristol. We walked to the very last row, which was rare.

Michel turned off the tractor and jumped down. He and Pop grabbed the first dowel and turned it on its end. Leaning it vertically against the first post, Luisa and I were instructed to walk down one side of the row, pulling the heavy five-foot-high cylinder along with us. Luisa took one end and I held the other. The material struggled to unravel as we tried to move forward, and it took all our strength to spin the heavy roll. It constantly fell onto the ground and got caught in the tall grass. We had to stop and clean it off and try again. It was a long and arduous process. The thin plastic mesh cut into our tender hands, and our fingernails snagged on the awful material.

This was definitely another bad idea.

After completing the first step of unraveling the netting, we were then supposed to pull it up to the trellis wire to cover the entire vine. The vines had grown above our heads, and Pop soon realized this would be an impossible task for our small arms. Instead, he instructed us to just protect as much of the plant as possible. We used short wire ties, similar to what you'd get it if you bought sliced bread at a normal market, and connected the netting to the trellis. Stopping every three feet, at the bottom and at the top of the mesh, we twisted the wires as one of us tried to hold the mesh on to the trellis wire. It was difficult and took us hours to cover just one side of a row. Michel and Pop worked on the opposite side of us at a quicker pace. It was easy for Pop to realize they'd have to finish the project as Luisa and I simply didn't have the strength or height. The following month was consumed with installing the netting. It was the worst.

Weeks later, after watching a swarm of birds fly into the vineyard, I was curious to see if any of our work paid off. Mom and I hiked down a row together. Glancing at the vines, we spotted a bird's nest that had been skillfully constructed just inside the netting, right next to the plant. It looked like we'd successfully created a safe place for the hungry bird to live in the middle of grape heaven. No longer did the birds have to fly in and out for the fruit; they could live permanently in luxury accommodations. I giggled, thinking how wise the birds were and how silly we humans were. Defeated again.

Mom grumbled over another failed attempt at protecting our precious grapes, and I feared the inevitable, knowing at some point we'd be told to bring all that netting down.

My parents continued to investigate options for frightening away the birds and deer. In one of Pop's books he read about the use of a propane cannon. A loud blast from this machine could be programmed to go off every three to seven minutes to disrupt the birds. It sounded like a reasonable solution. Pop made another purchase and positioned one of the cannons in the middle of the vineyard. Every five minutes, a blast would thunder through the vines, and starlings would suddenly fly to the surrounding fir trees. They'd nestle there for a few moments, munching on fresh berries. When finished, they would fly back into the grapes for more. This rather comic routine went on all day. Every five minutes: blast, retreat, and return. Out of all the methods we tried, even though it wasn't perfect, this one seemed most effective. At least we didn't have to go out and bang pots anymore.

TREASURE HUNT

I heard birds singing outside my window when I woke to another day of summer. My eyes opened to the familiar view of the valley, and my parents' voices carried up the stairs from the open kitchen. Even though I couldn't make out their words, knowing they were up and in the house was comforting and meant breakfast. I climbed down from my bunk, feeling the cold wood steps of the ladder against my bare feet until I touched the carpet. I didn't sense the usual bustle of activity either inside or outside the house. It was a rare feeling.

I found Mom and Pop sitting at the kitchen table with their coffee and newspaper covering the entire surface.

Mom looked up. "Good morning, honey."

"Morning." I slid down into an empty chair next to my father. "What's happening today?"

"Would you like to run an errand with me?" Pop folded his newspaper in half and looked at me, finishing up his last sip of coffee.

"Sure. What are you doing?" I felt fortunate to be the first one up, stealing Pop's full attention. Whatever he was going to do would be fun, because he made it that way. The simplest errand usually turned into some kind of an adventure, and I was always up for that.

"I'll explain later. Get some breakfast, then meet me at the truck." He left the table as I took a bowl of fresh granola, adding a spoonful of honey for a touch of sweetness and a large scoop of my mother's homemade yogurt. I rushed through the bowl and tossed back a glass of goat's milk and patted Bristol's fluffy head, and then I was off to join Pop in the banana truck.

He smiled at me with a twinkle in his eye. "Okay! Let's go."

"So, where are we headed?"

"Well, we're going on a little treasure hunt." He turned the key, and we were soon bouncing down the dirt road.

About fifteen minutes later, we pulled off the highway into a wrecking yard near Tualatin. We parked in front of acres of junk. Enormous piles of scrap metal and smashed cars balanced on top of each other were stretched out as far as I could see. I found it a bit creepy to see so many destroyed vehicles and tried not to think of the people who probably didn't survive those accidents.

Pop seemed less impressed as we headed into the mountains of steel and sheets of used metal. I followed him around, wondering what he was looking for among all this garbage. It was such a strange place.

I bet nobody else spends their Saturdays walking around a place like this. Do normal people even know junkyards exist?

At least I wasn't waiting for him to find something at the Tigard plumbing store, which is where I thought we might be headed. This is where I often amused myself by meandering through the rows of merchandise, wondering who would ever buy a neon green toilet seat while my father looked for a fitting he referred to as either "male" or "female."

I almost got distracted peering at a smashed Fiat convertible when I spied Pop down a long stretch of scrap metal.

"Here! This is it!" In his hand was a large, smooth piece of metal. Obviously, this was exactly what he was hoping to find. He was beaming.

"It's perfect. This is great. Now I can get back to work." He grabbed his metal treasure with both hands, and we walked back to the cashier station together. Pop always made sure I was nearby and rarely walked in front of me unless he was after some treasure. After paying a few dollars for the find, we climbed back into the banana truck. I slammed the heavy door and slid in closer to Pop.

"So, what are you going to do with that?"

"It's for the destemmer I'm working on." I had no idea what he was talking about, but I didn't ask any more questions. It sounded boring.

"*Oh okay.*" I sat in silence, leaning my head up against his warm chest. He reached over and pulled me a little closer, pleased with his morning hunt.

"Just one more stop before heading home."

Petrich's General Store was a frequent destination. It was the only store in Scholls, a kind of community landmark, critical for nearby families, who often needed gas, milk, or animal feed. The original crumbling wooden stairs to the front doors were built right next to the busy highway. Whenever I walked up those stairs, I considered how neat it was that they were the same ones from a hundred years ago. They'd been on Scholls Ferry Road when horses used to pull carts from Kinton to Scholls to Newberg. The family store had been operating since 1918.

Petrich's was the best. My favorite part of the general store was their penny candy, conveniently located next to the register. The red gummy cinnamon bears, butterscotch, peppermints, and Smart Tarts always made my mouth water. Sometimes, Pop allowed Michel to get a large jawbreaker from one of the two large gumball machines, but I preferred the brightly colored gumballs.

Petrich's was the everything store. It served as the local pharmacy, grocery, feed, hardware, and plumbing supply store, all under one roof. Salsa was stocked next to the toilet paper, which was just around the corner from the chicken scratch, which was just down an aisle from the Coca-Cola and potato chips. Pop usually found what he was looking for at the rear of the store, hunting for a particular bolt, screw, washer, or some plastic fitting. I would stand in the aisle for what seemed like hours while he dug through small containers, searching for the right part. Our visits weren't specific to any single project, as we nearly always found ourselves there when we were on a treasure hunt. On this day, my father had selected a small handful of tiny screws for himself and a bright-blue gumball for me.

Arriving home, he immediately resumed work on his latest project. He wheeled out his trusty welding machine, put on his protective welding hat, and slid down the face shield to begin. I watched the first few minutes of sparks flying before I walked closer, hoping he'd notice me. He stopped and pulled back his mask.

"What are you making?"

"This is one of the most important pieces of winemaking," he began. "After we pick the grapes, we will need to crush them before the juice goes into the fermenter. But instead of mashing the fruit, I want to carefully shake the berries off the clusters, keeping the berries whole. I think if we do it this way, the wine will have better flavor."

"Why is that so important?" I asked, trying to sound curious only because he seemed so interested.

"You have to understand Pinot Noir," he patiently explained. "This grape is very, very delicate. In fact, it is one of the most fragile of all wine grapes. In order to get the best flavor from it, we need to treat the little berries like jewels—very gently, with respect." His face lit up as he spoke. I tried to understand his excitement but didn't get it.

What's the big deal about? Aren't they just grapes?

When he talked like that, I immediately thought of my Italian grandmother, Nonna, Pop's immigrant mother who had also relocated from Michigan to California, with her husband in the late 1960s. This second marriage was to an Eastern European, John Pondzo, who shared Nonna's lack of English. It made for an interesting union. Although she initially resisted leaving the Sunshine State following her husband's death, my parents encouraged her to move near us when they found a perfect little home in Hillsboro. It was conveniently located near the Catholic church and the town's modest Main Street. She never learned to drive, so this central location was ideal. Just fifteen minutes from our farm, she lived a simple life with her cherished dog, Skippy. The garden in her backyard was always full of fresh basil, ripe tomatoes, and a couple of plum trees. Her single lemon tree reminded her of sunnier days in California.

My grandmother, Nonna, was born in the States, but soon after her birth, her father died and she moved back to Italy with her mother. She was just sixteen years old when she returned to resettle in New Castle, Pennsylvania, where she met my grandfather. What followed were many difficult years of abuse and living off a meager income. Despite her daily struggles, she remained a devoted mother. She was committed to raising healthy children, which included lots of chicken soup and a good dose of castor oil for each boy every Sunday morning.

Nonna spoke with a very strong Italian accent and showed her love through a firm hand holding your wrist and quick slaps on the top of your hand if you touched food she prepared before it was ready. She rarely smiled, but when she did, her dark-brown eyes softened, and the single black mole near her mouth curved up. Her smile often broke into laughter, and in those rare moments, you could sense a joyful spirit. I imagined her as a free-spirited person whose challenging past forced her to bury that characteristic. We recognized Nonna as a woman of strength, intensity, and tireless energy who offered straight-forward advice, but only when asked.

Hearing Pop talk about this Pinot Noir grape reminded me of how she talked about food. Whether she was making tomato sauce or kneading pasta dough, she was focused, precise, and serious. The food was very important.

"Letta it rest," she would say, placing the fresh pizza dough in a large ceramic bowl to let it rise for two hours. "Now doncha you touch it." She turned and looked right through me with her dark eyes. She had gently slapped my hand enough for me to know she meant it. She treated all her ingredients with respect and did not move quickly in the kitchen, but methodically and with purpose. Just like Pop. Now, I watched as he worked with the same concentration on his metal destemmer.

"Sounds neat, Pop." I gave him a hug from behind and walked away. This was all too common. My father was fully engaged in one of his many projects, and it was time for me to disappear. In his private world of discovery, he had the free-dom to do what he loved the most: taking an idea or being presented with a problem, then developing a solution and tweaking it until it was completely resolved. He was a master of problem-solving. He never rushed. Instead, his actions were thoughtful and deliberate.

FIRST HARVEST

All summer long, we watched as our precious Pinot Noir grapes transformed from tight green clusters to vibrant pink ones and then finally to small, deep-purple grapes. The clusters were beautiful, popping bursts of color from the otherwise massive backdrop of green leaves and brown canes. In contrast, the Chardonnay berries turned deep gold and developed larger clusters than the Pinot Noir. The other white grapes, all planted closest to the house, had ripened into varying shades of yellow and green. Only now did each plant reveal how they differed from each other.

By mid-September, about a week after we started school again, I noticed Pop heading into the vineyard early in the evenings after returning home from work. For the past two weeks, he had been armed with his refractometer, a tool I learned was used to check the grape's sugar content. I also noticed he would often pop a few berries in his mouth and spit out the seeds and skin. He explained to me that he could tell if the fruit was ready to pick by biting into them. If the seeds were still bitter, the grapes needed more time. The less bitter, the more mature the fruit. Unlike the cherished, huge green seedless grapes my mother forbade us to purchase due to California's Delano grape boycott, our little wine grapes were more about seeds than flesh. I realized this was probably why we were referred to as "winegrowers" instead of "grape growers," which always seemed odd to me. The abundance of seeds also prevented us from snacking on our crop.

By the end of September, Pop announced it was time to harvest our first crop. Of course, Mom was planning a large celebration to mark the occasion. I figured it was just another great excuse for her to have our friends over again, but as I learned more about what "harvest" meant, I realized it may have been because there really was no way the five of us could pick our entire vineyard before the rains came. We needed help.

Mom and I had created a special invitation, explaining what a grape harvest was, since nobody had ever heard of one. We told our friends they had to bring their pruning shears, wear work clothes and boots, and be prepared for the weather, most likely rain. We created a guest list, which included our closest friends, the Grimms and the Downs, whose large families would be key to the enormous task. Age didn't matter—the more hands, the better. In my mother's typical creative fashion, the printed invitation involved a poem pronouncing harvest as a symbol of life, the awakening of the land, and the importance of celebrating Earth's bounty with friends and family. I didn't grasp most of it, but thought the card was pretty since Mom had sketched a twisted vine on it. Once the date was announced and the invitation was printed, Luisa and I helped fold all thirty of them and walked the bundle to the mailbox.

The kitchen phone rang off the hook as our friends received their mail, thrilled to be invited to the inaugural affair. They all asked for more information on what to expect and how to prepare. Excitement ran through the house in anticipation of the big day.

I woke up early on the special Sunday. It felt like Christmas morning, as excitement had been building for weeks. Grandma and Grandpa were picking up Nonna in Hillsboro on their way out to the farm. As I made my way down the shag-carpeted staircase, I saw Mom already kneading a huge mound of dough on the kitchen table.

"Good morning, honey," she sang to me with her green eyes sparkling. "How did you sleep? Are you ready for today?"

"Yeah. I guess," I responded sleepily. I watched as she rolled out the dough, cutting it into long strips. She put her fingers in a small bowl of soft butter, scooping out the creamy substance and spreading it evenly across the thin sheets of dough. Her greasy hands reached for a cup of brown sugar, and she sprinkled it over the buttered layer of pastry. Next came a handful of chopped walnuts. She was making one of our favorite breakfasts: delicious sticky buns, a contrast to her otherwise healthy baked goods. *Yum!*

"Wow, you're sure making a lot of those, Mom." I noticed five large, greased pans waiting on the counter.

"Yeah, we're expecting a lot of people today. I thought it would be nice to bring fresh sticky buns and hot coffee into the vineyard for everyone." She smiled, making all her labor seem effortless.

"Sounds good." My lack of enthusiasm conflicted with Mom's abundant energy. It seemed like a lot of extra effort on an already busy day.

"Why don't you help Pop set up the wine table outside on the lawn?" As usual, she resumed her standard "get to work" approach. "We'll need plenty of glasses and some fresh flowers too."

As I headed out into the dark morning to find Pop, I heard the grinding of gravel in the driveway. It was only eight in the morning, but cars were already coming. Until then, the property had been completely still. The birds were still nesting in the firs, and a heavy dew sat on the vines. It was a typical Oregon morning. To think people would drive out this early, a thirty-minute trip from their comfortable city homes, seemed odd. Nevertheless, they began to unload from their vehicles with smiles planted on their faces, rubber boots on their feet, and shears in their hands. I was awestruck at their enthusiasm.

Mom asked me to show them where to pick while she and Pop continued to ready the grounds for the midday party that would follow the morning's picking. Michel fired up the tractor. He'd been assigned to haul the full boxes of grapes back to the garage. Luisa shadowed Mom in the kitchen. Once the sticky buns were in the oven, her next task was to make the tomato sauce so it could simmer all morning. Nonna had arrived and quickly became a fixture in the kitchen. She immediately tied on her apron and went straight to work mixing up another batch of dough for the pasta, placing heaps of flour into the center of the table. She used her hands to carve out a small divot in the middle of the flour and cracked several eggs in the center. She added some salt, then began to introduce the flour. Bringing the two ingredients together, she began to gently knead it with her strong hands as it slowly formed a mound. Once it was finished, the dough was placed into a large ceramic bowl, some olive oil was poured on top, and it was covered with a clean dishtowel.

It sat for two hours before Nonna returned to complete the steps. She rolled it out thinly and sliced it into narrow strips, using our well-worn pasta machine to create the noodles. Nonna spent most of the day in the kitchen, switching between pasta making to watching the tomato sauce simmer to helping

Grandma clean the pots, wipe down the counters, and sweep the floors. Like me, they always tried to minimize the chaos, especially on this day, as the kitchen quickly became crowded with curious guests gathering into the cozy place.

Mom had asked each of our guests to bring a dessert, which meant they all had to enter the kitchen upon arrival. Every group arrived at our front door with their sweet contribution, along with children, a random dog, wet rain jackets, and boots. It was a mess, but Mom loved it. She greeted each person with a smile and a hug. Always chatting, she'd effortlessly move to check the sticky buns in the oven, and when the yellow phone on the wall rang, she'd give directions while putting on another pot of coffee to brew. For me, the kitchen scene was too crazy, so I escaped to the vineyard and assumed my role of being a nine-year-old "row boss."

I approached a crowd of people chatting in the vineyard road.

"Hey, Maria!" Joan Grimm shouted to me. "Where do we get started?"

"Yeah, and how do you want us to do this anyhow?" her sister Sarah asked.

"Should we cut everything? Even the green ones?" Jeanne Roy asked thoughtfully.

"Is it okay if I start on this row?" Gloria Mathies politely asked.

Everyone was eager to jump in. They must have figured that since I lived on the property, I was the expert, even though this was also my first time picking grapes. Pop had shown me the day before how to gently hold the cluster and use my pruning shears to clip the green stem just above it, snapping the fruit off. He also explained if I pulled off some of the leaves, I could see the cluster more clearly, and how it was important

not to cut grapes that were underripe or damaged. Now I had
to explain all of this to the crowd.

"Okay," I began, "first, be careful you don't cut your fingers,
or your neighbor's fingers, because it's sometimes hard to see
through the vines. Also don't pick anything that is too small
or green."

"What about this?" Jere Grimm reached into the canopy
and opened it to show a small cluster about the size of an egg,
with mixed purple and green grapes.

"No. Don't pick that. Just the ripe ones. The dark-purple
ones." I thought that was obvious, but I realized they were taking the whole thing seriously, so I supposed I should too.

Michel brought out a bunch of wooden prune boxes with
the tractor and left them at the end of each row. Pop got a great
price on these small crates from a local cherry farmer and felt
they'd be perfect for collecting the grapes. I started handing
them out to the workers.

Sounds of the bustling vineyard began to echo beyond the
boundaries of our property. The stillness of the morning was
broken by shears snipping, people chattering, babies crying,
dogs barking, and the roar of the tractor engine. The sun was
just beginning to sift through the clouds.

About an hour into picking, the mist began to clear, and I
heard a squeaky, piercing sound coming from the far end of the
vineyard. I turned toward it, trying to make out what it could
be. Three old men in skirts, silhouetted against the dark mist,
were walking up a row. They marched together along the slight
incline, and as I looked closer, I could see they were each wearing a bagpipe. Everyone stopped working and left their places
to catch a glimpse of the captivating scene. They paraded up
and down the rows for about an hour, entertaining our hardworking guests. Mom never shared with us this little secret she
had planned for the crew.

By ten o'clock, the bustle had quieted to a soft murmur when I heard footsteps down the main vineyard road. I peered out beyond the end post to see Mom heading down the lane with her warm sticky buns tucked inside a beautiful basket tray. Luisa followed her, carrying two thermoses of coffee in her hands and a bag of paper cups under her arm. Bristol was at her heels.

"Oh, Mom. Those smell so good!" I jumped into the road to help.

It didn't take long for the crew to smell the freshly baked cinnamon and sugar, and work came to a quick halt. People flocked to the main vineyard lane, and their sticky, dirty hands reached out for the warm pastries.

"Oh my! So delicious!" exclaimed Erma, one of our eldest pickers. She had turned her prune box over and sat on its bottom. "Nancy! You are amazing."

Their filthy fingers didn't seem to bother our working friends as they sank their teeth into the delicate, sweet layers, washing the sugary, toasted walnuts down with strong coffee. Our harvesters were happy, and Mom was beaming with delight.

By noon, the sun was high in the sky, and our crew began to feel the heat as they crouched in the vineyard rows, snipping away. By now, most everyone had taken off their first layer, hanging sweatshirts and rain jackets on the top of end posts. Gloves came off and were left strewn on the ground. Pruning shears and paper cups had been discarded along the road. The youngest kids had left their work to chase each other around the lawn and play with the goats near the barn. Luisa and Mom had taken the empty baskets and thermoses back to the house to prepare for the next meal. I tried to rally some pickers to keep working, but it looked like I had lost most of them.

There were a few hearty workers who remained, as I heard the clipping of shears and the clusters being dropped into boxes. As I walked down the aisles of grapes, I noticed how picking methods varied from person to person, depending on age, height, and eagerness. Some people bent down from the waist, while others preferred to squat in front of each vine. But everyone took care with the fruit, placing each bundle gently into their wooden crates. I helped by carrying the thirty-pound containers to the end of each row, staging them for Michel to pick up with the tractor. Just after noon, most of the boxes were full, and Mom and Pop decided we should break.

"Time to come in, everyone!" Mom announced.

"Time for pasta!" Pop shouted into the rows.

I was struck with concern as I realized we had only picked about a third of the vineyard. I wondered how the rest of the fruit would be harvested since we had school the next day. I stayed in the vineyard, pulling various items off the end posts as the guests filed out and moved abandoned crates out of the rows. As I carried one last full box to the main road, I searched for Michel. If he didn't come soon, the birds would take away our hard work.

As I leaned against an end post waiting for him, I felt my body ache. I recognized the signs of physical labor. I had become familiar with how the soreness remained in my body throughout the night and into the following week, unwilling to wear off until the next weekend, when it would start all over again.

"Here you go!" I spied Michel. He climbed down and started loading the boxes onto the empty pallet on the back of our tractor. Then he hopped back on and drove down the main road, grabbing crates along the way. Once the tractor was fully loaded, he drove to the garage, where Pop was waiting.

"Right here." My father directed him to park near the front doors.

Pop and his good friend Ray leaned down to taste the grapes. "Hmm. Nice and sweet," Pop stated proudly.

"Yeah. Tasty, but lots of seeds," Ray agreed, as he spit some onto the ground.

Pop placed one crate upon a small wooden scale he'd borrowed from a nearby hazelnut farmer for the day's work. Michel checked the weight on the scale and wrote it down on a piece of paper attached to a clipboard. Then Ray removed the crate and carried it into the garage, where the crushing station was staged.

This was the heart of the operation; how we broke the berries was critical. My father emphatically believed this part of the process would determine the final quality of the wine. For the past several weeks, he had been tinkering with a used destemmer he'd purchased through a catalog. After researching all available home winemaking equipment, he determined the options were either too big or too small or would crush the fruit too much. The most common destemmer at the time was made by SIPI, an Italian manufacturer. The problem with the SIPI was that it was too expensive, and it wasn't made from stainless steel. As a solution, he ordered the smaller version, then used the stainless steel sheet from the junkyard, his welding, and some help from the machine shop at PCC, he repurposed it. He created an entirely new machine, perfectly adapted as he had envisioned.

Pop positioned his machine above a four-by-four plastic-lined tote. The totes were rented from maraschino cherry producers near Forest Grove. The boxes of grapes would be turned out on top of the plastic rollers that received the fruit, then the steel spokes below would separate the berries from the stems. All the stems and leaves caught by the spokes were funneled into a wooden crate, leaving only the remaining and most important ingredients: whole berries, seeds, and juice to flow down and collect into the plastic tote. Pop never lost his focus on this part of the process. It went on for decades. He continued to adapt and fine-tune this equipment nearly every vintage.

That day, though, each crate was weighed, then carefully moved atop his small contraption while he managed the amount of fruit and the speed of the machine. He analyzed each step as each box of fruit dropped from above.

"I think it's working pretty well," he observed. "But we may be crushing the fruit a bit too much. Hang on." He turned off the motor and used a wrench to loosen the rollers, creating less pressure on the berries. Ray and Michel resumed dumping the crates of grapes into the machine. Pop was constantly adjusting it, slowing down the speed of the motor, tapping the spokes inside, and opening or closing the rollers.

As each box of grapes moved through the destemmer, the plastic tote below began to fill, capturing the extract. The scent of fresh grape juice filled the garage, fleshy and sweet. The stems and leaves were tossed out, forming a large mound on the cold concrete floor. Luisa took a flat shovel and cleared the pile into another empty tote. The juice continued to flow into the half-ton fermenter.

While Pop was lost in the grape processing, Mom was focused on feeding our tired work crew. A large buffet table sat in front of our home, beautifully dressed in a bright red-and-white checked tablecloth with a large vase of happy sunflowers in the middle. Grandma placed a heaping basket of freshly baked bread on the table, and Nonna followed with her fresh pasta and delicious marinara sauce. The hot Italian sausages were presented on another enormous platter and were placed next to the sauce. A crisp autumn breeze carried the inviting aromas across the yard. Mom had prepared a huge salad from romaine and red leaf lettuce, lemon cucumbers, and heirloom tomatoes from her garden. Luisa garnished the salad with bright-yellow and orange nasturtiums. Everyone from the vineyard now surrounded the festive table, and a long line formed as the hungry workers waited patiently for their reward.

For our midday entertainment, Mom had asked a local guitarist and fiddler to perform. Without the means to pay for any of this entertainment, she enticed them with free wine and a hearty meal. They were as curious to join a "grape harvest" as the rest of the group and happily accepted. As the musicians played on our front porch, blankets were spread across our lumpy grass, dogs sniffed the open picnic, and jubilant families reveled in the festive scene.

Another small table was set next to the buffet, creating a kind of bar. It quickly appeared as though every single bottle had been opened and was being consumed by our friends, who began to dance on the lawn. There were half-empty glasses of wine sitting in the grass, on the porch, and in the hands of our joyful guests. The eating, dancing, and drinking lasted until late in the afternoon.

At last, the sun began to set over the top of our vineyard, signaling it was time for our friends to leave. I was relieved to see the last car finally drive away. But it wasn't over.

Before dark, I combed through the vineyard one last time and found abandoned jackets and hats, cutters, tissues, and paper cups littered among the rows. Unused boxes had to be collected and brought to the garage to be washed. On the lawn, the linens were pulled up, the vases put in storage, and the tables brought inside. Empty and partial cases of wine and dirty glasses were strewn all over the place.

I saw Nonna at the sink washing dishes when I stepped inside with an empty ice chest from the wine table. I set it down and crept behind her for a hug.

"Hi, Nonna."

She shook her wet hands and dried them on her apron.

"Oh, mya sweetie. That wasa lotta people. I tella-you itsa lotta works, this is. Itsa alotta work, this."

"I know, Nonna. I know." We understood each other.

The kitchen counters were piled with dirty pots, wooden spoons, and wineglasses. Leftover food covered the table without enough space left in the refrigerator. Grandma was mopping the hallway that was marked with dirty boots and dog tracks. The towels in my parents' bathroom were stained dark-purple and brown. Grandpa was taking full garbage bags outside. Our home was completely trashed.

Grandma joined us in the kitchen.

"How you doing, Maria?"

"Tired. That was a long day."

"Yes, it was." She nodded and started drying the clean pots.

The grandfather clock in the hall struck nine: bedtime.

I walked back over to the garage to say good night to Pop. There, I found more of the day's carnage: garden hoses with sprayer nozzles on the cold concrete among various sizes of plastic tubing, random buckets, and boxes. There was a layer of tacky juice and smashed grape skins under everything. My tennis shoes stuck to the floor as I passed trying to avoid puddles of water and discarded leaves. I found Pop standing in front of our fermenter of Pinot Noir. He was glowing with pride.

"You going to bed?"

"Yeah. School tomorrow," I said and leaned in for a hug.

He put his arm around me.

"Hey. Thanks for all your help today. It was fun, huh?"

I nodded slowly. *Sure.*

"We made two hundred and forty gallons of Pinot Noir. Our first wine!" he exclaimed.

"Yeah, that's great, Pop," I said, less than enthused.

"Well, good job, honey." He kissed me on the cheek. "I'll come up a bit later to tuck you in. Good night."

He turned back to his prized container of grape juice as I dragged myself back to the house. I gave Mom a kiss on the cheek as she continued to put food away. I dragged myself up the stairs and nestled under my warm comforter.

Finally done. This whole wine thing is exhausting.

WINEMAKING
101

Before heading out to teach class each morning, my father
would first duck into the garage to check on his project. He
had added some yeast he mail-ordered from a hobby winemaking shop in California, mixed it with some grape juice into a
small bucket, and then slowly added it to the fermenter. The
concoction would turn the juice into wine as the grape's natural sugar converted to alcohol. During this process, the juice
was integrating with the seeds and skins inside the fermenter.
I learned this was when the wine received most of its flavor and
color. It was called "cold maceration" and usually lasted about a
week. Pop explained it to me with the confidence of an expert,
but I was pretty sure he was just reciting from *Guidelines to
Practical Winemaking.*

In order to get deeper color and more intense flavor, Pop
had to move the skins and seeds around in the juice. He called
the top of the fermenter a "cap." The cap was where all the
skins and seeds floated together, creating a hard surface several inches thick. The tool he used to break the cap looked a

lot like a big toilet plunger. Walking around the two-foot-high fermenter, he raised the plunger into the air, then brought it straight down, using his strength to break through the tight layer of drying organic matter with the tool's round disc. He repeated this twice a day, once before heading to his real job in the morning and again when he got home each evening. He called it "punch down."

It seemed the sleepy tote was alive. Pop told me carbon dioxide was being released. All I understood was it was important to leave the door open for at least three weeks until the transformation was complete. Now it smelled like eggs in the garage.

My father regularly checked the sweetness by drawing a sample of the liquid into a narrow plastic beaker and dropping what looked like a big thermometer into it. He called this tool a hydrometer, and it gave him information on the sugar level as the juice transitioned into alcohol. He also monitored its temperature each day, as the juice naturally warmed up during the fermentation process. For the next couple weeks, Pop paid close attention to our little batch of wine, constantly tending to it morning and night.

Three weeks later, Pop determined the juice had finished fermentation. It was now officially wine. Pressing was the next step. A cap remained on the top of the fermenter, but it wasn't as tight as before. It was time to remove those skins and extract the wine from beneath and move it to barrels.

It was another Saturday without play as Pop gathered our motley crew of three into the garage. My hair was pulled back in its usual messy ponytail, and I was wearing a red-and-blue-striped T-shirt over a pair of khakis that were too short to reach my scuffed tennis shoes. My lack of interest would have been obvious as I stood next to Luisa and Michel, who had similar attitudes, waiting in the cold garage for instructions. I was pretty sure Luann was selling Girl Scout cookies in front of the grocery store. *Lucky.*

"It's a big day. Today we'll move the wine into barrels—and it begins with buckets."

My father leaned over the fermenter with a white five-gallon bucket, dug it into the mixture of juice and skins, and pulled it up, bringing with it heavy skins, seeds, and wine. He lugged it over to our small basket press. It was the same one we'd used to make wine in California. Pop had told me how he made this treasure entirely by hand. The slightly bent pieces of wood sat vertically, creating the basket. Each one of the staves had been hand cut and sanded to the perfect dimension. The two-inch steel bands wrapped around the wooden perimeter were hand-chiseled and rounded. Each and every screw and bolt had been meticulously handcrafted by Pop.

We all watched, but nobody moved. We were all thinking the same thing: *this is going to take forever.*

"Okay, Michel. Why don't you give it a try." Pop handed his son another bucket. Michel moved timidly, dipped the vessel into the vat, and managed to collect about four inches of material.

"Try harder," Pop directed.

Michel dug deeper into the bin and pulled out half a bucket. The purple wine dripped down the outside.

"There you go! Much better."

My brother lugged the juice over to the basket press. As he stepped up onto the couple wooden boxes Pop had stacked for us, he focused on the top of the press. He lifted the bucket above his chest and tipped it into the opening, spilling some wine outside of the wooden cage. I watched as more red juice dripped down the wooden staves and onto the concrete floor.

Then it was my turn. Michel handed me the sticky bucket. The wet handle stained my hand, and its cold metal roused me into work mode. I moved a bit faster than my brother, but with the same reluctance. When I pulled the bucket back up, the cold juice poured down my arm and under my sleeve. *Nice.* My bucket was about a third full, and I tried to balance it coming out of the bin. I felt the contents splash onto my pants as I hauled it over to the press, trying to stabilize the weight and walk at the same time.

"Good job, Maria," Pop encouraged.

My eyes were focused on reaching the press. *I really hate this.*

Once the press was full of skins and juice, Michel pulled slow and hard on its steel handle. He cranked down on the press, and its round metal plate met the skins, pressing the wine through the wooden staves. I watched as the liquid oozed through the smooth slats, holding back the used grapes while the wine dripped down through the trough and was captured beneath in a rubber basin. Instead of using a pump, Pop had simply attached some small PVC pipe to the basin and run it along the concrete floor, directing the tubes down the basement staircase to the dark cellar. He utilized gravity to move the wine into the few oak barrels we had stored below. Pop had been deliberate about this process to ensure it was as gentle as possible. A pump could have easily been attached to the hose, accelerating the movement and completing the task, but that wasn't his objective.

"Never rush the process," he'd say.

At the other end of the hose, Pop had attached an even smaller plastic tube with a valve at its opening to turn it off and on. After we dumped about ten or twelve buckets into the press, the process was complete, and the initial wine had been moved into one of the oak barrels. Pop was downstairs with the barrels.

"Hey, Maria!" He shouted from below. "I need you down here."

I stopped staring at my brother, who was staring at my sister, and followed his voice. As I stepped down the dark stairs, the warm sun disappeared behind me. I found Pop among our five empty barrels in the cold cellar. Each of these had been purchased from France, and I understood they were very expensive. Two heavy wooden beams were on the floor with a three-foot aisle in between them, and the barrels were arranged on top of the planks, turned onto their sides, each one open to the ceiling.

"Here you go." My father handed me a mini flashlight and two plastic tubes, one slightly larger than the other, and offered me confusing directions:

"Okay, so the wine will come through this large hose, so keep it in the barrel. With your right hand, shine this flashlight into the top of the barrel. Then take this," he said, holding a thin flexible tube about ten inches long. "Stick one end into your mouth, the other into the top of the barrel. You'll use both the flashlight and the tubing in your mouth to see how close the wine is to the top. Once you see the wine rising, keep the tube in the barrel and suck. When you taste wine, pull the main hose above your head. This will break the suction. If you don't raise it high enough over your head, the wine will continue to flow. Got it?" He turned back to the stairs, forgetting to wait for my answer.

What?! What am I supposed to do?

A minute later, Pop yelled from the top of the stairs. "Okay, Maria, here it comes!"

I tried to remember the directions. I had the light in one hand, a large hose in the other, and the small tubing in my mouth. As I waited for the wine, I adjusted all the items crammed into the barrel hole and started sucking air through the plastic. I smashed it between my teeth, feeling anxious and overwhelmed. I had no idea what I was doing. I changed my hold on the flashlight, hoping it wouldn't fall inside the barrel. A second later, it seemed like the main hose started to vibrate.

Wait. Oh no.

It was difficult to keep the light shining down into the small barrel hole. I couldn't see anything except for the dark wood inside. I tried to stick the flashlight in farther to get a better view, but the large hose wouldn't allow it, and it was getting heavier in my hand. To get a better look, I took the tubing out of my mouth and bent down, putting my face right over the barrel. I was holding the hose right next to my face when cold wine hit my cheek like a baseball and went straight into my eye.

"Ahh!" I shrieked and closed my eyes. I managed to shove the hose of gushing red wine back into the barrel. My cheek and eye were throbbing and dripping with cold wine.

"Oh my God!" I wiped my sleeve across my eye, not sure if I wanted to cry or scream. I was still holding on to the hose and the wine continuing to gush when I realized the tiny tubing had fallen to the floor during the accident. I dropped the flashlight onto the ground, grabbed the small tubing, and put it back in my mouth.

Bending over the barrel again, I placed the other end of the plastic tubing into the barrel. As the wine flowed into the barrel, I started to suck air from inside of it. The wine continued to fill the barrel. I continued to suck air—waiting. Then suddenly there was liquid—my signal the barrel was full! I pulled up quick and hard on the main hose, thrusting it above my head.

"Stop! Stop! Stop!" I shrieked as loudly as I could. The wine finally stopped coming.

I looked down at my wet, stained shirt. The cold liquid dripped down my neck, and I watched as it overflowed down the outside of the barrel. I hadn't pulled up on the hose fast enough to stop the suction as he instructed.

Pop rushed down the dark stairs.

"What happened?"

"Sorry, Pop. I just didn't see it coming."

He looked at me and laughed. "Oh boy. That's okay. Go clean up. I'll take it from here."

"Really sorry, Pop. It was just so dark."

He chuckled. "It's okay, honey. No problem. Go wash up."

Relieved but disappointed I'd let him down, I handed over the tubing, hose, and flashlight and headed up the concrete stairs, back into the daylight. *That was just stupid.*

MAKING IT REAL

Steam swirled off the stack of freshly made crepes that were set on the table next to a small glass dish of sour cream and Mom's homemade strawberry jam. She had staged a light-blue ceramic vase of yellow garden roses and a lit candle near the meal for ambiance. This was one of our very favorite breakfasts, and in my sleepy state, I was aware something must be up. Mom was known for making yummy breakfast treats on either holidays, someone's birthday, or before making us do some awful chore.

Bristol was stationed under the kitchen table as usual. I was quick to find the chair closest to him so I could dig my frigid feet under his heavy coat. My parents liked to keep the house cold. They told us it made us healthy. I took my first crepe, spreading the sour cream and jam together across its thin surface. As I began to delicately roll it up, Pop came around the corner from his bedroom with piles of paper and set them on the table.

"Okay, we need your help in naming the winery today," Mom announced. She pulled a chair up to the table. I relaxed, realizing this may not be as painful as I imagined.

"Oh boy, do we have to?" said Michel, reaching down to pet the dog under the table. "Todd and I were going to hunt for arrowheads today." His best friend lived at the end of a dead-end road, about a twenty-minute walk through the fields surrounding our house. They'd often meet halfway and search the area for native treasures.

Luisa joined us, her hair untouched as she'd rushed down from her bunk in fear she might miss out on the fresh crepes.

"What's happening?" she asked, rubbing sleep from her eyes.

"It shouldn't take long," Mom responded, handing Michel a couple more warm cakes on his plate.

"So, what are the choices?" I inquired, somewhat intrigued.

"Well . . ." Pop pulled out handfuls of paper from a well-worn file folder. There were white-ruled notebook sheets and pieces of yellow scratch paper, along with cocktail napkins and used envelopes. Each contained scribbled words, some circled, others crossed out. He placed them all on the table in front of us.

"We're thinking of calling it something that represents the place. Like Kinton or the Tualatin Valley."

Kinton was the name of our township within the Scholls community. It mostly consisted of a rarely used old grange and a windowless, condemned schoolhouse that leaned to one side. Not super inspiring.

The second option, as Mom explained, was the region where we lived, the Tualatin Valley, but I never heard of it and thought that sounded boring.

"Anything else?" I asked.

She recited names like Crystal Creek, inspired by the small creek behind our house that flowed into the Tualatin River, or Bachelor Button, for the blue flowers that covered our fields in the summertime. There were a few other words that had some connection to our property. But nothing was very interesting.

Luisa and Michel both rolled their eyes. "No, those are all dumb," Michel said emphatically.

"We agree. We like them, but they feel too common. They could be said about any other farm in the area, right? So, Dad and I were thinking of just naming it *Ponzi* Vineyards. What do you think of that?"

"Yeah, I like it," I said.

"Sounds good," Michel and Luisa chimed in agreement.

My parents looked at each other. It was a big decision, but they both seemed confident in their choice.

Regardless, she wanted to justify their decision. "Europe's most serious producers farm vineyards they own and make wines themselves, and they are most frequently recognized by their family name. We feel using our name will signify we are winegrowers, winemakers, and family-owned. Hopefully, this way, they will take us as seriously as the Europeans."

My father nodded, and three of us joined in agreement as we continued to spread jam on our crepes.

FORMAL
MEETINGS

By 1975, there were fourteen wineries in Oregon. The small band of wine people had grown so large that fitting everyone around one dining table wouldn't work. People from outside our neighborhood were also interested in getting involved. Residents of McMinnville, Amity, Salem, and even farther north near Mount Hood and south to Roseburg were intrigued with the fledgling wine industry. It was time to find a bigger meeting venue.

No matter the meeting location, it seemed everyone would have to commit to long drives. Fortunately for Mom and Pop, the group decided to meet at the Tigard fire hall, which wasn't far from us. The modest building was situated off Highway 99, the main stretch that connected the nearby towns of Tigard, Sherwood, Newberg, Dundee, and McMinnville. It was also the route most winemakers took when they headed into Portland for their regular day jobs, so it seemed like a convenient place for everyone to get together at the end of the workday.

The brown walls and gray carpet conflicted with the colorful and dynamic characters who filled the hall the second Monday of each month. The place immediately came alive once the "Pinot Obsessed" entered to exchange passionate opinions and have boisterous conversations. I was happy to learn they wouldn't meet at our house anymore, so we could sleep again.

This group became the first official wine organization in Oregon, and Pop was its first president. The original members of the Oregon Winegrowers Council included my folks, Chuck and Shirley Coury, Bill and Susan Blosser, Bill and Virginia Fuller, Marj and Ron Vuylsteke, Paul Bjelland, and Richard Sommer. The mission of the council was to serve as a research body for all vinifera grape growing in the state, with its future sights on creating a marketing and promotions arm. Since the group lacked support from the Department of Agriculture or any other state agency, it was up to them to organize themselves.

The plan was to meet regularly and discuss how to improve the valley's viticutural practices. They began developing the first "Grape Day," an event where anyone could come and learn more about the new industry and get tips on how to grow wine grapes. Several farmers in the area were showing interest in the possibility of converting their current crops over to grapes. Over the past five years or so, whispers of a budding wine industry had started filtering through the area, and those with curious minds wanted to learn more. Thus Grape Day was born.

I noticed Mom was using her Olivetti 22 typewriter more frequently, and I assumed it had to do with promoting this event since it was all my parents could talk about in the weeks leading up to it. She spent hours drafting press releases about the big day, mailing them to all the local newspapers. She hoped anyone with a burgeoning interest in Oregon viticulture would attend. Because the inaugural event was solely funded by the council members, the pressure was on to ensure its success.

Pop was unusually anxious in anticipation of the big day. It would be where he and the other men would assume roles of the first "regional wine experts." They'd share why they selected their vineyard sites and talk passionately about why certain wine grapes have great potential for success in our cool valley. They would also discuss some of their mutual challenges, including bird control, concern over unquarantined plants, and the fear of phylloxera. Hours and hours of presentations would explain how to prepare the soil for planting, how to manage weeds, what fertilizers worked, how to prune, what type of trellising should be considered, and eventually how to harvest the fruit. As president, my father was the opening speaker and moderated most of the seminars. Other featured speakers the first year were Chuck Coury, Bill Blosser, Gary Fuqua, Dick Erath, and David Adelsheim. The success of the first event prompted the group to continue organizing future affairs. Grape Day demonstrated the interest and the need for having broader conversations and the importance of getting together to share ideas and experiments. It was all about doing this thing together.

THE
WINEMAKER'S
PROJECT

One thing that came out of those discussions was finding out more about *the type* of Pinot Noir that would thrive in our region. Most of the original Pinot Noir cuttings came from UC Davis, since it was one of the few sources for cool-climate vinifera material. But, apparently, the university's stock was limited since Cabernet dominated the nearby Napa Valley's commercial wine industry, and Pinot Noir was extremely rare and relatively unknown. The "Pinot Obsessed" knew several different types or clones of Pinot Noir existed. Each one would respond differently, depending on where it was planted. I kept hearing the names of the two most popular: Pommard and Wadenswil.

Pop, Adelsheim, and Erath considered there may be other Pinot Noir clones better suited to the valley and wanted to investigate. Through his contacts in Burgundy and with the help of Oregon State University, Adelsheim was able to bring additional clones to the valley for evaluation. By 1978, the Wine Advisory Board had started to work cooperatively with OSU and fund research projects. Clonal research was one of the earliest projects that demonstrated a state interest in Oregon's budding wine industry. It was a big deal; it meant the "Pinot Obsessed" didn't have to come up with the money to fund the research, something to which they'd become accustomed.

Two blocks were selected for the experiment. One was near us in Hillsboro, and the other in Yamhill County atop Erath's Dundee hillside. At both two-acre sites, between thirteen and twenty Pinot Noir clones were mixed, creating a single block. These were the first multiclonal plantings of Pinot Noir in the valley. The test plots were monitored for years, with the men paying close attention to fruit quality, maturity, and eventually wine quality. They found the clones varied; one ripened sooner than another, another may have shown more spicy character in the wine than another, and another may have brought greater tannin. Both men realized that each plant did indeed bring different components to the wine, but ultimately, they both agreed that the original Wadenswil and Pommard performed best in both vineyards. The fruit ripened on time and maintained ideal flavor in the finished wines.

In 1980, my parents were fortunate to purchase the two acres of mixed clones, and we named the site Abetina Vineyard after the oak trees that majestically stood there. Soon after purchasing the vineyard, Pop began picking the entire block at once instead of separating the clones. He would harvest the fruit all at once, regardless of complete ripeness throughout the vineyard. The grapes were picked into a single bin, fermented, and barreled all together. My father found that after many years of working with Abetina Vineyard, in almost every single vintage, this barrel exceeded the quality of all the rest of his Pinot Noir. Abetina's aromatics, flavors, and depth of character seemed far superior, regardless of the vintage. It proved itself as a remarkable experiment and gave terrific insight into the impact of clones to site.

DESIGN PHASE

Back in the garage, as the wine continued to age, my enterprising parents began to consider how they were going to sell it. There was a lot to discuss. Packaging now became the topic of our conversations at the dinner table, in the car going to Grandma and Grandpa's house, and in the kitchen as we cleaned the dishes. Mom heard many of the "Pinot Obsessed" were working with artist friends or had even hired professionals to design their labels. Mom and Pop heard about a guy they thought could help us named Jack Meyers.

Apparently, Meyers was a friend of a friend who considered himself a graphic designer. I didn't know what that was exactly, so Mom tried to explain it: an artist who creates logos and marketing materials for businesses. It sounded groovy. Meyers also liked wine, so Mom and Pop decided he'd be perfect for the job since he was willing to trade for his creativity.

The three of them sat down at the kitchen table one afternoon and began discussing what message they wanted to convey through the label. They sifted through different paper samples and talked about each one's "weight" and "texture." I had no idea it was possible to talk about paper for so long. Then they moved on to discuss different "fonts." Should the type be sans serif or just serif? Should it be foiled or embossed? It was obvious this discussion wasn't ending anytime soon. I escaped out the back door to find the litter of kittens Michel told me had been born in the barn.

Returning to the house a few hours later, I walked by the dining table now cluttered with a mess of papers. Curious, I sifted through the penciled sketches, reviewing the different illustrations, elaborate letter styles, and paper types. Mom spotted me and walked over.

"So, what do you think?"

"I don't know. What's the plan?"

"Well, we're considering a pretty traditional look. We need the label to feel serious, sophisticated, like the Europeans, so our customers have the same confidence when selecting our wine. The package also needs to look appropriate sitting on a white linen tablecloth in a nice restaurant or in a five-star-hotel. We like the idea of having an illustration of the property since it's important they can see the place where it's made."

"Uh-huh." I nodded. I was intrigued. I grabbed a chair and sat down, sifting through the designs as she further explained the concept.

"We don't want it to look like a standard California label. No gold foil on the label, for example. We want it to feel more natural —like it's connected to the earth. And simple is always best. This is the one we like a lot." She reached down and picked up a pencil drawing on a piece of tracing paper.

Basically, it was the view from the mailbox. It showed our home surrounded by the vineyard, featuring the five large poplar trees that lined the driveway. I always felt the five trees symbolized the five members of our family. In the drawing, the vineyard sprawled out in front of the house, and the tall fir trees framed it from behind the house. But as I looked closer, I saw something I didn't recognize.

"What's this, Mom?" I pointed to a small structure nestled in between a grouping of trees, to the left of our home.

"Oh, that!" She smiled. "That's your father thinking ahead. We asked Jack to sketch in where we think the winery will be built someday."

"That's kind of weird. Where the old garage is now?" Mom nodded. It felt a bit like we were lying by eliminating our little house and instead presenting a large roof that didn't even exist.

My parents tweaked the label for several weeks, and there were constant meetings with Meyers over the design. Every night, they debated the multiple options. Discussions at dinner had completely shifted from the exhausting topics of pruning techniques, ideal fermentation temperatures, and clones to government rules regarding label specifications and what it would take to get the label "approved."

"The BATF (TTB) requires we put a government warning on it, Nancy," Pop pleaded. He was trying to explain to my mother, who, as usual, was resisting proper procedures.

"Well, it's just wrong," Mom responded to the requirement of making room on the back label for a paragraph stating how wine was harmful to pregnant women's health.

"Mom, what's the BATF, and what's the warning all about?" I interrupted.

"It's the federal agency that controls and regulates alcohol, tobacco, and firearms."

"Firearms? You mean like guns?"

"Yes. Guns and cigarettes. Because wine is alcohol, it's considered equally as dangerous," she explained.

"What?! You're kidding me! That's so crazy." I laughed. For the first time, I realized we weren't just making wine—we were making alcohol. I never really thought of it that way. It wasn't hard to understand alcohol was frowned upon from the way the kids in school judged us. But, until now, I hadn't seen it as something as harmful as a semiautomatic weapon or as unhealthy as a cigarette. It alarmed me that what we did was considered so terribly dark.

"And what's this about pregnant women?"

"Well, unfortunately, our government also believes drinking wine causes birth defects in unborn babies. I disagree with this statement as women all over the world, for generations, have managed to have healthy babies while enjoying wine moderately." She continued, "If there must be a warning, it should be about the harmful effects of excessive drinking—by anyone!"

I couldn't shake the conversation. I lay awake that night, watching the car lights flash across the valley as I reflected on how this recent information so directly conflicted with our lives. I couldn't believe our society viewed wine so negatively. In contrast, my parents believed wine was healthy—which was why it fit so well into our lifestyle. Obviously, the government did not understand our way of life.

BOARD
DISCUSSIONS

We weren't the only ones struggling with the label stuff. I heard Mom talking on the phone with the other "Pinot Obsessed," grumbling over the subject. Pop decided to make it the main agenda item at an Oregon Winegrowers Council meeting. Since Mom and Pop both wanted to attend this important discussion, they dragged us with them that night, which meant we had to sit through the lengthy and tedious dialogue. We brought our coloring and comic books and sat in the back of the room and waited.

Since table wines had never been produced in the region, it meant there was an open slate for what an Oregon label would look like. My parents and especially David Adelsheim saw this as a great opportunity to set a unique high standard for our winegrowing region. Passionate discussions commenced.

"As we approach the subject of labeling our wines, I feel we should be honest with our information," Pop said as he introduced the topic. "We need to set Oregon wines apart from other wine areas."

"Well, that's why I'm here and not in California," growled Coury, blowing cigarette smoke from his mouth.

"And we all know this is the only place to grow real Pinot Noir. That's for certain," Lett declared.

"I think we should do something completely different than California. I think we should call our wines by their true varietal names," Adelsheim suggested. "For example, instead of calling our Chardonnay 'Chablis,' it should be called 'Oregon Chardonnay.' And instead of referring to our Pinot Noir as 'Hearty Burgundy,' it should be known as 'Oregon Pinot Noir.'"

The room was quiet as his idea was contemplated.

"That's right," Mom agreed, always one of the more assertive women among the group of mainly men.

"Well, it stands to reason since we aren't in Chablis or Burgundy, France, after all," Susan Sokol Blosser respectfully agreed. Susan, originally from Wisconsin, and her husband at the time were both Stanford graduates. Bill had a master's degree in city and regional planning, and Susan was considering a teaching job at Reed College when they arrived in Oregon. They found their property just outside of Dundee. It was an abandoned prune orchard before they cleared it and planted their first eighteen acres in 1971. Like many of us, they faced bitter opposition from neighboring fundamentalists when it came time to build their winery. It took persistence and diplomacy, but they were finally able to establish their vineyard property. They had three kids, just like us, who experienced most of the work.

"And, while we respect the French, we don't want to make French wines," Pat Campbell, another bold woman, agreed. "We're making Oregon wines."

Eventually, it was decided the group would submit their labels to the BATF, noting Oregon in front of the varietal name. Because Oregon would be the first region in the country to submit labels with true varietal identifiers, the group was aware they might face closer scrutiny from the authorities. But it was unanimous: Oregon needed to stand out. The "Pinot Obsessed" wanted to make the point the wines were from a very different place and things would be different here. It was clear: being authentic was a core value these wine revolutionaries all shared.

In 1977, ORS 471 passed. Among other things, it most importantly mandated that all Oregon wine would be made from 90 percent of one varietal. By doing so, the move created the most restrictive labeling laws in the country. It was intended to dissuade others from reducing the integrity of Pinot Noir and strengthened Oregon's unique position in the marketplace.

REALITY

I walked into Mom's bedroom one Sunday morning and was startled when I found her sitting on the edge of her bed with her head down, her hands covering her face. She was usually up at the crack of dawn, cheerful and ready to start her daily chores, but that morning it was clear something was wrong. I hesitated, respecting her privacy, but I was also concerned. When she noticed me, she looked up and dried her eyes with her hand. She had been silently crying. I had never seen my mother in despair; this was completely out of character.

"I'm fine, honey," she said quickly, recognizing my surprise.

"Mom, what's wrong?" I sat down next to her, unsure what to do.

"Oh, it's nothing really."

"Come on, Mom," I insisted. I put my hand on her thigh.

"Oh, it's just the house."

What? The house? It was new!

"I just want some shelves in the basement. But your father doesn't seem to have time to build them."

Shelves? Mom is upset about not having shelves?

"It's really not a big thing." She lightly patted her nose with her hand.

But it was definitely a very big thing to her. I couldn't figure it out. I'd never seen this side of her. It always seemed she loved the chaos. Desiring shelves sounded much too basic and ordinary for my mother. It must be something else.

I sat on the edge of the bed with her and considered that maybe her sadness had more to do with her overwhelming environment. After all, she was taking care of the animals, all of us, the house, and the laundry, plus doing the grocery shopping, the cooking, the gardening, and the vineyard work. There had also been more meetings in the evenings and on the weekends as she was part of the PTA, the ECFC, and the Jacktown Women's Association.

My mother was busy, but until that moment I hadn't realized the extent of her responsibilities. The vineyard alone was plenty. For the past six years, she'd committed daily to working the twelve-acre vineyard. When we left in the morning for school and Pop headed to PCC, she was the one left to tend to it. In the winter, she'd pruned and pulled away the dead canes and tied down the remaining ones. In the spring, she'd train the growing vines along the trellis and hoe the weeds from their bases. The list of vineyard tasks never seemed to stop, day after day, from one week to the next, one season to the next. And although my father spent many hours out there working in the evenings and on the weekends as well, Mom was a one-person crew most of the time.

I still couldn't completely understand why the shelves were so important to her, but I had an idea it had something to do with more than just maintaining the household.

I leaned over and gave her a kiss on her soft cheek. "I love you, Mom. I'm sure it'll be okay."

"I know, honey. It will. Thanks."

It was 1975, and the reality of our life as winegrowers was having an effect on my folks. It had been six years since we planted the nursery row and almost two years since our first harvest. As I rushed by the kitchen table one evening on my way up to watch my two favorite TV shows, *Happy Days* followed by *Laverne and Shirley*, I noticed my parents looking serious. The table's surface was another mess of paper: open envelopes, bills, bank statements, a calendar, and their checkbook. Their conversation was calm, but there was a level of intensity I'd rarely seen. It was clear I shouldn't stick around, so I quickly headed for the stairs to the TV room.

"You need to stop worrying, Nancy. Things are going to get better," I overheard Pop say in his reassuring voice. I dug my toes into the thick carpet as I slowly climbed the stairs, still eavesdropping. "The wine is almost ready to sell, and then things will start to ease up. We just have to be patient."

"I understand, but I'm getting concerned. I wonder if we should try to borrow some money."

"Ha! Yeah." They both silently chuckled, remembering the last time they asked one of the local banks for a loan. They had been immediately ridiculed for their naïveté. Who would loan money to a couple of inexperienced hippies who thought they could grow wine grapes in cold Oregon?

The modest savings from my father's previous paychecks from California were depleted, and his teacher's salary was barely keeping up with the daily costs of caring for the family. Bills had been piling up. First there were grape cuttings, posts, wire, the used tractor, and all the broken implements, but things had gotten more serious now with wine in production. More materials were needed. Payments were due for the French oak barrels that Pop insisted were critical to making the finest Pinot Noir. Apparently, the flavor from American oak was too strong for this type of wine, so these expensive, custom-made barrels imported from France were necessary. Then there were the bottles, corks, lead foils, and fancy labels. We were fully invested, but there was no return. And the demands kept coming.

My parents seemed to be dealing with multiple challenges, but the primary one was how to raise a family while starting a business with very little money. Regardless, they remained committed to doing something they'd never done before and were convinced that people would be interested in it. It was all a leap of faith. Pop only had one chance a year to try a different technique, attempt a new experiment, or work through another idea. One year at a time. One vintage at a time.

Nothing was certain. Would the grapes even ripen? Maybe it would rain too much, or hail, or there would be a devastating frost. Maybe we should pick earlier, or maybe later. Did we prune too much, or too little? Is our soil any good? Is there better soil somewhere else in the valley? Should we plant at a higher elevation? How can we trellis to capture more sun exposure? Should we be using a spray to protect against mildew?

There were similar questions in the winery as well. What should we do if the fruit is damaged by rain or mildew? How long should we ferment? What is the correct temperature, and how can we control it? What is the best fermenter size? Does it exist? And if so, can we afford them? How do we move the wine from fermentation to the barrel? Are we using the right barrel, and how long should the wine age? When should we bottle and how?

Unlimited questions—all unresolved.

What Mom and Pop did have was determination, energy, and a belief they could make something happen. They were forced to be patient, take on more risk, and remain frugal—all things that occasionally made Mom anxious.

"Nancy, it's true that things are going to be tight for a while. We just need to keep working at it," my father stated quietly and confidently. He reached over and gave his wife a hug and a kiss on the cheek.

"I know." She smiled at him, reassured. The adventure would continue.

At the top of the stairs, I slipped into the TV room. Luisa was laughing at Squiggy and Lenny while I was immediately distracted with figuring out how I could get my sweater mono-grammed with an enormous *M* like Laverne's *L*. *That would be so cool.*

THE PRECIOUS
PACKAGE

That summer, Mom and Pop decided to rent our original home to a nice college student they met through the Grimm family. His name was Dale Rawls, and he agreed to pay a meager fee to live in the tiny building. His contribution helped to store a few extra dollars away for animal food and Michel's never-ending piano lessons.

I liked Dale. He was about ten years older than me, had long hair and glasses, and wore tie-dyed T-shirts and bell-bottom jeans. He was an art student, so his paintings, brushes, paint tubes, and sketches were found all over the place. When I wasn't working in the vineyard, we made granola in the small kitchen together and listened to Cat Stevens. Dale seemed to be in a constant good mood and was always ready to help with our various projects.

It was fortunate we had him around to help bottle our first wine when Pop announced the 1974 Pinot Noir was finally ready. For almost two years, he'd visit the cellar to check on his beloved wine. Almost weekly, using a slender glass vessel called a wine thief, he'd draw wine from the barrel to sample its progress, analyzing its flavors and color. He was finally satisfied with how it had developed and was confident it was ready to be bottled. It was perfect timing because the 1976 harvest was coming, and we needed to make room in the garage for the next vintage.

Bottling required equipment we didn't own, so we would need to ask our "Pinot Obsessed" friends for help. Fortunately the Vuylsteke family wasn't far away. Marj and her husband, Ron, lived with their six children near Hillsboro, just minutes from our home. Like many farming wives at the time with limited income, Marj was mainly concerned with finding ways to provide for her large family. Her summers were devoted to harvesting and canning in preparation for the upcoming winter months. Her pantry shelves, like many in the valley, were packed with jams, pickled vegetables, canned peaches, and plenty of dried walnuts.

I heard it was in the late 1960s when Marj discovered an interest in winemaking. She dug up anything she could find on the subject and discussed the idea with a writer from the *Oregonian*, who encouraged Marj to add brandy to her large crop of fresh blackberries and mash it together one day. They joked this was one way to have instant wine. Then she got serious.

She used strawberries and raspberries for her initial trials, then advanced to peaches, dandelions, pumpkins, and even carrots. She learned it was possible to make wine from just about anything. After her few successes, she encouraged her husband to purchase some property off Burkhalter Road, which was home to a small dairy built in 1917. It turned out the milking parlor was ideal for a start-up winery. The Vuylstekes had a filler, and they were happy to loan it to us for our first bottling project.

Another vital instrument we needed was a corker. This tool would push corks into the filled bottles of wine. Again, we didn't own one, so Pop called around until he learned the Campbells had one we could borrow. Pat and Joe Campbell moved their small family, three kids packed in a trailer, to Gaston in 1973. Pat's great-grandfather was a Swiss immigrant to Oregon who grew grapes and made wine prior to Prohibition. When the family discovered a dilapidated piece of property outside of Forest Grove overrun with blackberries and abandoned prune and hazelnut trees, it was her father who remarked the only crop with a minor chance of survival would be wine grapes. They decided to give it a try. Pat's husband, Joe, took medical classes at night while teaching himself the science of winemaking.

With the borrowed filler from the Vuylstekes, a corker from the Campbells, and adding onto Erath's order of glass and corks, we were able to bottle our first vintage. Working collectively this first year, and in the years that followed, was significant since our volume of wine was so small. It was difficult to justify making a large purchase ourselves, nor did we have the means to do so.

The assembly line was set up in the basement. Michel, Luisa, Mom, and I were on hand while Pop figured out the system. As usual, all the tasks usually started with a lot of waiting, and when we were forced to hang out in the cold and dark, I became restless. It was hard for me to stand around, so I'd start stacking buckets, coiling hoses, and collecting wet rags. I found stuff stashed everywhere. Nobody else seemed to mind the mess, but it drove me nuts, and the cleaning gave me something to do.

Glancing over at Pop, I could see he was now fooling around with something called the filler. This contraption sat on the ground and consisted of a large steel-covered basin and six stainless steel nozzles stationed underneath. The barrel of wine sat above the basin, and a hose was inserted into the top. Instead of using a pump to move the wine into the filler, Pop used gravity once again. He sucked hard on the one end of the hose to draw the wine from the barrel to the basin. Once the filler was full, he would break the siphon by pulling up on the hose and close its lid. Directions followed.

"Maria, you'll be over here at the filling station. Michel, you're on corks, and Luisa, you help Mom seal the cases."

"What can I do, Dick?" Dale asked. He was always willing to lend a hand.

"Hang on, Dale. Once we get started, I'll let you know. Okay, everyone ready?"

I squatted down in front of the filler, ready for my next instructions.

"Wait, Maria. Let's get you more comfortable." Pop brought over a wooden crate for me to sit on. "There. That's better." He was constantly trying to improve things.

I positioned myself again in front of the filler, realizing how similar it was to how Mom milked the goats. I immediately felt the weight of this unknown responsibility and as usual felt a rush of anxiety. I watched as wine from the basin began to flow down into the steel rods. At the end of each rod was a nipple with a small opening. Pop showed me what to do; he leaned over, hooked a bottle on a rod, and then reached for another empty one. Repeating the steps, one after the other, he hooked six bottles on until all six nozzles were flowing. Once the first bottle was filled, he would carefully move it off and replace it with a fresh one. After completing a case of bottles, he stepped away.

"Okay, Maria, now it's your turn."

I nervously moved the box a little closer to the machine and grabbed an empty bottle in my right hand. I tried to mimic

Pop's method, hooking it onto the first nozzle and reaching for another one. I tried to shake off my nervousness, focusing on my work. I kept hooking on empty bottles when I noticed the first one was already full. I felt a rush of adrenaline. If I didn't pull them off quickly, they would overflow. I refocused and tried to remain calm, carefully lifting up and pulling off the first full bottle, setting it down onto the ground next to me. I continued to pull off the full bottles with one hand while hooking on an empty one to replace it. My weight shifted on the box as I tried to keep my balance and create some consistent speed to keep up with the pace of the filler.

Soon, I had mastered a routine and managed to keep up with the quick tempo, filling all six bottles at a steady rate. Accurate and efficient—just the way my father liked it. He hovered, but allowed me to operate the equipment.

"Move the case of bottles closer to the filler," he prompted Dale. "Good job, Maria. Keep your eye on the bottles. Be sure you don't overfill." The assembly line would never be complete without my father's perfecting and gentle reminders.

As I pulled off each full bottle, Dale would carry them to Michel, who would take each one and slip it under the corker. This blue apparatus allowed the bottle to be placed on top of a metal platform with a strong spring underneath it. Once secured, the bottle rose up and connected with a steel mouthpiece that housed a cork inside. A heavy steel arm hovered over the two parts. Michel steadied the bottle on the platform with his left hand and pulled the arm down with his right, compressing the cork and squeezing it into the mouth of the glass bottle beneath it. It was important to be accurate lest the cork pop out or the glass top break.

Like me, he began to find a rhythm, and within the first hour, we were Pop's well-oiled machine. My mind drifted: *I wonder if the sun is up? I wish I was riding my bike. Why is it always so cold in here?*

Luisa and Mom completed the final step, taking the finished bottles of wine, turning each one upside down (to keep the cork moist), and placing them inside an empty case. Mom sealed each case with strapping tape and stacked them on a small pallet. Luisa followed with a rubber stamp, marking the date on each box. We worked for hours as one efficient, well-coordinated crew.

Eventually, Mom interrupted our work for a quick tuna sandwich lunch. We climbed up the dark basement stairs as the sunlight blinded us, waking us from our trance, flooding the space, and warming our chilled bodies. My eyes squinted in the harsh light as it began to reinvigorate me. We flopped down onto the lawn and scarfed down the bulky sandwiches and juicy orange slices. Then, licking our fingers, we shuffled back down into our cave to resume the drill. I seemed to be doomed for a dark, cold summer. We bottled a hundred cases of Pinot Noir that day.

MARKET TO MARKET

Two pallets of wine were now carefully stacked in the corner of the garage. Our treasure. At last, there was something tangible to show for our years of labor. The basement cellar, once bustling with activity, was eerily quiet. Pop rinsed out the empty barrels with water, and the clean hoses were hung across the empty barrels to drain. The activity now moved upstairs.

Two cases of our newly printed labels sat adjacent to the pallets of wine. The garage now reeked of ink, replacing the odor of sweet grape juice. I loved this scent. It smelled so fresh. I couldn't help myself from opening one of the tightly sealed boxes. When I pulled away the cardboard top, I found neatly wrapped sets of labels. I inhaled deeply and looked at the contents.

Wow. So fancy. I picked up a packet and pulled away the plastic wrap. Our name, Ponzi, was centered in the middle of the crisp paper in large black Art Deco letters. The words "Oregon Pinot Noir Table Wine" were etched below it, and at the bottom was the elegant illustration Mom and Pop had worked so hard to perfect. It was simple and sophisticated with its varying shades of green watercolor. Even though I still felt it was a bit devious to boast a building that didn't exist, I had to admit it looked pretty professional. I felt a gush of pride as I returned the label and closed the box. For the first time, I felt we were doing something pretty special.

Our next obstacle was how to apply paper labels and lead capsules to the bottles. Pop first called Myron on the phone, asking to borrow some of his glue pellets. Then he called Coury, requesting to use his labeling machine, and he called the Vuylstekes to see if their capsule spinner was available. The fact was, we were all trying to label our wines around the same time, so we had to coordinate our efforts. But, as usual, everyone was flexible and willing to share.

Once all the components were secured, they were loaded haphazardly into the garage. I moped around with Michel, waiting for instructions as we stood in the cold space. I tried to ignore the summer sunshine tempting me to go outside. Our grandparents also gathered with us. Luisa snuck in later, holding a stray kitten that had recently shown up at our place, as they sometimes did in the country.

The smell of hot glue permeated through the small space. Mom and Pop were busy moving things around to create another assembly line with an L-shaped group of tables. The pallet of Pinot Noir sat next to the end of one table, the labeler was staged in the center, and a stack of the freshly printed labels were situated next to it. The new paper seemed to sparkle among the other battered, rusty equipment. I quietly hoped I'd be assigned a job with the labels.

The spinner sat below the labeler with a box of new capsules by its side. The shiny red lead tops were stacked upon each other, creating several tubes piled high in the box. Like the labels, the shiny towers of color seemed to brighten the otherwise drab setting. I loved the newness. I thought Pop must have selected the dark-red color to decorate the top of our bottles since they resembled those of the great wines from Burgundy. I remembered Mom explaining it was important our package appear as prestigious as European wines.

"So, here's how this will work," Pop began. "Michel, please take your hands out of your pockets. Now, I want you to take a bottle out of the case and hold it over the labeling machine."

This small but heavy metal machine was positioned on the table. When it was turned on, a large, flat roller rotated around a cylinder. A basin with hot glue stood directly under the roller, and as each label was inserted, it threaded itself along the roller, pulling hot glue from the basin and adhering it to the back of the label. The sticky label was spit out on the other side and attached itself to the wine bottle.

Thirteen-year-old Michel looked less than thrilled, his greasy hair covering most of his adolescent face. He nodded, signaling he understood, but his hands remained behind his back. Michel rarely saw the need to rush. His preference was to wait until it was really time to engage. He liked to conserve his energy.

"Then, Luisa . . ." Pop spun around, looking for his youngest child. "Put the kitten down. Your job is to take the labeled bottle and place a capsule on top of it."

"Okay, Pop!" She set the pet down, wiped her hands on her jeans, and grabbed a stack of the brightly colored caps. She stood next to the table and began pulling them off.

"Maria."

I stepped up as he called my name.

"Once Luisa is done, I want you to take the bottle and push it slowly into the capsule spinner—like this." He turned the machine on. It resembled a large electric pencil sharpener, but instead of shredding the inserted object, its strong plastic wheels spun around the bottle's mouth, twisting the foil around it and smoothing out any creases as it was pulled back out. The result left a shiny decorative top on each bottle.

"You have to get it just right," my father explained. "If you don't, the capsule will ripple or fold in places. It must come out smooth." He pulled one out from the spinner—perfectly crease free.

He handed me a bottle. "Try it."

"Okay, sure." I tapped a cap onto its top and pushed it into the machine. It vibrated in my hand, and I struggled to steady the glass while pulling it out. It felt like the bottle was under attack until I yanked it out of the machine. The foil was badly folded. Pop grabbed the bottle and ripped off the top, tossing the wasted capsule onto the floor.

"Now, try again, but this time, don't hesitate. Push against the pressure."

I tapped another new capsule on and took a deep breath as I inserted the bottle into the vicious spinning wheels. I held tightly as it knocked around inside the machine and slowly pulled it out.

"Not bad." Pop patted me on the back. "Good. Just keep working at it. You'll get it. But try not to make any mistakes. These capsules are very expensive. Same thing with the labels, Michel. Those cost about ten cents each. Watch what you're doing and take your time. You'll get it."

He stepped away to observe the operation. Grandma and Nonna took the finished bottles from me and returned them to their cases. Grandpa used strapping tape to seal them and began stacking them on an empty pallet. Mom slapped a wet label on the outside of each case announcing its special contents. Pop made his usual rounds. He adjusted the spinner, added more glue to the label trough, and restocked the bottles at the start of the line. He often pulled a bottle when he didn't feel it was perfect. Poorly labeled bottles were placed in a bucket of warm water so the label could be soaked off. Crumbled capsules were tossed on the floor. Everything had to be just right. He even checked the cases on the pallet to make sure the layers were locked in and straight.

Over the following hours, I attempted to perfect my work. *No folding allowed. Watch the creases.* Eventually, I became comfortable with the process and peered over to the finished pallet of wine. I wanted to see how much we had accomplished. When I pulled the next bottle from the spinner, I glanced at my Timex and attempted to do some math. It looked like we were packaging ten cases an hour. I was pretty sure at this rate we'd be here all day. I settled back into my zone and dreamed about life outside the garage.

EDUCATION

With our third harvest now aging in the basement and most of our first vintage still packaged and waiting in the upper garage, the dinner conversations once again changed to another new wine-related subject.

"Hey, can we please not talk about wine tonight?" I tried to divert the typical chatter to something else. I was desperate for any other topic.

But Mom and Pop just kept talking about the most recent happenings down in Dundee. Erath had just received a new press, and everyone was excited about it.

I pressed on, interrupting the banter. "Mom, there's a carnival at school this weekend. Can I go?"

"Maybe," she said, placing a green salad on the table. "Michel, please come to the table. Luisa! Where are you? Dinner is ready."

Pop served the steaming rigatoni covered in rich marinara sauce, dividing the homemade meatballs equally among us.

I pushed on. "I think it sounds like fun. They're supposed to have a go-fish stand and a bubble gum–blowing contest."

"Fun!" Mom said, passing the Parmesan cheese to Luisa.

"I think they even pass out ribbons! Maybe I'll win something!"

She nodded as she placed her napkin on her lap. The nod translated to acknowledgment, not agreement. Mom had never been one for competition or sports. I recalled the argument she and Michel had over his desire to play Little League baseball when he was ten years old. She told him if he was interested in athletics, he could bike himself the five miles to practice. Apparently, she didn't have time for baseball, but there always seemed time for his piano lessons.

"That sounds great, Maria," Pop said, seeming to sense my excitement. Then he quickly steered the conversation back to wine stuff, something about blue signs being installed along the roads to direct visitors to the wineries. I wanted to tell them about my new crush at school, that the cutest guy in my class had asked me to go to the carnival. But that would have to wait, once again.

My parents had received notice earlier that week that our business license would allow for a winery tasting room. Tasting rooms existed all over Napa Valley, but there was nothing like them in Oregon. Serving alcohol on farmland seemed odd to me, and I wondered how our skeptical neighbors would view the new concept. Mom and Pop, however, were thrilled with the idea, as it would open up an entirely new opportunity for us. Having a place where we could engage with the public, share our wines with them, and explain what we were doing was exciting. The state had decided to fabricate and install directional signs for travelers to navigate their way to these new attractions.

The days that followed were filled with soft chatter as Mom was constantly on the family phone with the "wine women:" Shirley Coury, Marj Vuylsteke, Virginia Fuller, Linda Shafer, Pat Campbell, and Corinne Gross. She'd pull the cord across the kitchen counter, taking notes and cooking at the same time. We always knew Mom was working on something important when a tuna fish casserole appeared on the table and was served by Pop.

"Where's Mom?" I asked one such evening.

"She's over with the girls discussing how to promote the new tasting rooms. With the new highway signs going up soon, we're hoping to see some traffic." My father brought the smelly tuna fish from the oven to the table.

Not again. *Hot tuna is so gross.*

Summertime meant a relatively clean garage, as all the wine was down below, aging in barrels. Pop moved the harvesting and labeling equipment to the opposite side of the space to allow room for a tasting bar. He sat two empty wine barrels on end about six feet from each other in the center of the room. Dale brought over a door he found at the back of the barn. After he removed the doorknob and placed it across the barrel tops, the makeshift structure was the perfect bar.

Mom still hadn't found the ideal wineglass despite flipping through stacks of restaurant equipment catalogs. She and I finally went into Portland to visit a restaurant wholesale store. Much like my father in the plumbing store, my mother was overwhelmed with her options, so I amused myself walking down aisles and aisles of glasses, plastic bowls, and serving utensils. We ended up buying a few boxes of short, stubby ones made by Libbey. We both agreed they were uninteresting, but they would have to do since the price was right.

Back at home, Mom chose a blue-and-white checkered table linen to spread over the unfinished door and set the new stemware on top. I thought it looked pretty professional.

"Maria, could you and Luisa go cut some flowers?"

"Sure!" Luisa and I were always happy to wander around the property in search of colorful blooms. I snitched some daisies from the vineyard row, and she found some purple and blue wildflowers near the barn. We brought them back to Mom in a vase.

"So pretty! Just what we needed." She placed them on the bar next to the wineglasses and a bottle each of our Pinot Noir and Riesling. There were also several bottles of each wine on the other side of the table with a price tag in front of them. A small box holding some cash and a cork puller sat just behind the two sample bottles. We were set.

"It looks really nice, Mom. Like a little wineshop."

"Thanks. I think so too." She smiled and took my hand as we walked out of the garage. "Now all we need are people."

Because of our proximity to Portland, my mother felt we had a strong chance of attracting visitors. Pop had installed a wooden sign at the intersection of Vandermost and Scholls Ferry Roads to guide the traffic to us. The handsome sign had been hand-carved and boasted a large Ponzi logo, followed by letters painted in gold and black that read "Oregon Table Wine—Tasting Room Open Weekends 12–5 PM." I was surprised when I learned they had paid someone else to make it. It was rare for them to buy anything new, so when they did, we all noticed. It felt different.

The next weekend, the long-awaited blue directional signs were up, and they seemed to shout to the world: "We make wine!" Like a billboard, the secret was out—now everyone would know we were there and produced alcohol. It made me uneasy.

But nothing happened. A week went by, then another, and nobody showed up. Every weekend I changed out the flowers, reset the glasses, and dusted off the bottles. We wondered if anyone would ever come, and Mom and Pop pondered what more they could do.

One Sunday afternoon, I passed by the "lookout" upstairs, and something caught my eye. The lookout was a narrow, single-paned window positioned at the top of the stairs in the house, across from the single bathroom. It faced the front of our property: the driveway, vineyard, and lawn. I stepped back to take a second look. Dust billowed from a vehicle headed down our dirt road, but it wasn't our car, it wasn't the banana truck, and it wasn't Grandma and Grandpa. In fact, I didn't recognize it at all. Then I panicked as I thought of the tasting room and realized Mom wasn't in the house.

"Hey, Michel! There's a car coming down the road. Hurry!"

No response.

"Michel?!" I shrieked.

"What? What are you talking about?" He grumbled from his bedroom.

"I don't know." I looked again. "It's some beat-up old truck!"

"Oh, probably someone's just lost," he said.

Luisa glanced at my anxious face and climbed back into her bunk with a comic book.

I watched as the car pulled up to the house and parked.

"Mom!" I shouted, running down the stairs and nearly falling down the last five steps. I caught myself. *Where is she?*

I tried to avoid the glass front door at the base of the stairs, but the couple had already made it onto the porch. They saw me and our eyes met. I had no choice. I had to greet them.

Why are we the only people with glass doors?

My hand trembled as I turned the doorknob and tried to smile. "Hi." I slowly opened the door. "I need to get my mom. Just a minute."

Leaving the door open, I darted away, desperate to find her. I headed out the back door.

"Mom! Mom!" I ran outside in a frenzy. She was in the garden, bent over at the waist, pulling weeds. She looked up, her blue bandanna holding her hair back, and wiped her brow with her dirty glove.

"What's up, honey?" She stood up slowly.

"Mom! There are people here! I think they're here to taste wine. I don't know what to do! Hurry!" I was out of breath.

"Oh, that's great!" She smiled as she began untangling herself from the tomato plants. "Tell them I'll be right there!"

"Okay." Relieved, I turned and ran back to the front door. Our guests were still there on the porch, talking to each other and looking at the vineyard. Bristol had found them and rubbed up against the man's leg.

"She'll be right here!" I blushed. They nodded and continued to look around our property. *What are they even looking at?*

Mom came up behind me, striding through the kitchen to the bathroom. She washed her hands and face and adjusted the bandanna on her head. Then she brushed the loose dirt from her jeans, grabbed a fresh cotton blouse, and slipped it on as she headed for the front door.

Smiling, she graciously greeted our guests. "Hi! It's so nice to have you! Thanks for waiting. Let's go into the tasting room." She led them down the porch, chatting until they reached the garage.

Mom returned about an hour later. I had waited for her on the stairs the whole time, petting Bristol's thick hair.

"So, what happened?"

"It was good! We tasted the wines and talked about why these grapes grow well here, and I explained how we're just starting out."

Then she explained some rules. If this happened again, I should be friendly, allow the people inside the house if she wasn't there, and offer them water. The master bathroom was available, and I was to direct them there if they needed to use it. Even though Michel and Luisa listened to these same instructions, I could tell it was all up to me. There was no way Michel would do it—he didn't even answer the phone—and Luisa, at nine years old, was just too young to care.

After that day, a few other people would occasionally drive up to the house. I figured they were in the country to pick berries, peaches, or cherries, and we were just a side attraction. It was uncomfortable having strangers at our house, but we slowly became accustomed to it. We'd watch from the lookout on weekends, waiting to see if anyone would invade our home. We'd make up stories about who was in each car and place bets if they would buy wine or just take away a lot of Mom's precious time.

By the end of the summer, I gathered enough courage to follow Mom into the garage and listen to her talk to some guests. I busied myself with straightening the bottles behind the bar as I listened in on their conversation.

"So, what is a table wine?" The question came from a tall, long-haired woman wearing bell-bottom flower-embroidered blue jeans, a red turtleneck, and lots of heavy jewelry.

"We think of wine the way Europeans do—as food. We feel wine should be a part of the meal, at the table every night."

"Interesting. And why are you making wine here? Don't grapes grow better in California?"

"It depends on the type of grape. Oregon has a much cooler climate, so it's better for growing certain types of wine." My mother attempted to patiently explain as she poured a taste of Riesling for the woman.

"Huh, it seems like it'd rain too much." She swirled the glass and took a sip.

"It's true it does rain a lot, but that's actually all right for these grape varieties." Mom smiled, trying to connect with her potential customer.

"Do you have any sweet wines?" Apparently, the woman wasn't too impressed with her first taste of dry Riesling.

"No, we only make wines to pair with foods, but Oak Knoll Winery makes some sweeter wines you might like. They're just a few minutes away, near Hillsboro."

There were so many questions, and it felt like Mom had to defend everything. Why do we do this? Do we know what we're doing? What were the wines called? How do you pronounce them?

I found it interesting, but I mostly enjoyed listening to Mom. She was eager to explain to those who knew little about our work. She was so patient, so poised. She made it look easy. I often stayed behind to remove the dirty glasses and restock a bottle if someone actually bought one. When a purchase was made, Mom's face lit up, but it rarely happened. She spent most of her time educating people and smiling. It seemed exhausting.

WINE SALES 101

My jeans spent more time in the sauna than I did. The hot closet worked well to dry clothes I'd forgotten to put in the dryer the night before. My parents never used it anyway. On my way to grab a pair of jeans one morning, I caught sight of Mom pulling up the long zipper of her knee-length boots, the soft brown leather hugging her sun-kissed legs. She looked up at me and smiled. The soft morning light filtered through her bedroom window, hitting her cheek like a spotlight. I always thought she was so pretty, but in that moment, she was beautiful. She wore a well-fitted burnt-orange V-neck sweater, a brown tweed skirt, and tall boots. It looked like an outfit the actress in the Charlie perfume commercials would wear. Her long hair, usually tightly pulled back into a bun, fell down her shoulders. It was softly curled and swept off her freckled face. Her green eyes shone. I thought she looked like a movie star.

"Wow. You look great, Mom."

"Thanks, honey." She slipped on her favorite gold hoop earrings, the ones Pop had bought for her on a trip to Italy, and brightened her lips with a light shade of bronze.

"Where are you going?" It was obvious she wasn't staying home.

"I'm off to sell wine!" Her eyes sparkled as she anticipated this next adventure. "Since you have the day off, do you want to come along?" It was a workday for the teachers, which meant I was free. The idea of hanging out with my mother in the city sounded fun.

"Really? Could I?"

"Sure. I don't know how long I'll be, but I'd love your company." She grabbed her red-and-brown beaded macramé bag, took one last look in the mirror, and turned to the door.

"Let me go change." I ran upstairs, cleaned myself up, and met her in the car.

We were off by nine a.m. I could see that in her groovy handbag she had crammed the essential tools of a wine sales professional: sample bottles of our Pinot Noir, Chardonnay, and Riesling and a wine opener. We took the traditional route into the city, passing green pastures and orchards before hitting the freeway leading closer to our target: Portland's best restaurants.

I could sense her anxiety along the way. The drive allowed time to concentrate on her talking points and presentation. First, Pop's reminder to focus on explaining a table wine—wines meant to accompany food and be enjoyed at the dinner table. Secondly, the unique similarity between our wine-growing area and Burgundy. And thirdly, and perhaps most importantly, that we were local producers.

The most popular restaurant in Portland was French and every wine family recognized the key opportunity it presented. L'Auberge was located in northwest Portland and occupied a large old home built in the 1920s. Its dark wood interiors and stained-glassed windows set the stage for a very sophisticated dining experience. The wine list was almost exclusively expensive Bordeaux wines and a couple of well-respected California Cabernets.

As we pulled into the side parking lot at L'Auberge, Mom took a deep breath.

"Well, this is it!" she exclaimed, looking at me. "Let's see what happens." With nearly seven years of hard work behind us, now was the moment that really mattered. It was time to present our wine to the experts. There were only about five high-end restaurants in the city, making Mom's target list short. This meant every introduction and every presentation was important.

She parked the car and reached for her bag, checking herself one last time in the rearview mirror. "Okay, let's go."

I straightened my hair as well and looked down at my red pants, hoping they were clean. I brushed off my Nikes. Mom opened the door and took another deep breath. We climbed the concrete stairs off the busy street to the front door. As she opened the door, the dining room opened in front of us. The crisp white tablecloths were elegant—and intimidating. I noticed Mom push her shoulders back a little further. I slid behind her, feeling my presence was inappropriate.

"May I speak with Bill McLaughlin?" she asked the host. "I scheduled an appointment with him last week."

"Sure." The young man took us to a table in the dining room and offered us a seat while he found the sommelier. She pulled open her bag and carefully placed the three bottles of wine on the linen and set the wine key in front of her. She straightened her skirt. I pulled in my chair, and we both quietly soaked in the handsome space and waited.

"Hello." A tall, burly man strode up to the table. "I'm Bill. You must be Nancy."

"Yes, hi!" She stood up and reached out her hand with a smile. "I'm Nancy Ponzi."

"How can I help you?" He sat down in the chair across from her, only glancing at me. It was clear he wanted to get right to the point. I was obviously invisible to him.

"Well, my husband and I moved up from California and planted a vineyard near Beaverton almost seven years ago. My husband, Dick, gave up his job as a mechanical engineer, and we moved our three children up here to make wine. This is Maria." She turned to me proudly.

I looked down. *This guy doesn't care, Mom,* I thought.

"Uh-huh." He glanced at the bottles on the table, then at his watch as he noticed a server arriving late for work.

My mother persisted. "So, we've been working really hard at this and think our Pinot Noir is an excellent example of what can be produced right here in our own valley."

He smiled smugly and chuckled. "Really? You *really* think you can make wine here?"

"Yes." Unshaken, she continued. "We are confident certain grapes like Pinot Noir have great potential here. Would you like to taste ours?"

The man stared back at her in disbelief. I was shocked by his demeanor.

"Honestly, Nancy, I have no interest in these wines. I have a great list of French wines, and our diners appreciate only the very best from Europe. These just wouldn't sell. We have a very high-end clientele with international taste."

I could tell Mom was taken aback by the abrupt response, and especially with his lack of interest in even tasting the wines. She hadn't anticipated this reaction. My mother had naturally assumed the local market would embrace the local wines and the budding wine industry.

"I understand, but we're right outside of Portland, in Beaverton, just a few minutes away," she stressed.

"Yes, but I'm just not interested. My wine list makes money for the restaurant. The wines on that list need to sell." He pushed his chair back and got up to leave, reaching out for a handshake. "I wish you the best." Then with a sideways grin, he strode out of the room.

Stunned, Mom packed up her bottles and wine key and stuffed everything back into her hippie bag.

"Well, let's go, honey," she said to me quietly, and we stepped out of the dining room. I trailed behind her, feeling her disappointment. Back in the car, she considered her next stop.

"I know where we'll go next," she said, shaking off the setback. "This is a place I'm certain we'll have better luck." I felt bad for Mom. I knew how much she wanted our wines at that French restaurant.

David Adelsheim, one of our "Pinot Obsessed" friends, had just taken a job working as the wine steward at L'Omelette after previous positions at a bank and with the art museum. His role at L'Omelette was pivotal as it was the only other important French restaurant with a stellar reputation in Portland. Hearing guests' opinions of different wines allowed Adelsheim good insight into the interests of the local market. He also had the advantage of learning how distributors operated, what wine prices were most successful, and how the competition worked.

David was an army brat before moving to the Willamette Valley with his wife, an artist named Ginny. Like many of the folks we met, they were inspired with wine following a visit to Europe. Although much younger than my parents, the couple shared the same drive and dream of living off the land and had purchased a small piece of land in Newberg even though neither of them had ever farmed. They planted their first nineteen acres of Riesling and Pinot Noir in 1971, and Adelsheim worked with Lett on his 1973 harvest. He got the position at L'Omelette following a trip to Burgundy in 1974, where he went to expand his winemaking experience.

My mother hoped this visit would be more positive since he was one of our own. It was known around the wine circle Adelsheim had been asked to create one of the city's first Oregon wine lists. He enthusiastically met us as we waited in the foyer.

"Hi, Nancy. So glad you decided to stop by!" Always genuinely friendly, he gave me and Mom a hug, and we sat down together at a table near the front of the dining room.

"Great to see you too, David." She opened the wines for him and poured a sample of our Riesling into a sparkling clean wineglass. Mom couldn't stop from sharing how the previous visit went and what a disappointment it had been.

"They will get it soon enough." He empathized with the rejection. "It will take time. Your wines are all delicious."

"Thank you, David," she replied.

"Yours will now make the tenth Oregon winery on my list!" He was so pleased as this made L'Omelette the first Portland restaurant to present so many local wines. I couldn't help but compare his reaction to the one we had earlier. We drove home later that afternoon and reflected on the day.

"It looks like not everyone's that excited about the wines, Mom." I began.

"Yeah. Unfortunately."

I could sense her dismay.

"They're not taking us seriously. Maybe it's because I'm a woman, and they assume I don't know anything about wine-making, farming, or managing a business."

"Yeah," I agreed, aware that women in general weren't taken very seriously in any field at this time, especially in the alcohol industry.

"I'm getting pretty tired of people thinking this is just a hobby."

As we entered the front door, I heard the phone ring and grabbed it. It was Bill McLaughlin. I handed it to Mom.

"Hello?" she answered reluctantly.

I stood by her side, anxious to hear the conversation. She was quiet for some time, only nodding. Then finally she responded.

"Oh, thank you, Bill," she said quietly. "We really appreciate it. Thank you. Thank you so much." She hung up and turned to me.

"So, what happened?"

"I guess he decided to take a chance on us, after all," she announced, still shocked. "He said a wine had sold out, and he needed to fill the space right away. He thought he'd give our Pinot Noir a shot, but cautioned me it wasn't going to be easy. At least he's going to put it on!" She smiled and gave me a hug. As the months and years went on, Bill McLaughlin became a true champion of Oregon wines, ensuring they were always represented on his list.

At dinner that night, Pop shared the story of Bill Fuller, who, despite being a male, was also struggling with wine sales. Fuller, a UCD graduate, and his wife, Virginia, had arrived in the valley with a similar dream of making wine. A brainy, stocky guy with black-rimmed glasses and less hair than his hippie comrades, Fuller had a business savvy our other wine friends didn't possess. He was an assistant winemaker at Louis

Martini Winery in St. Helena, California, and like Coury and Lett, had majored in winemaking at the university.

After working nine years at Martini, Fuller left the winery and ventured north, where he purchased 160 acres outside of Forest Grove and founded Tualatin Valley Vineyards in 1973. From my limited perspective, Fuller seemed brighter and wealthier than the other "Pinot Obsessed." Maybe it was because he bought all that land or maybe it was because I learned that instead of waiting for his fruit to mature like the rest of us, he purchased white wine grapes from eastern Washington, enabling him to make and sell wine immediately.

"Maybe Fuller has the right idea," Mom said. "While we're targeting restaurants, he's targeting grocery stores that will give his brand more exposure and bring in more sales quickly."

Like Mom, Bill loaded his truck with wine in the morning and would spend the entire day in the city, preaching the greatness of Oregon wines. But his targets were the Safeway stores. It was an important chain as the regional stores had decent wine departments, and the markets were scattered all over the Northwest.

"He told me there is just one buyer who makes the wine decisions for all the stores, and her office is in Salem. Fuller has been taking the ninety-minute drive every three weeks for nearly ten months, pitching his wines, but having no success."

"Oh dear," Mom replied. "We've got to be so persistent."

"Well, I guess he finally won her over with one caveat: that the cases would need to be packed with six bottles instead of the standard twelve. She's concerned the product won't sell, and she doesn't want to hold extra inventory. I guess he got his kids to repack the seventy-case order, and he got the sale."

"That's fantastic!" Mom remarked. "Great news for all of us."

Following the successful announcement, my father later shared the second part of the story. Apparently on a random day while lobbying on behalf of the industry in Salem, Fuller dropped by one of the Safeway stores to check on his wine. He was surprised when he didn't see it on the shelf and asked to speak with the wine department manager. When he found her in the back, tasting wines with a California producer, he kindly asked where his wines could be found. She responded by explaining she was waiting for her Gallo rep to come in to place them on the shelf. Fuller was taken aback with the news. After months of work finalizing the sale, now it was in the hands of a California winery to merchandise it. This signified the power Gallo had in the marketplace. Selling wine was much trickier than anticipated.

AFTER-SCHOOL CALLS

Mom was late again. She was supposed to be at school twenty minutes ago. Luisa and I had gotten used to sitting on the cold steps after all the buses and cars had left. We would wait, watching the ladybugs and ants crawl along the front drive, until we'd catch a glimpse of our family car pulling up to meet us. Luisa and I would climb into the back seat of the car since Michel would already be in the front. Mom would have picked him up earlier from the middle school in Hillsboro. Today, I noticed wine in the back of the wagon.

Oh no. It's going to be one of those afternoons.

Mom had lugged three cases of wine in the back of our 1976 Datsun 710. She was very proud of her new car, since it was the ideal transport for wine deliveries. Grandma and Grandpa bought the car as a gift to my parents since Grandma felt strongly that Mom needed a reliable car if she was going to drive so frequently to and from Portland. The old Chrysler kept breaking down. My father was initially humiliated by the gesture, but soon realized the benefits of the upgrade.

"Sorry, guys, but I need to deliver an order to Strohecker's today," Mom began.

Then why can't I go to the Girl Scouts meeting with my friends instead?

"Ah, Mom, do we have to?" I whined.

"Yes. Then we'll take Michel to his piano lesson right after."

Great. An afternoon wasted.

We drove into Portland's West Hills to a favorite local market where Mom had become a fixture. The shop was owned by the Strohecker family. Wes and Wayne were at the helm of the operation, and Mom had become close with Wayne, who shared her love for conversation and wine. He had been responsible for transforming the entire basement of the family's market into a wine cellar to satisfy his obsession. Many of the best bottles in the city were found there.

We pulled into the familiar lot and parked near the loading dock. An unhappy man wearing a baseball cap nodded us through from his perch on a stool that was surrounded by dumpsters and stacks of empty cardboard boxes.

Each of us picked up a case and followed Mom through the back doors. The hall reeked of stinky old cheese, stale meat, vegetable waste, and whatever else had dropped, dripped, or been smashed on the concrete floor. Passing through the narrow stretch, I held my breath until we reached another set of doors that opened into the wine cellar. The ceilings were low, the worn carpet was burgundy, and the crowded room was packed solid with aisles of wine cases and wooden crates.

"Hey, Nancy!" a cheerful Wayne exclaimed, rushing over to greet us from behind the stack of cases. He welcomed our little crew with a smile, a hug for each of us girls, and a handshake for Michel.

"So, how is everyone today? Everyone is looking so good!" His sparkling blue eyes lit up the dark space.

Wayne always made us feel like what we were doing wasn't silly at all. Somehow, when we stood in his wineshop, it felt like we belonged. He always wanted to know what we were doing. "How's the vineyard? Are the vines all right with all this cold weather? What other wines have you tasted recently? Have you met this guy, Myron Redford? I love his white wines, and his Gamay is so good! Wow." He never stopped gushing about wine. Especially Oregon wines. He was a real fan. He loved being in the center of this movement, delighted to share his enthusiasm with his customers.

"Your Pinot Noir is something really special, Nancy. Dick really nailed it with those earthy notes, that bright cherry fruit, and the acid is beautiful. Really. You guys are doing it right!" He rambled on about the remarkable flavors, textures, and layers of our wine. These descriptors were becoming familiar to me, and it seemed like Wayne understood my parents' vision. I walked around the space, the way I did with Pop at the plumbing store, the junkyard, and Petrich's. But at Strohecker's I was enamored by the elegant candles, fancy wine keys, and clever cocktail napkins.

As I passed the shelves of wine, I searched for ours and finally spotted it. A bottle was situated on the bottom shelf, next to a bunch of French wines, collecting dust. It seemed unfair. There was no way anyone could see it, hiding so low to the ground.

I walked over to Mom and nudged her.

"Yes, Maria?"

I whispered, hoping Wayne didn't hear. "I think our wine is too low on that shelf. Nobody will see it. Don't you think it should be moved up?"

"Maybe, sweetie," she replied, clearly not hearing me.

She turned back to her conversation with Wayne, and I headed back to the walls of wine. I saw our Chardonnay in another section with a bunch of Napa Valley Chardonnay. The bottle was turned with the label facing the wall. I turned it so it faced forward. I went back and moved our Pinot Noir next to it, now on the middle shelf.

Much better, I thought. If they talked less and paid more attention to the displays, we'd probably have more success.

IN SEARCH OF SUPPORT

One night, Mom raised a new topic, albeit still about wine. After she placed a steaming platter of pepper steak and rice on the table, she filled two wineglasses with Pinot Noir and the other three with goat's milk. She lit a candle and sat down. Then my mother retold her L'Auberge story and how humiliated she felt and how she thought something had to be done to change the perception of Oregon wine in Portland.

"I think it's time we get some support. We need more people talking about what we're doing. I don't think we'll ever sell wine unless wine drinkers believe what we're doing is worth it. Sommeliers aren't willing to place an order unless there's demand."

"Aren't we doing that with the tasting room, Mom?" I asked. "People are tasting our wines there."

"Yes, but it's not enough. We need to get hold of people who influence the wine buyers. We need to meet the wine press. We need to introduce ourselves to them and change the market's perception of Oregon wine."

"That's true," Pop agreed. "But I also believe we need to work together to sell our wines outside the state. I know a lot of the guys are thinking the same thing. We're not having success here because the wines haven't received recognition nationally. We need that credibility."

"I guess we need to do both." The familiar wine chatter continued.

Were other people's dinners so long?

"Mom, I'm tired. Can I please be excused?" I jumped in when there was a break.

"Me too?" Luisa chimed in, bored as well.

"Sure." They looked at us as if they'd forgotten we were still there. We stood up with our dirty plates and headed for the kitchen. Michel moved to the piano and began practicing Scott Joplin—again—as my parents continued to discuss a plan. After finishing all the dishes, Luisa and I headed up to bed. My parents' conversation echoed up the stairs and continued well into the night, finally putting me to sleep.

The other "Pinot Obsessed" shared the same concerns. By now there were nearly ten wineries in the state: Coury, Erath, Eyrie, Oak Knoll, Sokol Blosser, Tualatin, Mount Hood Winery, Honeywood, and us. There were about thirty-five acres of vineyards planted. Most of the group realized the importance of promotion as the only way to keep things moving forward.

Initial shoestring budgets had been depleted, but the bills continued. By now, marriages were being tested, and emotions were at an all-time high. Workloads were never ending with minimal returns. It was obvious that the men's day jobs were insufficient. In order to survive, everyone would need to get involved with marketing. A strong community campaign was essential since nobody had the means to do it alone.

Mom jumped back on the phone and scheduled meetings with the neighboring wine women. These local women established themselves as the Washington County Wineries Association back in 1975, making it Oregon's first wine marketing group. They began to gather on a regular basis to discuss ways to more effectively market their wines and wineries.

I traveled with Mom to one of the meetings held in Marj Vuylsteke's living room after school one day and watched as these ambitious women sipped coffee and nibbled on freshly baked cookies. As a young girl, I listened and became inspired by their energy and courage. All were involved with the local community while still raising families and growing their family businesses. I sat on the comfy couch, overhearing the conversation, and I was reminded of the poster hanging in my bedroom: "Girls are expected to do twice as much as boys to be considered only half as good. Fortunately, that's not difficult." These women inspired me.

Mom continued to write for the *Hillsboro Argus*, sat on the board of the Jacktown Women's Club, and was the president of the Groner PTA. The other wine women were equally as busy. They discussed how to use their individual networks to inform their colleagues about the local wine industry and help spread the word.

"Our greatest challenge is that the general public doesn't understand the wine style," Mom stated. "There's a feeling that wine is simply a path to drunkenness. Most folks don't even know about fine wines, about dry wines. We need to educate them. They need to understand."

"I agree," Virginia Fuller chimed in. She was a soft-spoken woman with a tall, lean frame. "Maybe the thing to do is get people into the cellar, have them experience that environment, and taste the wines there?"

"I like it," Marj agreed. "Perhaps even more interesting would be inviting them to taste the wine before its time?"

The women laughed, as one of the most successful ad campaigns running at the time was Gallo's message of just the opposite: "We will sell no wine before its time."

"Hmm, that's interesting. You mean taste straight from the barrels?" Mom said. She leaned forward.

"Yes! Exactly. What better way for them to learn?" Marj continued.

"I like it." Virginia grinned. "Maybe we should do something special on the Fourth of July?"

And so it was agreed: the first group promotion would be suitably held on our nation's day of independence. The holiday provided the ideal opportunity for people to get out and enjoy local attractions. Each winery would open their tiny cellars and allow interested visitors to taste wine directly from the barrels. Tasks and all costs for the promotion would be shared equally among the group.

From my young perspective, it seemed like a bad idea for a few reasons. Firstly, none of the wineries had many barrels. Secondly, why show something unfinished? Thirdly, shouldn't we charge for our wine instead of giving it away? But of course, I said nothing. What did I know? I was only twelve years old. I snatched another cookie.

We hung large American flags on the cellar walls and bought smaller ones to put in the floral arrangements on the bar. On the warm Saturday following the national holiday, we swung open the doors and welcomed our guests inside. People flocked to our cellar for this unusual experience. Pop was staged in the cellar, pulling Pinot Noir samples, one by one, with his wine thief. Mom was stationed behind our makeshift bar, selling bottles of our current vintages to the merry guests. These novice wine enthusiasts loved tasting wine in such an unconventional way, with the winemaker who made it right there to talk about it. This activity attracted the attention of many locals who otherwise may have never come to one of the new wineries.

A couple weeks after the inaugural event, the wine women reconvened at Marj's home. It was time to decide if the event met their expectations.

"It was amazing!" Marj asserted, as we sat around her pine coffee table with embroidered doilies under a teapot and a plate of warm molasses cookies. "We probably had a hundred people here! And we sold wine! At full markup! I think we should do more events together and more frequently."

Mom nodded. "Yes, it was successful, but we went through a lot of wine. I wonder if we could avoid pouring free wine from our few barrels. We have so little." By this time, we had grown our wine production to about a hundred barrels (2,500 cases) that included mainly Pinot Noir, Chardonnay, and a little Riesling.

"Why not just have an open house?" Corinne Gross of Cooper Mountain Vineyard offered. "We could all have our tasting rooms open but map a loop around the area. At each winery, visitors would receive a tasting of whatever wines we select."

"Sounds easy enough," Mom said. "Perhaps there could be an incentive for them to visit more than one of our wineries?"

"What if we create a sort of passport where the visitor gets a stamp at each winery? If they visit three tasting rooms, they could take home a logoed wineglass or something," Shirley Coury said.

This became the first guided winery loop in the state and launched over Memorial Day weekend. It was such a success, the group decided to host a similar event over the Thanksgiving holiday weekend. The second wine tour loop had a different incentive: those who visited at least three wineries over the weekend received a handcrafted cork Christmas tree ornament. I thought the ornaments were awful, but our guests loved them. They were made at a factory in Hillsboro that employed disabled people, and the group was able to get them for only two cents each. They were made from used wine corks, pipe cleaners, eye bobbles, ribbon, and other crafty items. Once glued together, each one resembled a snowman, reindeer, elf, or some other holiday caricature. They were a hit, as was the passport concept, and the open house weekends became a holiday tradition well into the future.

These successful campaigns were significant as they demonstrated the impact that could result from simple collaboration and limited resources. While most of the men continued to work on perfecting their wines and were forced to maintain their day jobs to support their families and growing operations, the women's marketing contributions became increasingly important.

I felt their work was even more significant since most married women at this time lost their birth names and identities to their husbands. For example, my mother was recognized as Mrs. Richard Ponzi. This is how a married woman would sign a household check, completely abandoning her first and maiden name. She was also unable to access bank information or apply for a credit card without her husband's consent. By quietly taking control of some of the business demands, the women felt valued, but it was no small feat. They often worked behind the scenes, swallowing pride when they were expected to draft important letters, only later to be told their signatures wouldn't be necessary. Men still handled all the important details.

Because these first marketing efforts were spearheaded by women, the messages were sometimes misunderstood. People often categorized the new wineries as simple hobby projects. We were labeled "cute," "adorable," and "fun." It was difficult for the women to emphasize that our livelihoods were dependent on the success of selling our product. Meanwhile, the men were devoted to mastering it, committed to the fact that the wine quality was most critical. From my perspective, however, it seemed the women understood that marketing and sales were equally as important.

CONSTANT CARE

Dinner was late again. I think Mom had all the best intentions of serving dinner by seven, like most American families, but somehow it was often closer to nine before we were all seated.

"Maria!" Mom shouted from the bottom of the stairs. "Can I get you to set the table and maybe help with the salad dressing?"

Again? Where is Luisa or Michel? Why is it always me?

"Yeah! Sure." I put away the letter I was writing to my pen pal in Paris and marched down the hall, kicking Luisa's garbage out of my way. She was in her bunk bed, reading a *CRICKET Magazine*.

"You really should clean up your room. It's disgusting," I said flatly. She didn't look up.

I continued down the stairs. My mood changed when I smelled dinner: beef stroganoff. My favorite.

"Yum!" I grabbed place mats, napkins, dishes, silverware, and candles. Mom always insisted upon a nice table. The ritual felt like church, even though we weren't religious and I'd never attended a church. The most important components—flowers, candles, and music—were mandatory and expected to be perfect. I enjoyed setting the table, choosing the color of candles to match the place mats, and taking time to properly fold the cloth napkins. Fresh flowers were common, as was Chopin or Mozart playing softly in the background. Once the table was set, I would move on to my famous vinaigrette dressing. I performed these two tasks like clockwork most evenings. There was something comforting about being around my mother in the kitchen. Even though I never paid much attention to how she was making the food, which was more Luisa's interest, I enjoyed being near her. I was drawn to her grace and competency.

Dinner finished around ten. As usual, Luisa and I hopped up to wash the dishes while Michel shifted over to play an Elton John piece on the piano. Mom and Pop stayed at the table to talk. After our chores, I headed upstairs to my most cherished place: my bedroom, where I would snuggle under the warm blankets and wait for Pop. He never forgot to tuck us in with a kiss each night.

"Hey, sweetie," he said, pulling open my large drape to enter my room. He climbed my ladder a couple rungs.

"Hi, Pop." I leaned over and gave him a hug. "You going to bed?"

"I will a little later. I still have some work to do in the winery."

"What? Pop, it's so late. What do you need to do?"

"I'm concerned the fermenters aren't heating up fast enough. It's been so cold. I'm going to wrap them with electric blankets to get the ferments moving."

"Oh boy. You're crazy." I leaned over and gave him another kiss on the cheek.

"Good night." He reached around and tucked the blankets all the way under my body down to my toes, then kissed my head.

The fall of 1977 was one of the coldest we'd experienced since moving to Oregon. And nobody had temperature-controlled fermenters. They didn't exist. Instead, most of us had plastic bins that did nothing to control the fermenting temperatures—one of the most important steps of quality winemaking.

While we were all snug in bed, I imagined my father heading back into the dark, wet night, carrying a heavy load of electric blankets in his arms. He told me the next day how he'd used extension cords to connect them together, securing them around each bin with several large bungee cords. Then the blankets were plugged into the wall, and he cranked the heat as high as possible. The hope was it would be enough to kick the yeast into gear and start the fermentation. If the ferments didn't come alive soon, we could lose the entire vintage. I knew Pop was worried, and I imagined him lying awake in his bed that night, considering his options and problem-solving. It seemed to never end.

WINERY

By the fall of 1978, we were headed into our fifth harvest and needed more room to make the wine. The plan was relatively simple: move from the current garage to the old one. Pop always imagined the garage adjacent to our first home (the shack) would become the main winery. By now, our small production of wine had increased to nearly five hundred cases, and Mom had grown tired of restaging the tasting room in the garage following each harvest. It was time to expand. The banks were still apprehensive when it came to the young wine industry. Therefore, as usual, Pop was forced to get creative.

From his visits to the wine regions of Europe, he knew he wanted to create a structure that conveyed a similar sense of permanence while maintaining an authentic connection to the Willamette Valley. He particularly admired the works of legendary architect Frank Lloyd Wright. Wright's handsome rooflines and use of local wood and stone were components Pop wanted to incorporate in his building. His time at Disneyland also influenced the design: keep the facade impressive and the rear simple. He felt we should invest money in front but keep costs down in back.

The general idea was to bring the original garage together with the shack to create a single structure. The garage was ideal for a winery: open space, concrete floors, a small shop, and an attic. Even though Dale still lived in the shack, Mom and Pop saw the potential for a permanent future tasting room there. That would come later, but for now, the two buildings, sitting so close to each other, provided an idyllic setting for a small winery.

The first step required stone. My father felt an exterior rock wall would evoke a sense of permanence, mimicking some of the world's most admired producers. There was something exotic about stone that would demonstrate the sophistication he desired for our winery. Even though rock wasn't nearly as common in the valley as timber, there happened to be a quarry just minutes from our house. Pop decided to stop in one day and have a look. He spoke to some of the workers there, who told him there was often a collection of rejected basalt that was of no use to them. Pop knew an opportunity when he saw one.

Later that week, he took Michel and the banana truck out to the pit and filled it with as many pieces of flat basalt as possible. The truck inched down the driveway; its four tires flat from the weight of the valuable material.

"What a find!" Mom exclaimed as the truck came to a stop in front of the old garage.

I knew we were destined for another work party. My cousins were visiting for the summer, and I knew they'd want to attend the big event.

"I've already called the Downs, the Grimms, my folks, and your mother," Mom announced. "And Dale can help first thing in the morning."

I dreaded the next day. *Lots* of people and more work.

* * *

I woke to the familiar sound of nails pounding into wood echoing across the property. Pop had risen before us, completing the necessary forms for the stone wall. I peeked out to the fields past my window and then pulled the warm covers toward my chest.

"Time to get up!" Mom's voice traveled up from the bottom of the stairs. I waited for the second call.

"Come on, kids!" There it was. I pushed the cozy blanket aside and lifted myself over the edge of the bed. *Another day of crazy.*

"This is going to be so great!" Pop exclaimed, meeting us outside near the garage. His blue eyes were twinkling, and his rosy cheeks were alive with the fresh morning air.

"Come hold on to this corner. This should be it." Luisa and I reached over and held two boards at a ninety-degree angle so he could hammer nails into the final form. He had already built a frame outlining the wall. It looked cool, though I couldn't tell how it was all going to come together.

The familiar cars began to roll in. First, the Grimms. Ray wouldn't have missed this for anything. He jumped out of his little green Subaru, quickly walking toward the building and scanning the scene through his wire-rimmed glasses. His speckled beard, gray beret, and brown clogs were paired with a well-worn blue sweater. He was appropriately dressed like an art professor.

"You already started?" he shouted to Pop. "Hey, are you sure these two-by-fours are going to be strong enough? When does the concrete come?"

Pop looked up from his work, happy to see his good friend already questioning his decisions. These two were masters of consideration and loved to exhaust all the possibilities of how something could be done. Their discussions often lasted for hours until ultimately they'd choose one path and move on to the logistics and the fun of making it happen. They both reveled in the adventure.

"Yep. We're all set. It should arrive soon."

The Wysongs pulled up with their older boys, and Derek and his family were next. Pop began to organize.

"Once the concrete arrives, we're going to need to work quickly, but carefully." He smiled at everyone, then continued. "I'll need a couple people lifting the stones up to the others who will place them into the concrete and hold them while the pour comes. I will monitor the flow of concrete coming from the trough. Those of you on ladders placing the stones, be sure the largest surface of stone is positioned so the nice side faces out." He winked as everyone recognized his eye for detail.

Everyone nodded. I moved to the back of the crowd, thinking I might be able to get out of the work, after all, as it sounded like a lot of heavy lifting and there were plenty of other people around to help.

I heard the gravel grind as an enormous cement truck rolled toward us. Its massive rear end spinning with the heavy weight of wet concrete mesmerized me. Everyone got in place, and the truck began to pour the heavy gray liquid into the wooden frame while the crew held stones to the outside edges. Feeling the dangerous mix of too many people in proximity to heavy cement and big rocks, I stepped back and watched safely from the lawn.

As expected, the end of the day concluded with lively conversation despite aching backs, rough bare hands, and random bruises. Mom had made everyone lasagna the night before, and our hearty group now gathered together, eating and drinking wine and soaking in the satisfaction of the day's efforts.

Pop waited several weeks for the concrete to cure before removing the outside frame. As he and Michel finally started breaking it away, the stone wall began to reveal itself. The next step required a chisel to break off the rough parts, resulting in a beautiful smooth face of stone that stood about five feet tall. To complete the look, Mom and Pop brought in a couple loads of fresh dirt to mound in front of its base. Mom couldn't wait to plant lavender in front of it the way she'd admired the French and Italian estates.

The modern look of cor-ten steel seemed a likely material for the roof. Pop loved its texture and the way it weathered, turning from rusty orange to dark-chocolate brown. He thought it would fit well into the Northwest landscape, especially nestled among the old-growth fir trees that surrounded the site. It was a significant investment, and I overheard many late-night conversations over whether it was worth it. In the end, my parents concluded this was where they needed to splurge. The roof required renting a small crane to lift each heavy section into place. Once they were positioned, my father secured the sheets onto massive beams he'd recovered from a nearby collapsed barn. These refurbished beams supported the roof as well as determined the length of the building.

Pop worked every day, all summer long, completing the project. His finishing touch was a large, handsome front door he had carefully designed and made from paneled fir. As was sometimes typical for my pop, he didn't always finish the final step: a lock to the premises. He didn't feel it was that necessary, so it was never installed. Our makeshift solution was a two-by-four that sat upon two steel braces behind the stately front. This served as our security system for years.

By the end of summer, we had a fully dedicated space to grow the operation. The room was multifunctional. It received the harvested fruit, staged the destemmer, and housed the press, all our fermenters, and oak barrels. Following harvest, we used it to bottle and label the wine, and during the off-season, we entertained visitors and tasted wines with them there. This new building was life changing and continued to be the center of our operation for many decades.

Completing the expansion required adapting the original shack to a tasting room. Dale was just married, and he and his new wife, Barb, felt they should move out. It was perfect timing as Mom and Pop were ready to move the tasting room away from family activities. We'd grown tired of strangers coming into our house, using the bathroom, and hanging out on our porch. It was our first attempt to designate family life from work life. *Ha!*

Every weekend, we worked on the new tasting room. We removed that terrible sliding glass door, tiled the floor, and opened the space by demolishing most of the hall and kitchen. Pop hired a local cabinetmaker to construct a small oak bar that would allow at least eight people to stand and taste. It seemed so slick to have a real bar after using doors for so long! Pop installed two bathrooms in the rear, where our old bedroom used to be, which also felt quite elaborate. We rolled in empty barrels, using them to merchandise the wine, and hung photographs of Pinot Noir grape clusters on the walls.

Having this new tasting room meant we could bring in other items to sell beyond wine. My father was reluctant when Mom suggested we sell wineglasses and T-shirts with our logo. He didn't feel it was necessary to promote anything but wine. "This room is to educate and present our wines, not silly T-shirts," he proclaimed. Regardless, Mom placed a small order with the local printshop, and when they began to sell, he realized the potential of the wineshop. It was beginning to feel like a real business.

WHITE WINES RULE

By the late 1970s, it had become increasingly apparent that white wines were going to become very important to us. Unlike Pinot Noir, which required two years of aging in expensive French oak barrels, white wines could ferment and finish in stainless steel barrels in less than six months. This meant we could sell the whites much earlier and at a lower price than Pinot Noir. It was a critical discovery at a point when cash continued to be tight. Mom was still taking us to Goodwill for back-to-school clothes, and lentil soup had unfortunately become a signature dinner dish.

For the past four years, we had been working with the Alsatian varieties of Riesling, Müller-Thurgau, Gewürztraminer, Sylvaner, and Muscat. These all came from the original vines we planted in front of our house. Mom and Pop realized after the first couple of vintages most of these wines didn't excite them nearly as much as Pinot Noir, but they felt they might be easier to sell than our red. So, they got clever.

Since the varieties were not enjoyed individually, the idea of blending came to mind. Perhaps by putting the grapes together, the wine would be more interesting, and we could create a "volume" product. "The Oregon Harvest Wine" was born. This blended white also answered my mother's question of how to enter the Portland restaurant scene. The wine was bottled into gallon jugs and sold to some of the top restaurants in the city as an inexpensive glass pour, a kind of current "keg wine."

Based on the success of the Oregon Harvest Wine, my parents later created a similar product named Marisa—a combination of my name and Luisa's. Instead of jugs, Marisa was packaged as something very special and was adorned with a floral wallpaper aesthetic and elegant script. Despite its attractive label and price, the wine inside was less impressive, and the project didn't live past its first vintage. I was disappointed our namesake wine flopped and made a note to be careful when naming something after loved ones.

I overheard my parents' conversations, and I learned there was another sign of hope during this period of white wine discovery. A relatively unknown variety, Pinot Gris, also recognized as Tokay d'Alsace in Alsace and Pinot Grigio in Italy, showed promise in the cool valley. Mom and Pop had been introduced to the wine on one of their earlier trips to Alsace. They couldn't help but notice whenever they sat down with local vintners, they poured this wine at the end of a meal as something very special. Whether Pinot Gris would reap any commercial value in our area was an entirely separate topic, but a few of us were willing to give it a try.

"I hear Lett planted a few Pinot Gris cuttings in his original site," Pop started one evening while Mom pulled some slightly burned garlic bread from the oven. "I'll see if he's willing to sell us some cuttings."

"Well, I love this wine, and if it ripens well and we can get it to market quickly, I think it's a great idea." Mom was always ready to try something new, especially if it meant seeing a return.

Unfortunately, Lett was unable to share the few cuttings he had, so Pop ended up purchasing a couple hundred from UCD. He built a small greenhouse onto the rear of the garage that housed the plants until spring. To accelerate the process, they also decided to graft some of the Pinot Gris cuttings onto about two acres of the existing white varieties in our vineyard. This required taking the base of a current plant, cutting a V into it, inserting the grafted plant on top, and sealing it together like a splint. Doing this would expedite the growth, meaning we would have grapes a year earlier than those planted on their own roots.

In addition to the grafted acres, Mom and Pop cleared an acre on the north end of our vineyard and two acres on the south end of our property. This expanded our small vineyard by an additional three acres. In total, we now had nearly five acres of Pinot Gris and the remaining ten acres planted in Pinot Noir, Riesling, and Chardonnay.

My father spied three empty stainless steel Coca-Cola barrels sitting in an empty warehouse one day and brought five of them home for less than twenty dollars each. His mind was on Pinot Gris. This wine, unlike Chardonnay and Pinot Noir, wasn't meant to have a lot of tannin or structure, so oak barrels were unnecessary. Instead, Mom and Pop said the wine should be fresh and lively—to be enjoyed with lighter dishes.

Three years later, we released our first commercial bottling of 1981 Pinot Gris. It was a small amount, just a hundred half bottles, and we sold them that summer for five dollars each. The idea was to get this new wine out to as many people as possible so they'd start talking about it. As expected, the Portland market was suspect: What is this wine and why should we buy it? Nobody had heard of it or even knew how to pronounce it. Our strategy would remain the same: educate.

Now that I was thirteen years old, Mom and Pop felt I could handle the tasting room myself, allowing them to focus on other projects. Although I was still afraid of any public interaction, I'd overcome middle school bullying, which toughened me up, and my involvement in school theater bolstered my courage, forcing me to face my greatest fear: public speaking. Through multiple performances, I felt myself transform in front of an audience, and slowly my fears of being on stage decreased. In fact, I started to dream of becoming an actress. Hours of reading scripts and rehearsing acts forced me to become great at memorization too. All of this came in handy when I was asked to stand behind the bar and talk about our new wine.

"'Gris' means 'gray' in French," I'd begin. "This is how the grape gets its name. The cluster is small, with purple-gray berries. When the fruit is pressed, the juice is white. We ferment it in stainless steel so the flavors are retained and the resulting wine is fresh and clean." The words rolled off my tongue so easily, most people probably thought I actually drank it.

"But what's the name of the grape?" a confused visitor asked.

"Pinot Gris. The wine has the same name as the grape."

"You mean it's not a blend?"

"No, we don't blend many varieties in Oregon," I replied.

"Why do you put it in such a small bottle?"

"We don't make much of it. In fact, we're only one of three producers in the country that make this wine," I explained easily. *Listen to me. What a pro.*

"Wow. That's pretty neat." Then they'd walk out of the room, amused by my little story about this unusual grape we were trying to grow in our "hobby" vineyard.

* * *

After two years of producing Pinot Gris, David Adelsheim, David Lett, and Pop all decided it had significant potential. They loved that it naturally ripened in the vineyard and fermented with ease in the cellar. Best of all, the flavors were well matched with those of a traditional Tokay d'Alsace, making it another food-friendly wine, elegant and well balanced. Mom loved we didn't have to wait two years to sell it, and the price was less than both our Chardonnay and Pinot Noir. She happily added it to her wine bag to present it alongside our more expensive wines—eight dollars for the Pinot Noir.

It was at this point that the three winemakers decided to get out of the state to tell the story of Oregon Pinot Gris—and the Willamette Valley. Unless we started showing it to the trade like our other wines, the market would never be interested in our region. Adelsheim, Lett, and Pop would use Pinot Gris as a vehicle to tell our story and invite the opportunity to discuss our coveted Pinot Noir. The three men began traveling as a trio across the nation, often seeing themselves as educators more than winemakers. Together, the wineries produced less than a thousand cases of Pinot Gris.

BOUTIQUE BULK

The 1978 vintage was tough. While 1977 was wet and cold, 1978 was hot. The summer was considered one of the warmest in Willamette Valley history. Temperatures in July and August reached as high as 98 to 100 degrees. The winemakers believed without the common cool temperatures, ranging from the high 70s to mid-80s, the grapes would not retain good acidity. These hot temperatures would also mean high sugar levels, which translated into high alcohol. Attaining the balance of fruit character, acidity, and sugar content was the winemaker's focus, and cool temperatures were at the core of creating elegant wines.

We struggled through the harvest, attempting to cool down the fermentations and generally slow the process. It was almost impossible. Winemakers feared the resulting wines would be clumsy and uninteresting. They were concerned they wouldn't depict the true wines of the region, and for the many inexperienced vintners, it was considered a failed vintage. The question on everyone's mind was how could we show the world the region's potential if we couldn't produce beautiful wines every year? For fear of harming the developing reputation of the valley, many producers chose not to sell their wines that year.

Having cases of inferior wine left my parents anxious. We had to sell something. Mom and Pop had to find a way to make it work. They struggled with a solution for several weeks before finally coming up with a plan.

Mom and I were folding the laundry at the kitchen table when she started explaining the dilemma. As usual, I was more concerned that my favorite pair of jeans were wrinkled because too many clothes had been crammed into the dryer—again. *Don't people understand? You can't overpack a dryer!*

Mom was going on and on about how the wine may not be up to standard, but how we had to find a way to sell it. We couldn't afford to simply pass on an entire vintage.

"So, I'm thinking we will call it Boutique Bulk," she exclaimed.

"I don't get it," I said, trying to process the words. "What does that even mean?"

My father walked by the table.

"We are a boutique winery, but we just made wine of bulk quality!"

Both Pop and I were quiet for a moment, but then he responded, "That's actually brilliant, Nancy." She looked up at him and giggled. "Yes, I think that might work."

Mom continued with her marketing plan. "I'll ask Jere to design a unique label just for this wine, and we can create a story around it. The packaging itself will be so appealing, it will surely sell despite the wine's poor quality."

It seemed a little shady to me, like the building on our label that didn't exist. But then again, what did I know? I didn't even understand what "boutique" or "bulk" meant. And I surely didn't know what made a wine good or bad. Even when I tried the ones everyone said they loved, I felt they were awful.

Mom and Pop nailed it. Once the wine released in 1980, we successfully sold it. People raved about the creative packaging, colorful and bold. Nobody seemed to mind the quality, and few even asked the meaning of the unusual name.

Throughout those years, though my parents were always concerned about the lack of cash, they did a great job of hiding their worries from us. I later learned they had been trading wine for basic needs. Somehow, they'd found a group of hippies whose mission was to exchange products and services instead of money. One of the greatest trades my parents scored was for dental care. The five of us were well cared for by a local dentist for years through several cases of Riesling. Luisa even got braces out of the deal. Before Western Airlines morphed into Delta Airlines, one of their stellar employees and a family friend would occasionally snag my parents a plane ticket in exchange for some cases of Chardonnay. Pop loved this tack.

While my parents were worrying over money, the weather, and how to achieve consistent wine quality, for me, the late 1970s was all about how to achieve "the look." Golden-haired, tanned, blue-eyed Farrah Fawcett was everywhere, and her bouncy blonde feathered hairstyle was the absolute rage. For a middle schooler in Hillsboro, following trends was vital, and the transition from Groner to Brown Junior High had been difficult. I was bullied my first year despite attempts to remain inconspicuous. My shyness did not help, nor did my thrift-store wardrobe at a time when brands were essential.

Hair became a focus. I had good hair, and if I styled it right, I felt I might have a chance of accomplishing my main goal of fitting in. To do so, I had to be in the bathroom well before Luisa and Michel. Fortunately, that was relatively easy since they both liked to sleep in and didn't require the beauty care I did. Following fifteen minutes of artful blow-drying and another ten minutes of meticulous curling, I would preserve my work with several heavy coats of Aqua Net. I never seemed to resemble Farrah despite my efforts, but at least I gave it a good shot. I found it didn't matter most days, since Oregon's constant drizzle would take down every curl before I even reached the bus stop, leaving me to enter school with my all-too-familiar frizz. *Oregon!*

By 1979, eleven years after our move to Oregon, we began to hear about more families moving to the area with the same plan of planting Pinot Noir. There seemed to be an unusual amount of activity south of us, near Myron's vineyard in Amity. Most folks in the wine trade by now had heard about the start-ups. Many of them had met Erath, Lett, or Pop and referred to them as "The Boys Up North." The story was if you had the courage, heartiness, and work ethic, you could still purchase property up there for a dime. So, if you didn't have a fortune to drop in the California wine country but still had a drive for making wine, the Willamette Valley held promise. But it was still in its infancy, unknown and unproven.

Twin brothers, Ted and Terry Casteel, and their wives were interested in growing wine grapes, despite their lack of experience or education in agriculture. Like the rest of us, they were in search of a simple life where they could raise their children and live off the land. The Casteels built both their homes, started raising their babies, and planted their fifty acres of vineyards in 1979. It seemed the Casteels were especially interested in farming and were drawn to the common philosophy of the "Pinot Obsessed" commitment to being good stewards to the land. Many years later, they were instrumental in bringing a certification for sustainable farming practices to the state.

While all this was going on, I was a teenager and blissfully unaware of most of it. I busied myself attending football games and meeting friends at the pizza parlor, where we played PacMan for hours. I made any excuse to avoid family activities. I was far more immersed in adjusting to junior high culture: how to buy strawberry-flavored Kissing Potion lip gloss and apply Maybelline blue eye shadow without Mom noticing. Occasionally, Pop would slip me a private note under my pillow with advice on how to manage some drama in my adolescent life. Even though we rarely had serious talks, he was always sensitive to how I was feeling without my even mentioning it. He and I had a special, quiet bond throughout my teenage years. I knew I could share my most intimate issues with him. Although he remained consumed with the wine thing and was constantly planning for his classes, I knew he was always there for me.

MARKETING
AND PR

We were producing around a thousand cases of wine in 1979, and my parents knew they couldn't sell it all themselves. Something had to give. Until this time, we were making deliveries in the Datsun all over Portland to our few supporters, which kept Mom constantly on the kitchen phone trying to set appointments with the handful of important local restaurants and grocery stores. Most of these accounts remained relatively uninterested in our product, rarely taking the time even to taste. The majority of Portland's drinkers remained devoted to California Cabernet and Chardonnay, and buyers could not be convinced to add local wines to their lists.

My parents were smart enough to know they needed sales expertise: people who were well respected in the industry and who had a far better chance at explaining why our wines, and Oregon wines in general, were worth considering. My mother sent a letter to one of the very few local wine wholesalers, Henny-Hinsdale Distributing, asking for their representation. The small firm was owned and operated by Karen and Howard

Hinsdale, a young couple who had established their distrib-utorship in the city selling predominately French Burgundies and Bordeaux. They said they would look at our wines, and after tasting the Pinot Noirs, they agreed to represent us for a small fee. It was a terrific relief to Mom and Pop knowing they had veteran wine salespeople on our side.

There was never-ending conversation at the table that night even after they announced the news to us. It went beyond the need for Oregon sales. They discussed the need for additional national exposure, and one method would be to involve our-selves in competitions.

Mom pointed out entering a wine contest meant having to have complete confidence in one's product. This was especially true if it was coming from an unknown area. Furthermore, Pop stressed that whatever resulted from the competition would naturally reflect on everyone from the unknown com-munity. They questioned whether the region was ready for this kind of brutal exposure. Some of the "Pinot Obsessed" hadn't quite garnered that level of confidence, but one woman who had been visiting Oregon for several years had become a fan of our region's wines and encouraged it.

Becky Wasserman, a French wine importer, returned to her Manhattan apartment following one of her many visits to the Willamette Valley with several bottles of rare Oregon Pinot Noir. When she heard about a wine competition sched-uled in Paris, she decided to participate.

This event came just three years after the famous Judgment of Paris in 1976, a tasting hosted by a British wine merchant, Steven Spurrier, who only sold French wines at the time. The results of the international blind tasting shocked the wine world when two California wines stole the show, ranking top in two categories: Cabernet and Chardonnay.

The competition was the 1979 Wine Olympics, organized by the French food and wine magazine *Gault-Millau*. A total of 330 wines were submitted from thirty-three countries and evaluated by sixty-two experts from ten nationalities. France dominated in both the number of wine entries and in the number of judges. All the wines were tasted blind. Wasserman submitted one of her favorite Oregon Pinot Noirs.

Wines from California won six of the top ten ranks in the Chardonnay judging and the Cabernet-Merlot blend category. But most importantly for all of us in Oregon, the 1975 Eyrie Vineyards South Block Reserve placed within the top ten wines in the Pinot Noir category. It was the first time an Oregon wine was recognized in a global setting, and the fact it was selected over some of Burgundy's finest producers was shocking.

Several Oregon producers were unaware the judging had taken place until word spread of the results. We were thrilled. It was a huge victory for Oregon. The French were so outraged, they insisted on a second judging the following year, when another Eyrie Pinot Noir placed just second behind a bottle from a prominent and well-respected Burgundian producer.

In addition to these international competitions, Mom and Pop also knew that recognition in New York would be equally important to bringing attention to the region. New York City was predominantly home to European wines and boasted the nation's most acclaimed restaurants and most knowledgeable wine drinkers at the time.

Mom began researching wine media. She scanned as many local and national newspapers and trade publications as she could get her hands on, building a lengthy list of important wine writers. Before Google, this meant visiting grocery stores, bookstores, and small magazine shops, hunting for contact information and talking to the "Pinot Obsessed" for any leads.

Simultaneously, Pop was developing a list of wine distributors across the country. Before email, websites, and social media, the search for wine wholesalers required calls to colleagues and friends in the wine business and wineshops across the nation. The next step was finding appropriate leads for those marketing fine wines, another layer of research. This daunting and tireless task would continue for decades. All the young Oregon wine families were doing similar work, and when anyone found anything of value, that information was often shared among the group.

At last Mom had compiled her long list of wine journalists.

"Here you go, Dick." They sat together and reviewed the roster of names she created. "I feel it's important we send samples to most of them. I know we don't have many bottles to spare, but we need to get them writing about Oregon and most importantly, about Pinot Noir."

My father agreed. "It's going to be difficult to give away free wine, but without any knowledge of the region, none of us have a chance beyond our backyard—and even that's not working."

"I don't see how else we're going to do this unless people taste the wines to realize the area's potential," Mom continued.

Both were willing to risk giving free product in hopes of receiving positive media coverage. But it wasn't just our wine they were interested in exposing; it was about gaining attention for all of us. We were in it together. One family's success was a win for everyone.

Mom sat down with her typewriter and wrote lengthy letters to the handful of select writers they felt would have the greatest influence. I read over her shoulder as she described the subtle attributes of the Pinot Noir grape and why it was so well suited to our climate. She wrote about Oregon's location and specifically about how the Willamette Valley was nestled between two mountain ranges, comparing it to Burgundy. I understood how she was painting a picture for them to better comprehend our region. She addressed how Oregon winegrowers were committed to producing wines of authenticity, noting how our wine labels defined the actual name of the grape varietal and the restriction we made to blending. She illustrated how we treated the juice gently, in small batches, without the use of pumps, and how we preferred slow, cool fermentations and only used the very best French oak barrels for aging. She made sure to explain how everything was done by hand to ensure the very highest quality. The letters were long and detailed, but necessary.

Later that week, Mom and I packed the samples on the kitchen table. I could sense her trepidation as she pulled bottles of our precious 1977 Pinot Noir from the case, hoping it would be enjoyed by someone in the press. We sent a dozen of these to the most important wine writers in the country.

Several weeks passed. My parents remained hopeful, but heard nothing back. Mom's follow-up phone calls went nowhere. They scanned the important trade publications weekly. The table became cluttered with stacks of wine magazines and newspapers opened to the "Wine Review" sections. But there were only the same rave reviews of French Bordeaux and Napa Valley Cabernet and Chardonnay. Nevertheless, they kept a keen eye on the most significant ones: the *New York Times* and the *San Francisco Examiner.*

And then it happened. We were seated at the dinner table, passing bowls of minestrone soup and warm frites, when Mom shared the news.

"Guess what, guys!" she exclaimed. Her smile was big, and her green eyes sparkled. Pop gave her a wink and grinned as he bit into the freshly fried bread.

"What?" I responded, intrigued by their excitement.

"We just got reviewed by Frank Prial!" Mom announced.

"Who's that?" Luisa asked as she pulled apart a frite.

"The wine writer at the *New York Times*! And guess what—he loved our wine!" Pop reached over and kissed Mom's cheek. He was beaming. Mom was beaming. Everyone stopped eating and put their spoons down. Something big had just happened.

There was absolute silence. Luisa, Michel, and I weren't really sure what this meant.

"You mean they wrote about our wine?"

"Yes! Not only did he write about it, but he *loved* it!"

"That is so cool!" I leaped from my chair and wrapped my arms around Pop. Luisa and Michel joined me, laughing in delight.

"Where is it?" Michel asked. Mom passed the folded newspaper to him.

"This is really great news. It's really good news for *all* of us," Pop said with confidence. We picked up our glasses and raised them, big smiles plastered on our faces.

It was our first real triumph, our first win. This was the acknowledgment Mom and Pop needed to keep moving forward. The published article, written by one of the country's most prominent wine professionals at the time gave them the confidence to keep pursuing their dream. We felt fulfilled knowing someone across the nation actually enjoyed our wine and didn't refer to us as crazy.

HILHI DAYS

Almost as soon as I started high school, our lives began to take on a different rhythm. I dove into all the extracurricular activities offered at Hillsboro High School. My time was spent writing and photographing for the school newspaper, editing and creating the yearbook, crafting arguments with the debate team, and participating in student government. I attempted to try out for cheerleading, but when Mom got word of that, she drove the forty minutes to school and pulled me off the gym floor before the auditions even began. My mother felt it was demeaning for young women to dress minimally and dance seductively in front of an audience. As a true feminist, she didn't want me to have anything to do with it. A similar opinion applied to typing classes. To Mom, both activities represented a kind of subservience. Instead, she encouraged my interests in writing and politics. I was swept away in all the activities, quite aware it meant more time at school and less time at home, where I'd be asked to do real work.

The second notable change my freshman year was that kids slowly warmed up to me. Instead of the usual bullying and teasing I'd grown accustomed to, kids now seemed to show a curiosity in me. Once my peers learned my home included a winery, they'd suggest I have parties there. This idea surprised me. I had never imagined anyone would want to come to my house since we lived so far away, on a farm out in the country. But when I realized they wanted to visit because we had a winery, it scared me. I'd always seen wine as precious, so the audacity of kids wanting to get drunk from it was incomprehensible. I wanted nothing to do with that and once again realized the familiar discomfort of being misunderstood by my classmates.

At home, everything seemed busier too. We were spending less time with the animals and the gardening. The ducks and geese my parents had added to the farm had been forgotten, foraging below the confines of our fenced pasture, left to fend for themselves among the local coyotes. Our forgotten Shetland pony, Donovan, who had been a favored pet years earlier, was also left alone in the field. The focus had turned from the farm to the growing demands of the vineyard, the winery, and school activities.

Things were progressing with the "Pinot Obsessed," and demands on my parents continued to increase, but as we were learning, generally any setback or success relating to the wines developed at a slow pace. There was very little, if any, immediate gratification. After seven vintages, Pop was only beginning to gain confidence in his winemaking skills. It was challenging to navigate the varying vintages; a wet year followed by a warmer one meant treating the vines and wines much differently.

Pop's focus remained, as always, on making improvements. He took what he learned from one vintage and applied those results to the next. One year at a time. With each vintage he discovered a little more. He considered each part of the process: Should the juice spend more time on the skins or less time? Should we punch the cap down more or less? What yeast strain is showing the best results? Which barrel is best for the wine? Does the barrel cooperage make a difference? How do the different oak forests affect the wine? Could one barrel affect a vineyard block differently than another?

There were so many components to the puzzle. It was clearly not a profession for people who relied on set formulas and procedures. It was a craft for rare individuals who thrived on tackling new challenges and who could adapt, stay flexible, and above all be patient. It seemed the questions would only be answered with time.

Meanwhile, Mom continued to dedicate herself to the public relations efforts. She, like Pop, was learning it was vital for her to be creative and think broadly despite limited resources. Attracting visitors to the winery was increasingly important as we sold the wine at retail prices here, and the cash was immediate. In addition to those benefits, Mom believed the on-site experience was the best opportunity to educate and excite the public about table wine, a term most people still didn't understand. But at the core of all the efforts was the nagging sense that few people still took us seriously.

Once summer officially began, Luisa, Michel, and I were found in one of two places: the strawberry fields or the vineyards. Neither place suited me, but it was expected, and I was enticed by the chance to make money. The strawberry fields were near our home, and farmers needed as many hands as possible to quickly harvest the crop. Hiring country kids to do the work was common, earning us a dollar per flat. This took about thirty to forty minutes if you were a fast picker, focused, and chose the biggest berries. The best time of the day came when the row boss would call for lunch, and I would try to negotiate a Hostess Ding Dong from a friend. Strictly forbidden at home, the moist chocolate cake and sugary white frosting made the rest of my afternoon in the hot sun a little more bearable. On a good day, I would earn about five dollars.

After the strawberries were picked, we turned to the vineyard. By July, it was necessary for us all to help. The vines were filled with buds that quickly climbed the trellis, and the growth needed to be managed. My day would start by rubbing a generous amount of sweet-smelling Hawaiian Tropic sunscreen all over my face and body. I wished I was going to my friend's swimming pool, but instead I'd pull on my work jeans and a T-shirt and grab my Walkman. I'd wander into the stretch of vines laid out for what seemed like miles in front of the house.

Depending on how Pop was feeling, I was assigned one of two tasks. One of the most common was technically known as suckering: pulling off any small shoot that had started to grow at the base or along the trunk. He explained that we needed to remove this growth in order to keep the plant's energy directed to the main canes for quicker ripening. As the weeks passed and the vines' growth continued, it was also critical to train them along the trellis. I would lift each cane, press it against the main wire, pull out a wire tie from my apron, and twist it around both to secure. By doing this, the plant's small clusters were exposed to the sunlight and would ripen faster.

Row by row, I worked plant by plant. Like most of the tasks we were given, it became rhythmic, and the more I did it, the more efficient I became. Fortunately, Michael Jackson's latest album, *Off the Wall*, played in my head. In step with "Rock with Me," I quickly passed through the rows.

Thank you, M. J.

All the time in the vineyard also gave me plenty of time to think about what I was going to do with my life, my boy crushes, if I was going to make the lead in the school play, or if I would ever be as popular as the pretty girls at school. I did my best to sneak out of work, complaining of heatstroke or headaches from relentless temperatures in the mid-80s most days. Mom rarely took pity on me, but occasionally Pop would send me in for a quick break. Mainly, I did what was expected without much whining. When I did complain, reminding Mom, "I didn't ask for this life," her standard response was, "Well, this is what we're doing, and that's the way it is." And that was the end of the conversation.

TIME FOR JAZZ

Mom knew it wasn't enough to simply hope visitors would visit the tasting room on weekends. She decided that hosting more events might be the answer. In 1981, she was inspired by Michel's musical talent and created an attraction around it. As a high school junior, he'd formed a band that had been moonlighting at some of Portland's jazz clubs. It was difficult to imagine my shy brother performing at bars, especially because he was completely uninterested in alcohol and being around cigarette smoke, but the clubs provided an outlet for his music. Performances in the city introduced him to some of the most celebrated local musicians. My parents decided to take advantage of his connections and host a jazz concert. Although the concept of bringing live music to a vineyard wasn't groundbreaking in Napa Valley, it would be new to our valley. We decided to host the first concert in June before life got too busy with harvest and called it the Early Summer Jazz Concert.

The project started as usual with Mom at her typewriter. My favorite part. I pulled a chair up next to her as she settled in front of the machine, threading the white paper around the cylinder. She turned to me.

"We need to write a press release about the upcoming concert. Remember, it's important to tell the who, what, when, where, and why in the very first sentence. Be concise and always, always be sure what you're sending out is timely and interesting. Otherwise, nobody will even look at your piece." I nodded, listening carefully to her words.

She began tapping hard on the keys, the brass plates hitting the black-inked ribbon, etching letters onto the white cotton paper beneath. I loved the consistent clicking, the ringing of the return bar, and the fresh inky smell her work left on the page. I marveled at her speed and proficiency. As I watched her, I questioned why she'd prohibited me from taking a typing class, afraid I would end up working as a secretary for some man. Instead, I wished I could move the typewriter bar back and forth across the page as fast as she did. She wrote the release quickly, keeping it to one page, which was another one of her rules. Once she came to the end of the page, she ripped the paper out of the machine and passed it to me.

"Here. Why don't you read it over to be sure it's accurate and that my grammar and spelling is correct."

I appreciated that she valued my review. I read it over. "I think it sounds good, Mom. Should I fold and seal it?"

"Perfect. Thanks." She had gotten up from the table to start dinner. "You know, I think I'll hand-deliver it to the *Oregonian* tomorrow." I knew Mom liked any excuse to go into the Portland newsroom. It was an exciting place in the early 1980s, since everything anybody needed to know came out of that downtown building. It was the heart of the local, regional, and national news.

Mom tried to make friends wherever she went, spreading the word about our activities and the successes of our winery colleagues. She hoped her enthusiasm would fuel others to take notice, but Mom knew the most effective way to get attention was to be in print. She remained confident: any exposure about any of us in the wine community was good news for all of us.

After school the following day, I helped Mom put together the poster and flyer we planned to send out to our friends and local media inviting them to the concert. We sat at the kitchen table with her light box, glue, scissors, X-Acto knife, and paper and began creating our concert art around a vine sketch Jere had drawn.

"It looks great!" Mom exclaimed. "I'll take it to the printer tomorrow and ask them to run color copies we can distribute this weekend."

"Sounds good, Mom." I felt proud of our work and realized I enjoyed this part of the wine thing. I was drawn to the creation of working with paper, words, and images and loved bringing all the components together. I felt Mom was a master of the trade. Even without any previous experience or training, she worked like a true professional, and I followed her lead, intrigued by the process.

On Friday afternoon, as promised, Mom set the box of printed flyers on the kitchen counter. As usual, it was hard to resist opening the crisp white box to peer inside and review our finished work. I couldn't wait to send them out.

All three of us had sat down for an after-school snack of Tillamook cheddar cheese and saltine crackers when she made her announcement. "I'd like to get these flyers out this weekend, so I'll need your help tomorrow night, okay?" It wasn't a question, as it was more a warning. Whatever we may have had planned for Saturday night was about to change.

"Yeah, yeah," we groaned. Most kids were headed out to see the latest Star Wars movie or to the arcade to play pinball or Centipede all night. In contrast, our Saturday night now involved sitting on the floor of the TV room with stacks of marketing material in front of us.

Michel switched on the TV, clicking the knob in search of *The Incredible Hulk*, his favorite show. It wasn't on, so he was forced to watch *The Love Boat*. He despised it. Luisa and I loved it. While his Saturday night got worse, ours got a little better. We worked methodically through the stacks of paper as we folded, stuffed, and stamped all the letters and envelopes. The only break we took was during the commercials, when we would run to the bathroom to dampen the sponges we used to apply stamps. The two-hour job took us from *The Love Boat* all the way through the end of *Fantasy Island*.

Sunday was spent taking the few posters Mom had printed to some of her favorite places. Since she had relationships with the wine buyers at each stop, they were happy to help promote our first concert. As usual, each visit took hours: Mom had to first check the wine department to make sure our bottles were still on the shelf, then chat with the buyer and other employees. She would often make a purchase, demonstrating our mutual support for each other's small business. She was always thinking about how to build relationships.

"Hi, Bob!" She smiled as she called out to the produce manager, who was sorting through the navel oranges at Corno and Son's. "Don't miss our first jazz concert! Mel Brown is going to be there! It's going to be great. There will be plenty of food and wine!"

"Sounds fun, Nancy. I wouldn't miss it."

After weeks of promoting, the concert day finally arrived. As the morning light broke through the clouds, the house immediately came alive with activity. Michel and I took care of the farm animals, tossing the hay and quickly milking the goats. Mom didn't have time since she and Luisa were rushing around the kitchen in preparation for the guest arrivals. Luisa's excitement was fueled by the prospect of selling slices of home-made cheesecake. She got up early to mix large amounts of cream cheese and butter while Mom boiled sausages in three different large pots. Of course there had to be food presented along with the wine we planned to sell. Pop was outside, staging the event. He set up our grill in one of the vineyard rows and brought out a couple tables from the garage.

As usual, Grandpa and Grandma picked up Nonna, and upon arrival all three of them helped with the finishing touches outside. Grandpa finished mowing the grass along the edge of the vineyard while Nonna swept the entire driveway with our straw kitchen broom. Soon after the winery was complete, my parents decided to pave the driveway, an extravagant decision. I thought it symbolized normalcy and the rare possibility that we were making money. I loved that Nonna also took pride in our new asphalt by sweeping it whenever we were expecting guests. Grandma was setting up the makeshift tasting bar, bringing out glasses and cases of wine. I fetched fresh daffodils and some tulips for that always-essential bar detail.

The musicians began to arrive around eleven, a couple hours before the expected guests. Michel greeted them and helped haul all their cords and equipment to the stage. Pop had poured a ten-by-ten concrete pad to the left of the winery building, fabricating a small platform, and electrical outlets were installed nearby. It was as if this area was specifically made for the occasion.

On my way back inside, I passed the kitchen table and admired the cheesecakes Luisa had baked. She had selected fresh raspberries for the plain cheesecakes, placing each berry carefully around the perimeter, like a professional baker. To signify the chocolate ones, she shaved chocolate bars over the top. They resembled specialty cakes you would find at the finest bakeries in Portland. She managed to make three of each, and they were stunning. I helped her set up a table outside with a pretty linen. She was beaming with pride.

A few feet away was another table where we set up our friend, Fred Carlo. Carlo had recently moved from San Francisco to start a meat company in Portland named Salumeria di Carlo. We invited him to grill and sell his fresh sausages. Since he was new to the city and selling fresh charcuterie was novel at the time, he was thrilled to have the opportunity to introduce people to his business.

Grandma and Mom's admission table was set to collect the five-dollar fee per guest. Michel smiled, stationed at his keyboard with his musician friends, glowing at having local legends on his home turf. The region's most prominent jazz artists were in attendance: Ron Steen, Tom Grant, and Mel Brown.

As was typical, my parents were still running around when I yelled at them to come meet our early arrivals as the first car pulled in. *Why are we never ready?*

Within thirty minutes, our small lawn was covered with a crowd. Blankets, kids, and dogs were everywhere. Fred had a line in front of his table, and he was happily serving up his spicy sausages in warm buns. Luisa could barely keep up with the interest in her decadent cheesecakes, selling out by the second set. Mom beamed as she and Pop poured glasses of Chardonnay and Pinot Noir for the line that formed in front of the bar. Grandma and I wandered through the crowd, picking up empty glasses and dirty plates. Nonna washed the glasses as quickly as she could so I could run them back to the busy bar. Music carried over the property, mixed with laughter, barking dogs, and the frequent happy shrieks of kids running through the vineyard.

As I walked back to the house with another box of dirty glasses, I noticed Mom stuffing cash from the various tills into a brown paper bag. We had no way to run credit cards, so it was a strictly all-cash affair. She must have collected a couple bags full of cash that day, dropping each one on the kitchen table.

Like Nonna and me, Grandpa Charlie liked to keep the place clean. While Nonna managed the indoor space, Grandpa took it upon himself to manage the outdoors. As the event drew to a close, he started an open fire in the back of the house to burn all the garbage. Grandpa loved his fires. Once the guests left, we all took trips to the burn pile, tossing everything into the hot flames. I thought Grandpa's fire was a brilliant idea—so efficient!

At the end of the evening, our busy crew sat down at the kitchen table with cold glasses of water to discuss the busy day. It had been a huge success. We had more people attend than expected and sold out of both sausages and cheesecakes. Most importantly, we sold wine! Not just glasses, but bottles, and a few people even took home cases.

"How did we end up, Nancy?" Pop asked, looking at Mom.

"I was just going to get to that, but I can't find the bags."

"What bags?"

"I put all the cash in a couple of brown paper sacks and left them here on the table."

There was nothing on the table.

"Nonna, did you happen to move a couple paper bags from the table?" Mom's voice was concerned.

"Nev-erra saw em." Nonna shook her head.

"Luisa, did you take the brown bags from the table?" She was sitting on the stairs.

"Nope. Not me."

"Daddy?" Mom called out to Grandpa in the hall. "Hey, Daddy, did you happen to pick up a couple of bags when you were cleaning up?"

"I'm not sure. Everything I picked up just went into the fire."

A panic swept through my body.

Mom looked at Pop. Pop looked at her. We all knew what had happened. The money had gone up in flames. There was silence. All the work from the day—the setup, the cleanup, the promoting, those wine sales—all lost. Cash was never put in a paper sack again, and we all kept a closer eye on Grandpa's roaring fires.

Regardless of the monetary loss at our first event, we all knew that the Early Summer Jazz Festival was a huge success, and we continued to run them once a month until 1983. Having some of Portland's greatest musicians perform on our small lawn accomplished our main goal of exposing the public to our operation, our vineyard, and our wines. The buzz continued.

FREEDOM

On April 18, 1981, I turned sixteen. I was able to get my driver's license, which meant freedom. A license was my chance for mobility and independence from my isolated, labor-intensive homelife.

It was not to be taken lightly. I studied at my desk the entire week before the exam, and on the big day I easily passed both the written and driving tests. Because I had been driving for a year with a learner's permit, I had become relatively comfortable at the wheel. I was a cautious driver, aware that should anything ever happen to the car, it would have a significant impact on the family and our business.

After successfully receiving my license, my next step toward independence was finding a place to make money—away from the winery. Once we entered high school, Mom and Pop started to pay us a modest wage of two dollars per hour for any winery or vineyard work, but I wanted a more conventional setting. I wanted to meet normal people, with a job that provided air-conditioning and an organized, clean workplace.

Despite my guilt, I was motivated to pursue my ambition. I negotiated the family Datsun one Saturday, a big deal, and took the afternoon to search for my utopia. The hunt also gave me a great excuse to wear my "city" clothes. I chose a brightly colored, oversized neon-yellow blouse tucked into my favorite pair of high-waisted light-washed jeans and paired it with a wide white vinyl belt. I even teased my hair a bit and added the big gold hoop earrings I'd received as a birthday gift from Mom. I brushed off my coveted and only pair of stylish shoes: the newly released Nike Cortez, white with the famous brand's bright-red swoosh. I had saved enough money from working in the vineyard and picking strawberries to buy them. I loved them. I was ready to go.

I visited the two malls that existed within twenty minutes of our home: Beaverton Mall and Washington Square. I asked for job applications in nearly every retail store, crossing my fingers they'd like me. But it was on the way home that I noticed Baskin-Robbins. It was situated along Scholls Ferry Road near the grocery store Mom went to every week, and I was surprised I'd never noticed it. I pulled into the parking lot and found a spot right in front. I opened the shop door, and the scent of new paint and Windex blasted my face, followed by luxurious air-conditioning. Both welcomed me in from the hot, sticky day outside.

"Hi!" I smiled as I caught the eye of a girl about my age behind the counter. "Are you guys hiring, by chance?"

"Actually, yes! The store just opened, and they're looking for a couple other people."

"Great!" I surprised myself with my confidence. "Could I have an application, please?"

The girl responded with a broad smile revealing her perfectly straight teeth and handed me the required form. I sat down and eagerly filled it out as thirty-one flavors danced in my head. This is so perfect! Ice cream! So normal! And so close to home!

The kitchen phone rang a couple days later.

"Hello?"

"I'm looking for Maria Ponzi," a sterile voice said.

"Yes, this is Maria," I responded.

"I am calling to let you know that we would like you to come work with us at the home of thirty-one flavors."

"What? Really?!" I exclaimed.

"We will see you next Monday at four p.m.," the caller said.

"Great! I'll see you then." I hung up the phone. "Yes!" I shrieked, unable to contain my excitement. I would finally get to work for myself and meet people who would talk about topics other than wine! I couldn't wait. The toughest part would be breaking the news to my family.

"What?!" Mom replied in shock after I announced my accomplishment. "You did what?" She frowned, staring at me as if I'd told her I was smoking pot or had flunked a class.

"Yeah. I got a job working at Baskin-Robbins. The shop just opened down by the grocery store." I tried to garner her support. "I want to make some money this summer so I can buy school clothes next year or maybe even save up for a trip to Europe or something."

My explanation didn't change the look on her face.

"How do you expect to get there? How many days a week will you work? Does this include weekends? When do you start?"

I tried to calm her down while remaining sure of myself. "Well, I'll get my schedule next week, and then we'll have to coordinate trips with the car, I guess." I was determined to make this happen, determined to get myself out of the fields this summer.

She shrugged her shoulders and walked away. I knew I had let her down. I knew she needed my help with the work at home, and I felt her disappointment, but I remained confident in my decision. I had to shake off the shame.

Later that night, Mom came to my room while I was in bed. She climbed the ladder, leaned over, and lightly kissed my cheek. "I don't really understand why you have to go someplace else to make money, but I guess we'll give it a try. Congratulations." She gave me a hug and walked out of the room.

I imagined Pop had probably reasoned with her. He always supported me and had a way of looking past the winery demands to see me as my own person. I slept well, pleased with my demonstration of independence. I couldn't wait for school to be over so I could start work and clock lots of hours.

Anxiety hit when it was finally time for my first shift. Heavy guilt hung on my shoulders and settled in my gut as I pulled on my polyester brown pants and rainbow-striped top. I waited to put on the Baskin-Robbins hat until I arrived at the shop, already feeling awkward about walking through the house in my corporate uniform. It felt completely out of place in our rural environment. I ignored Luisa's sneer as I walked down the stairs and forced myself to ask Mom for the car keys. She looked at me with displeasure, gave a sigh, and handed them over. I released a deep breath as I walked out to the family car. I tried to ignore my selfishness for stealing our only car to go work someplace other than our home, especially when there was so much to be done. I straightened my shoulders and started the engine. *I'm doing this.* I started down the driveway, narrowing my stare to the road ahead and ignoring the demanding vineyard on my left.

It was a summer of disgrace. I was needed at home. I knew these months were the busiest of the entire year. Regardless, instead of working alongside my family in the vineyard, this season I was playing suburban girl, digging up scoops of Jamoca

Almond Fudge and pouring hot chocolate onto sundaes for the neighborhood. I took the job seriously, but for the rest of my family it was a joke. When the car was needed during one of my shifts, Pop would come in the banana truck, park right in front, and walk around the shop's large windows, making faces at me while I tried to serve customers. I knew Pop was just having fun, but I wanted to be left alone in my new, private world.

Having one car for the entire family became an issue. Michel needed it for band practice, Luisa needed to get to gymnastics class, and I needed it to serve ice cream. Mom was constantly frustrated with attempting to coordinate all the errands.

My mother's efforts were always focused on targeting sales in Portland. It remained exhausting work, and she was becoming more and more impatient. If she did get a sale and bring home a check, she'd discover the money had already been spent. I sensed the anxiety and saw that success was rare. The demands kept piling on. We were always preparing for the next harvest, the next bottling, the next release, the next review, the next sale, the next event. There never seemed to be an end to the work; it only escalated, with little to show for it. I heard one wine woman say, "It's like I'm pushing a huge boulder up the hill each day, and I can never reach the top." A year later, her marriage and their wine business failed.

One Saturday, while Michel and I were hanging out on the lawn, we heard a loud grinding and rumbling sound. We turned our heads toward the drive and caught sight of a shiny sedan. It was a beautiful buttercup-yellow Mercedes glowing in the sunlight. I assumed it was a tasting room visitor, but as it got closer, I saw Pop was in the driver's seat. Michel and I looked at each other and started to laugh. *What is going on here?*

My father looked out of place in such a luxurious vehicle. I thought he must have borrowed it from a work colleague. He smiled as he passed us, pulling right up to the front of the house. Mom came running out of the front door.

"On my! It's so beautiful!" She rushed up to Pop and gave him a huge hug and kiss. "This is so much better than a load of French oak barrels! I can't believe you did it. Thank you!"

Pop smiled, glowing with pride. "I thought you'd like the color. And look inside—leather seats!" He opened the heavy steel doors, and we all rushed over.

"Wow!" I climbed in the front seat, and the rich scent of worn leather overwhelmed me. I touched the thick, dark steering wheel, and then my fingers traveled across to the elegant burled walnut dashboard. As Michel walked around it outside, he stroked the shiny hood medallion. It was the real thing: an authentic Mercedes.

"Pop, this is really fancy. How did you afford it?" Michel couldn't help but react to this symbol of wealth.

"Well, it's actually a used car, so we should be able to manage the payments, and I thought it's about time your mother had something nice to drive."

It was true. Mom loved to drive, and she was doing plenty of it these days. To me, it seemed as though my father wanted to show his wife how much she was appreciated, but it seemed so extravagant when we were still struggling. Michel and I both driving had made running errands difficult for Mom, and this new possession would change things. We all felt proud to now own a European car. When Mom took deliveries into the city, at least now she would do it in style.

OUR CHAMPION

By the early 1980s, Mom and Pop understood the greatest challenge of their winemaking venture would be selling our wines to the national market. The high cost of flights, hotels, and meals made trips across the country prohibitively expensive. The phone calls made to random distributors across the country were futile and discouraging. Nothing went anywhere, nothing stuck. Real help was needed.

Fortunately, a strong soul stepped up to meet this most vital need: Stephen Cary. Cary was an Oregon boy turned Navy officer, who returned to the West Coast after the service and found a new career selling wine. He moved back to Portland in the early 1980s and met Howard and Karen Hinsdale of Henny-Hinsdale Distributing. At the time, the couple was interested in building their business to include the wines of California and Italy, and the Hinsdales hired Cary to grow their portfolio of fine wines.

My parents invited Cary over for dinner one night and quickly discovered he was a terrific storyteller. He shared his first experience tasting Oregon wines with us.

"I was fortunate to join the Hinsdales for a dinner they hosted in their Portland home one evening with an esteemed guest: Robert Drouhin," he began. "Drouhin was visiting the Portland market, promoting his family's wines. Karen decided to bring out an Oregon wine from their personal cellar and shared a 1970 HillCrest Pinot Noir made by Richard Sommer. They briefed Drouhin on the wine's background, noting it was the pioneer's seventh vintage of Oregon Pinot Noir."

My father nodded encouragingly as my mother poured herself another glass of wine, listening to the story.

"Karen mentioned all the newcomers to Oregon and said she was interested to learn what he thought of the wine," Cary continued. "Monsieur Drouhin swirls the wine, observes its color against the white linen tablecloth, and after a couple more swirls, lifts the glass to his lips, and in a way only the most elegant French wine connoisseur can, he brings air into his mouth, slurring the wine around his mouth, until he finally swallows it and gives a slight nod of his head, gesturing acknowledgment."

We all watched as Cary acted out the scene, making us giggle as we envisioned the gurgling of the wine and the French accent.

"And although Drouhin never commented aloud about the wine, I noticed that it was the one glass he kept reaching for throughout the meal. Both of us were very much intrigued by what we experienced that night. It was an eye-opening experience," Cary declared. "We couldn't have been more charmed by him. He understood the quality of well-made wines and was afraid to talk about it. He very quickly became a close friend."

Over the following three years, Henny-Hinsdale Wines grew from its original three-person crew to a forty-person staff. During that period, the Hinsdales began collecting Oregon wines, becoming a major source of Willamette Valley

Pinot Noir in the state. Since we joined their portfolio back in 1979, we had had these veteran wine salespeople working on our behalf in the Portland market, which helped to lift some weight off my parents. Although we had to compensate them for their efforts, there was comfort knowing there were others knocking on doors on a regular basis.

In 1983, Cary established Cary Oregon Wines. His agreement with Oregon wine families was to only sell outside of Oregon; in-state sales would be left for self-distribution or Hinsdale. The rest of the country would be his. It was an enormous undertaking for Cary. Until this time, the small wineries had been mostly unsuccessful in the national arena. In Cary's words, by excluding Oregon from his territory, he gave up the only market that had potential for any profit. The road was tough, but he remained a solid believer in the wines, and fortunately, for all of us, he was up to the enormous challenge.

Pop would later explain how Cary was only modestly armed with hundreds of Oregon Pinot Noir sample bottles and a well-worn Rolodex given to him years before. In addition to his local wineshop contacts from his earlier days as a salesperson, he had also developed strong relationships during his time as a wine buyer. Most notably among them was Michael Richmond, then of Acacia Wines in California. We learned how Cary relied heavily on his friend for referrals to wholesalers across the nation, which allowed him to begin his work. He called on those who already had a collection of Burgundies or a strong California portfolio with Hearty Burgundy as a prominent varietal. Ninety percent of his calls were met with rejection. When Cary would return from a sales trip, he would share his numerous encounters and rejections with us.

"What? What are you talking about? Pinot what?"

"Where the hell is Or-ee-gone anyway?"

"Hey, listen, I don't need any wine from the sticks. Get the hell out of here!"

"You've got to be kidding. Stop wasting my time!"

He'd tell us if he was ever lucky enough to land an appointment, even the most promising meetings often ended with: "Well, this may be good, but it's never going to be as good as Burgundy. I mean it's nice, but let's be honest—there's no way we can sell this stuff."

Fortunately, Cary never gave up. He remained confident in the local wines. Among his favorites was our Pinot Noir, along with those from Lett and Erath, and Sommer's dry Riesling. For weeks at a time, he'd board planes, navigate busy freeways, and march the sidewalks of New York, Chicago, and San Francisco with his wine bag full of Oregon wine samples. Wherever he went, his sole mission was to break down barriers and find opportunities. Like a warrior, he deflected hundreds of dead-end phone calls, closed doors, insults, and constant ridicule. Although his world was full of frequent rejection, he maintained a polished approach and optimistic attitude throughout the years, sharing our lofty vision for the region.

With Cary on the front lines of national sales, Mom refocused her efforts on local marketing, pumping out press releases on a regular basis. She reported on the happenings at our winery, announced the releases of new wines, and promoted various wine community events. She frequently reached out to the media, sending more samples for review and inviting journalists to visit and taste the wines. She and Cary collaborated, working together to build the brand of Oregon Pinot Noir. With their committed efforts in the front of the operation, Pop maintained a steady focus on making great wines on a consistent basis. The original wine families were convinced that if the quality didn't deliver in the bottle, nothing else mattered. It was simple: the wine had to be great to be noticed. The region would be nothing without quality. In order to be taken seriously, everything had to be the best. Everything mattered.

In June of 1983, I graduated from Hillsboro High School. I could not wait to move on with my life and avoid the next harvest party. I was going to study broadcast journalism at the University of Oregon in the fall. My parents were so involved with the winery, my college selection process was solitary. I simply announced one night I had been accepted into the U of O. I had learned earlier in my senior year that Grandma and Grandpa had purchased each of their grandchildren stock in Santa Fe Drilling Company with the intention of us using it for higher education. Certainly, Mom and Pop did not have the means to fund a college education, so we were fortunate to have this generous gift. Though my parents were excited about my acceptance and decision to attend the state university, business went on as usual.

As with most college freshman, the reality of living away from my parents started to settle in the closer my move-out date neared. During the two-hour drive to Eugene later that summer, I felt a pit in my stomach and wished we would never arrive. But once I was situated in my dorm room and met a few people, I became distracted with my new reality. Instead of never-ending conversations over Pinot Noir, I could finally focus on myself, my classes, late-night studying, boys, and football games. I packed my days with all the things I loved: aerobics, writing, and socializing. I was so immersed in my new situation that when I heard my folks were embarking on a new venture in Portland, I didn't initially grasp the levity of it.

ENGLISH ALE

By 1983, Pop was producing about seven thousand cases of wine, and it was increasingly difficult to keep up with all the work. The good part was we were starting to make a little money. It had been nearly ten years since our first harvest and fourteen since we established the nursery row. My father decided to make some changes. He slightly reduced his hours at PCC to teaching only two terms and decided to hire a young guy named Karl Ockert to help in the cellar.

Ockert was a fermentation graduate from UC Davis who loved the process. But unlike Pop, his real love was beer. He'd talk about it constantly while working in the winery. Back then, the only interesting beers in Portland were a few bottled European imports. Although Mom and Pop enjoyed these limited brews, they felt they were stale, possibly because of their long journey. I'd sensed a growing interest in the beer thing before I left for college, but I didn't think it would go anywhere.

"You know, Nancy," Pop interjected one evening, "we live near some of the cleanest water and some of the country's best hops." The town of Aurora, home to several family farms growing hops, was a quick thirty-minute drive from Scholls. "I wonder if we shouldn't give this beer-making thing a try?"

"From what I understand, you can make a batch of beer in a few hours, and if you don't like it, you can make another batch the same day, until you get it right," said Mom. As usual, she had done her research. "That sure sounds easier than waiting three years to see if you get the first step right." She grinned. "Besides, how great would it be to instantly make more product the next day if people like it, or pour it down the drain if they don't?"

Over the years, without any support from banks or other external sources, my parents had managed to save $45,000. Now, all of it would go toward establishing a microbrewery. Their hope was to make quick money that could help support the winery. Obviously, freshly made beer was a huge risk as it was another unknown product. Nobody in the country had heard of microbrews or handcrafted ales. The story sounded a little too familiar to me, and I was concerned. Fortunately, I was tucked away in Eugene, focused on my destiny, and only heard about the project when I called home.

What I learned was my parents had spent several weeks looking for an ideal building to set up what would eventually become the state's first craft brewery. They settled on an old rope warehouse in the industrial district of northwest Portland. My folks loved the old building's aesthetic: thick brick walls, heavy timbers, and a concrete floor. Being downtown presented the innovative enterprise with energy, exposure, and an unusual venue for Portlanders to experience a new beverage.

In traditional form, Pop went straight to work finding the appropriate equipment—or at least something he could adapt, which in this case was an old boiler, to start building the brewhouse. As usual, he salvaged all the parts: screens, wood slats, and the miscellaneous material needed to create an ideal kettle. This would eventually steam the wort—unfermented malt before becoming beer—as opposed to boiling it. This process would reveal the natural flavors of the finished beer. He hired a local company, JVNW, to design tanks for the brewhouse according to his specifications. Pop had previously worked with JVNW to fabricate stainless steel wine fermenters and asked if they'd look at his brewing needs before they moved on to the soda pop business as intended. Everything Pop designed was created custom for the building and developed specifically for beer production on a small scale. The vision, like our wine, was to craft a high-quality beverage. They sought to produce fresh, English-style ales. Whatever that meant.

While Pop was busy tinkering with craft brewing equipment, Mom researched different strains of hops, malts, and barleys and considered marketing efforts. They'd need to develop a company name and logo and announce the new product. Karl and Pop started brewing the initial trials. The process was similar to winemaking in terms of fermentation, but all the ingredients were different. It took weeks to craft a brew that tasted decent, but of course, the research and development was Pop's favorite part. He got a thrill from tweaking the equipment and experimenting with new recipes.

When I heard they had jumped into this beer project, I voiced my usual doubts. "Don't you have enough going on? Why start an entirely new business when we haven't got the first one down?" But there was no stopping them. They found this new adventure fascinating, and there was no curbing their enthusiasm. Of course, I couldn't deny my selfish pleasure at knowing there was no way they could rope me into their latest project since I was responsibly working toward my degree. As a student who always seemed to have to work harder than anyone else for a decent grade, I committed myself to finishing school in less than four years. My goal was to move as far from Oregon as possible and be my own person. I couldn't wait to start earning my own money and work independently. If I stayed, I feared I'd lose myself to the family business and all its chaos.

Columbia River Brewing Company opened its doors in 1984, and much like the wine industry, my parents soon discovered others with shared interest and drive. Portland was still a small town, and Mom met a similarly minded brewer on a ski bus one day. One of her many attempts to exercise was to join a group of skiers who drove up from Portland to Mount Hood on the weekends. They all boarded a bus at the Multnomah Athletic Club and sped the forty-five minutes to the mountain for an afternoon of downhill skiing. On one of these trips, Mom met Art Lawrence. Lawrence had been working for Grant's Brewery in Yakima, and they started talking about opening a small brewery in Portland. He introduced Mom and Pop to the "Brew Crew," an amateur home-brewers network. Within the year, my parents met other Oregon craft brew pioneers, including Kurt and Rob Widmer and Mike and Brian McMenamin.

Like the "Pinot Obsessed" who gathered to discuss ideas, all the beer guys (and Mom) met regularly to share issues and challenges. It started with the basics, like how to source the necessary equipment, find the best ingredients, and locate and transport kegs. Another common theme the wine and beer communities shared was a desire for successful marketing. Freshly brewed ales were also an entirely new product for the marketplace. They were not traditional Midwestern American beers, nor were they lagers from a can. Instead, these were English- and German-style ales poured from the keg. They were handcrafted and made in small batches from local ingredients, with richness and flavors few had ever experienced.

Nobody knew what to expect, and it was entirely possible that nobody would be interested. There was certainly no demand. Why would any American want a heavy beer when cold lagers were supremely popular across the nation? The situation sounded all too familiar.

Drawing from their wine pioneering background, Mom and Pop knew there would be a need to sample the new beverage, so naturally they went to work establishing legislation to allow for brewpubs. The pub idea mirrored the wine tasting room concept. The beer pioneers were unaware that pushing this agenda would prove more challenging than wine tasting rooms, as the major American beer brands weren't thrilled with the idea of local beer sold outside traditional means. The craft brewers, like the "Pinot Obsessed," banded together. I learned it took the same kind of tenacity and ingenuity my folks had been through earlier to see results.

"We didn't know if it was going to happen," Pop explained when I came home from Eugene for a weekend visit. "We thought our bill allowing pubs to operate next to breweries was a done deal. The McMenamins and I drove home together after a long day in Salem when we learned it was overturned while we were on the highway. We were blown away."

"What happened?"

"The big beer companies got involved. But we got creative and put it through another way. It ended up passing through some bed-and-breakfast legislation." He chuckled.

"No way!" I was impressed by their ingenuity and persistence. Their victory allowed tasting rooms and pubs to operate next to brewhouses. What seemed like simple legislation for Oregon at the time quickly became a model across the country, enabling small brewers to enjoy healthy profits by retailing their handcrafted products directly to visitors. As a result, popular brewpubs began to contribute to their local economies while exposing their publics to a new fresh beverage.

While I was home that same weekend, I visited the brewery. They had turned the front of the warehouse into a cozy space that mimicked an authentic English pub. The space smelled especially inviting as Mom had concocted a unique yeast from the beer wort to make a sweet, tangy dough for their signature pizza. The ovens were situated in the small kitchen they'd built behind the main bar. I thought it was brilliant they had limited the food options to only handcrafted pizza, maintaining the focus on the beer.

The bar housed three taps for the original fresh drafts and offered bar service only. My parents wanted to avoid the extra labor cost and headache of table service. The pub was also unusual in being one of the first to prohibit smoking and to allow children in a drinking space. People found one of the first brewpubs in the country intriguing. It had a down-to-earth vibe that attracted local urbanites, and it was easy for me to see why it had become a favorite haunt for many notable city leaders, including the mayor. Resulting from its novelty and simplicity—beer, pizza, and Ponzi wine—it had quickly become a sought-after destination. Mom explained how the low operating costs and relatively high margins made the pub business almost instantly lucrative, especially when compared to our meager wine profits. Unlike with the wine business, word of mouth about the beer spread quickly.

Despite a few neighborhood complaints on brewing days when pungent odors spilled out onto the city streets, craft beer was on the rise. Portlanders were intrigued by the fresh, flavorful new beverage called ale. It became so popular that by July 1988, the three major breweries at the time—Portland Brewing, Widmer Brothers, and our BridgePort Brewing Company—organized and hosted the first Oregon Brewers Festival. It was the brainchild of Mom, Kurt, and Art. At the inaugural affair, they organized over twenty-two microbreweries from across the country to celebrate the handcrafted beverage on Portland's Waterfront Park. They anticipated five thousand beer fans would attend the first-time three-day event, but more than fifteen thousand visitors came to sample the beers and celebrate in Portland. It was an overwhelming success and has continued to grow over the following years.

RECOGNITION

By 1984, the original Oregon Winegrowers Council had broken up due to constant tension between the producers in the north and south of the state. A new organization was formed, called the Oregon Wine Advisory Board (OWAB). It had two main goals: to promote all Oregon wines and provide research for the growing industry in its entirety. The founders agreed it was important for the industry to maintain long-term promotion and healthy research for the state's overall wine industry and its continued success. This meant they needed to guarantee funding. As a result, it was agreed that wineries would charge themselves twenty-five dollars per ton for grapes harvested in the state to support the OWAB. It was unusual for an industry to tax itself in such a way, but was paramount for a healthy future for the industry.

For more than a decade, the Oregon State Fair had been a main vehicle to help drive recognition for some of the region's wine. I was often humored by a gold or silver medallion hanging on one of our prized bottles of Riesling or Pinot Noir among a string of others, many of them made from raspberries or plums.

But now, the "Pinot Obsessed" sought out wine competitions across the nation and globe. Occasionally, some of these early contests brought terrific results. In particular, in 1984, Tualatin Valley Vineyards received Best of Show for both its 1981 Chardonnay and 1980 Pinot Noir at the London International Wine Competition, and Sokol Blosser received multiple awards for its wines submitted into the Seattle Enological Competitions, giving the Blossers regional recognition.

As usual, the group was thinking bolder. The 1983 vintage presented a terrific opportunity for nearly everyone in the valley. The fruit was ripe, and the finished wines were elegant and structured. Across our small region, nearly all wineries felt the wines demonstrated beautiful examples of Pinot Noir. Growing tired of the negative misperception, Cary discussed a brave idea with the OWAB to stage a judging of Oregon wines from 1983 against French Burgundies from the same year. It was agreed this vintage in particular demonstrated the true potential of Willamette Valley Pinot Noir. The OWAB agreed to help.

The International Wine Center (IWC) in Manhattan offered the ideal stage for such an affair. The IWC was one of the nation's few places for wine education at the time, and fortunately, Mary Mulligan, its owner and director, had become a friend of the Oregon winemakers. Mulligan proved to be instrumental in these early days as she believed in the wines, so when we asked for her help, she welcomed the idea.

Since our first vintage nearly fifteen years ago, there had been hundreds of informal comparative tastings between Oregon Pinot Noir and French Burgundy. And in nearly all of them, the winemakers and tasters were constantly surprised by the similarities between the two regions. They were convinced the domestic wine had promise, but breaking down the walls of market perception was another continual challenge. It was firmly believed that American wines would never be as good as those from Europe. When Cary suggested the idea of presenting the 1983s to the then–IWC President Al Hotchkin, he was told it would be a poor marketing strategy, but thanks to Cary's persistence and to Mulligan's encouragement, Hotchkin agreed to host the affair, and OWAB agreed to fund it.

Once Oregon winemakers received news of the project, they quickly submitted their wines, hoping to be selected for the international affair. The OWAB blindly selected ten of the twenty-seven wines submitted for the contest. Unfortunately, our wines didn't make the pick and were left out of the competition. Seven Burgundies were selected by the IWC, including top producers of Premier Cru, Grand Cru, and the Hospices de Beaune. IWC also selected the twenty-five judges without any influence from the OWAB. This prestigious group of judges was a collection of sommeliers, wholesalers, retailers, and reporters. All of them were well educated on the wines of Burgundy.

Once the Oregonians had shipped their wines to OWAB, all they could do was wait. They nestled into their small homes, garages, and makeshift wineries among the cool rolling hills of the quiet valley and hoped the critics in New York City would judge their latest work favorably.

About a month before the next harvest, on September 12, 1985, the panel of judges finally sat down to seventeen glasses of Pinot Noir. The setting, as with most formal wine judgings, was quiet, sterile, and serious. The twenty-five men sat behind a row of carefully buffed stemware placed upon white paper placemats. Each glass was filled to just one-third with each wine. The fill level would enable the taster to effectively swirl to observe color and clarity against the white backdrop. A pen was placed next to each setting, inviting each critic to carefully

note their experience. A glass of water and paper cup for spitting sat at the ready.

The tasting was moderated by Terry Robards of the *New
York Post*. He explained the objective: to simply select their
favorite wine and give its origin. An hour passed before all
judges had completed the task. Pens down. Robards carefully
uncovered each brown bag from the bottle, revealing its label.
The group responded with astonished gasps when the results
noted that 50 percent of the judges had selected the incor-
rect origin. Oregon wines took first, second, and third place.
The once-silent room stirred. Many judges began defending
the French wines, stating they required more time to show
their full potential and because of this were at a disadvantage
against the domestics.

When the triumphant news got back to Oregon, the "Pinot
Obsessed" were electrified. They prepared for their next vintage with renewed confidence and vigor.

The startling results left wine critics unsatisfied, and a second judging was organized two years later in February of 1987.
It was held again at the IWC, and the organizers selected a
slate of Burgundies and another panel of judges. Once again,
Ponzi missed being pulled as a selected wine by the OWAB,
but Oregon prevailed for a second time. Two Oregon wineries
shared first place, while two others swept second and third.
It was another riveting performance for our small region, and
although Oregon didn't get mentioned in the headline (it was
"Burgundy Fizzles Again"), our region was recognized.

Despite the less-than-favorable headline, as we all were
hoping for something like "Oregon Champions Pinot Noir,"
the results of the tasting spread quickly. Because the Oregon
Pinot Noirs were priced at nearly ten dollars less per bottle
than those from Europe, Oregon winemakers immediately
saw an increase in sales. Interestingly, for the first time, the

sales in Oregon and Washington saw an uptake equal to that on the East Coast. This swing clearly demonstrated the vital importance of having validation for our work from outside our backyard. These two judgings forced the nation to take notice.

When I heard the news from my Eugene apartment, I couldn't help but reflect on the irony behind these contests as I recalled how important the relationships were between the early Oregon winegrowers and the Burgundian producers. Their advice had been invaluable, and now we were presenting our wines alongside theirs in a rather desperate attempt to demonstrate our paralleled quality. These were honored friendships, and following this judging, the early Oregon winegrowers rarely went up against the Burgundians again.

Back in the Northwest, regional wine writers Matt Kramer from the *Oregonian* and Tom Stockley from the *Seattle Times* occasionally reviewed our wines. Kramer found it difficult to say anything positive about the local product while Stockley tended to embrace it. "Well, at least they're consistent!" my parents joked, knowing how the wines would likely fare when they considered sending out current samples. I was dumbfounded as to why our local wine critic didn't support our efforts, but instead raved about other domestic wines. It still felt odd the national press needed to take notice of our region before the region would acknowledge its own efforts. This was a different situation than other winegrowing regions, whereby a visitor would be hard-pressed to find anything but a local wine on local wine lists, and local papers would rave about local products. We got used to the drill.

Robert M. Parker Jr.'s the *Wine Advocate* was the country's most influential wine publication in the mid-1980s. Parker's interest was sparked by the tasting in New York, and he became the first critic outside the region to visit Oregon. In the spring of 1986, he requested a visit to taste wines from the barrel. I didn't understand what all the commotion was about when I called home.

"What are you guys up to this weekend?"

"Parker's coming!" Mom almost shouted in my ear.

"Who's that?"

"The most important man in wine. He's considered the Wine God. He can either make or break a winery. He's very powerful."

"Sounds like an egomaniac. What's the big deal?"

"He's never been here before, and he wants to taste the 1985 in barrel."

"You mean wine that isn't finished? That seems weird and kind of unfair."

"Yes, that's what he does. He makes projections on how the wine will taste once it's finished."

"I don't understand . . . but whatever. I hope Pop is ready, and it goes well," I responded.

News of Parker's arrival had the wine community on edge. I felt that having a wine expert taste unfinished wines was like having an art critic judge an unfinished painting or a food critic evaluate an uncooked meal. The result of the barrel tasting was as important for us as it was for the valley. It would be this prominent man's first impression of Willamette Valley Pinot Noir.

Parker had his eye on the 1985 Pinot Noir. Following an unseasonably warm vintage like 1984, experienced winegrowers knew that the following crop tended to struggle, resulting in low yields, but often delivering high-quality fruit. He would determine the verdict.

Pop described the scene to me over the phone as I quietly listened, taking it all in. I wished I could have witnessed it, as even my father seemed excited about his visit.

Apparently, Parker arrived late on the highly anticipated day. Pop assumed the previous vintner had tried his best to charm the Wine God, overextending his time allowance. Parker's car finally pulled into the lot, and a middle-aged, stocky man with a balding head and beady eyes unloaded himself from the vehicle. He slowly approached the tasting room with a red journal in hand. Not wanting to seem anxious, my parents waited for him inside the tasting room. After the usual small talk over the weather and how his visit was going, they invited the celebrity into our modest cellar. My mother stood next to the intimidating east coaster as my father readied himself with his trusty wine thief. He told me how he tried several barrels days beforehand to ensure only the best ones would be tasted during the visit. He had selected Pinot Noir from Abetina Vineyard, our most prized site, for the first impression. He drew a sample from deep within the barrel, dropping the glass tube of the thief down the hole with his thumb on top. Once plenty of wine had been captured, he raised his thumb and carefully released the deep-red liquid into Parker's wineglass.

All three of them studied it as it rushed into the crystal bowl. Parker took the stem and turned it slightly to its side, allowing light to filter through the glass. My father remained quiet as the critic reviewed the wine's color. He then expertly swirled the drink before positioning his large nose deep into the bowl. With the aromatics now expressed and evaluated, he pulled the glass back away, swiftly swirled and sniffed again, lifting the glass up and into his mouth. He slurped air into his mouth, creating additional aeration, and moved the wine across his palate before spitting it into the drain below his feet. I was told his face was expressionless as he repeated the sequence. Another sip, a swirl, a sniff, a good sloshing, and then a hearty spit. After the third and final spit, my father described how he made discreet notes in his red journal. He appeared unaffected by the experience.

My father kept his composure. Ignoring the formality and silence, he moved to another barrel, announcing the name of the vineyard, site location, date of planting, and age of barrel. I imagined the pretense and unease in the cellar must have been uncomfortable for Mom, as Pop told me she moved back into the tasting room. He pulled samples from at least eight barrels before concluding the affair. Parker never said a word; he just scribbled notes as they moved silently from barrel to barrel through the dimly lit room.

When Pop went back to the lab to put his thief away, Mom quietly returned to the cellar and saw Parker shaking his head, continuing to take notes, and mumbling to himself, "These guys don't know what they have here."

The results of the Parker tasting were unknown to my parents for several months since the magazine wouldn't be published for another year. The thick, multipage publication finally arrived. With immense trepidation Mom opened to the single page entitled "The Willamette Valley," and fewer than twelve wineries were listed. Mom and Pop scanned to their name, Ponzi. The suspense rushed through their bodies as Mom read his evaluation aloud.

His comments were impressive. The *Wine Advocate* reported that Pop's 1985 Pinot Noir was comparable to some of the best in Burgundy! Mom and Pop were overwhelmed. It was a phenomenal review and gave enormous credibility to our years of hard work. To have such an influential figure in the global wine world make this claim was remarkable and significant.

When they called me with the news, I reacted in disbelief. "How can that be? Is it really that good?" I couldn't wrap my head around this news.

"It *is* an exceptional vintage," Pop responded. "But we certainly didn't anticipate this kind of a review."

"Perhaps it's the result of such a small harvest," Mom chimed in. "Whatever it is, we are thrilled."

Once this press hit the newsstands, the kitchen phone started to ring off the hook. The wine trade and wine lovers across the country wanted our wine! The power of the press was overwhelming. I was amazed how one man's opinion could have such an effect, such influence. My parents were completely caught off guard, completely unaccustomed to this kind of popularity. Our greatest challenge was that the majority of wine had been previously released and most had already been sold. While Parker was right that the 1985 was a stellar vintage, it was also a short crop. Only a few hundred cases were produced, and once it was bottled, Pop had shipped most of it to the East Coast as those were the markets that had shown initial interest. We had only one pallet left at the winery. After a week of orders, Pop finally reported we were sold out.

Every bottle had been accounted for except for two cases. Only twenty-four bottles remained—all without labels. We'd run out before the end of packaging, so we decided to keep these in the cellar for ourselves. The reality of having no wine to sell created an unusual situation for my parents. Local accounts were furious they couldn't get the celebrated wine. Rumors began to swarm that we didn't care about the Oregon market. This tale of local disregard stuck with us for decades following the incident. "Oh, the Ponzis, yeah, I hear they sell everything to New York and DC. They must be too good for us."

Nevertheless, this incident significantly changed our future. At last, the wine market began to show an interest in our wines, and the press continued to prop them up with good reviews and high scores. In 1987, for the first time ever, the *Wine Spectator*, notoriously known at the time for predominately favoring California wines, listed the 1987 Ponzi Pinot Noir as a Top 100 Wine of the Year. It was another important achievement, especially since the vintage was considered by most critics a disaster for the region. To be featured among some of the most notable producers in the world in a tough year was another testament to my father's winemaking skills.

GLOBAL IMPACT

In June of 1987, I graduated from the University of Oregon's School of Journalism with a degree in public relations and broadcast journalism and a minor in Italian. Two weeks before graduation, I booked and paid for a flight to Boston. I'd leave Oregon one week after graduation. This was deliberately timed to avoid involving myself back in the family business. My parents seemed surprised when I abruptly announced my intention, but they were in the midst of planning the inaugural International Pinot Noir Celebration (IPNC), which left them sufficiently distracted.

The original idea behind the IPNC was to create a wine event that would benefit the economies of McMinnville and Yamhill County. After consulting with the Yamhill County Wineries Association and following the recent successful wine judgings in New York, the event planners were persuaded to create a noncompetitive event whereby French winemakers could be included.

The wine pioneers saw an opportunity whereby the Willamette Valley, and McMinnville in particular, could play center stage in celebrating Pinot Noir and regional food. As discussions continued, the potential of bringing international winemakers to the affair became increasingly appealing. The focus of the weekend would involve seminars and tastings to better understand the Pinot Noir grape. This celebration hoped to expose both the public and the media to our region's wines in a collaborative approach.

Fortunately, my parents' visits to Burgundy with Lett, Adelsheim, and others had created a bridge between the two regions, so they responded favorably when asked to attend the first IPNC. It became evident the Burgundians were as curious about us as we were about them. Although most of them were content to perfect and maintain their family legacies, some had become increasingly interested in this New World wine region. The IPNC was able to attract some of the most prestigious wine producers to the valley, including Maison Joseph Drouhin, Domaine Faiveley, and Domaine Dujac, all of whom had made previous visits to the Willamette Valley.

The first three-day event was held in 1987 on McMinnville's Linfield College campus, whose modest grounds created an idyllic place for frank discussions and developing friendships. A mutual bond naturally formed around Pinot Noir producers and its supporters in these early days as there was shared commonality over being thoughtful, connecting to the land, and for high quality standards.

Pop, Adelsheim, and Myron joined other speakers at the inaugural event, including wine celebrities Robert Drouhin of Maison Joseph Drouhin, Dominique Lafon of Comtes de Lafon, and Christophe Roumier of Domaine Georges Roumier, all from Burgundy. Richard Sanford of Sanford Vineyards of Santa Barbara, California, and Richard Graves of Calera in California's Central Coast also attended. There were three objectives: 1) learn from each other's varying regions and techniques, 2) take this information and attempt to make better wine, and 3) expose more consumers, trade, and the media to beautiful Pinot Noir. It was clear that was not a competition. Instead, the free exchange created an open forum for both winemakers and wine consumers, changing the quality and perception of Pinot Noir on a global level.

But there was another event that was having an even greater influence on elevating the quality of Pinot Noir across the globe: the Steamboat Conference. It was conceived of by two young wine friends who loved Pinot Noir. Stephen Cary and Mike Richmond had formed a deep friendship that set the stage for this kind of openness. Back in 1980, the two organized comparative wine tastings in Richmond's home in Carneros. Cary shared with me how they drank Pinot Noir from several producers, breaking down components, attempting to better understand why one wine could vary so much from another. They loved hosting these tastings and would often invite other winemakers to join. The tasting dates would change as would the location, but the men ensured they happened as they both felt they were invaluable.

In addition to their love for Pinot, both men were avid fly fishermen and spent time fishing the tranquil waters of Oregon's Umpqua River. While standing in the cold rushing river on one of these days, Cary explained how they couldn't imagine a more perfect place to combine their two pastimes. As a result, they occasionally moved their wine tastings to The Steamboat Inn, a quaint fishing resort on the Umpqua River. The gatherings continued for six years until the planners decided it would be easier to meet consistently in one place and even more interesting if they opened the tastings up to an international group. After learning the IPNC would be inviting a collection of global producers to Oregon, Cary and Richmond took advantage of the opportunity. The weekend before the IPNC, they invited a handful of respected wine friends and a few of the guest vintners to join them. The guests were carefully selected by Cary and had to meet his code of ethics and standards: the producer must be devoted to the Pinot Noir grape, must have made wine for several years, and would openly share information, be supportive, and provide constructive comments to others.

The event's purpose was to technically taste and analyze both finished and unfinished Pinot Noirs. The first wines and winemakers came mostly from Burgundy, Oregon, and California, but soon Pinot Noirs from New Zealand, Spain, Chile, Canada, and other regions of California began to arrive. The weekend at Steamboat quickly gained popularity, and the organizers soon realized they would have to tighten the guest list in order to keep the discussions open and honest as intended. Cary did this by blocking all media and marketers. Soon the roster included only winemakers and their families, making it clear it was an exclusive and serious event. Over the years, its reputation spread as it was a rare opportunity to access some of the most renowned wine producers in the world. Because it was held at an unassuming location on the banks of a remote river, discussions were lengthy and, at times, uncomfortably frank. I witnessed the gathering one summer.

"You mean you're fermenting in ten-ton fermenters?! Are you crazy?" a small Oregon producer remarked to a Californian producer during one session. "You need to reduce the size considerably if you ever want to make really great Pinot Noir."

"How long are you keeping your wine in barrel? All I taste is oak! You need to request less toast on the staves or maybe use fewer new barrels."

"Or try another cooper," another winemaker suggested.

"This wine is completely oxidized. How are you sealing your tanks?" questioned a peer from New Zealand.

The dialogue went on for hours. The intended focus was helping each other improve any flawed wines. Long days were filled with tastings and deep conversations, along with plenty of laughter and delicious meals from the kitchen. When there was a break in the collective sharing, the international group would often hike up to a favorite swimming hole and jump into the refreshing water. Many guests brought their kids and spent hours in the mountain streams and explored the nearby forest. I preferred to soak in any warm Oregon sunshine I could find, lounging on one of the many large, smooth boulders along the river's shore, blissfully unaware these weekends would become some of the most influential for raising the quality standards for Pinot Noir across the world.

MASSACHUSETTS

My girlfriends greeted me in Boston. It was June of 1987. I had met the group while on a semester exchange between the U of O and the University of Massachusetts Amherst during my senior year. I moved into a rental with them and went straight to work. Driven to launch my journalism career, I immediately started scanning the *Boston Globe* classifieds in search of a reporting job. Week after week, I was hopeful for an interview and outfitted myself in my latest investment: a black-and-white herringbone skirt and suit jacket. Once my checking account got down to twelve dollars, and there were no significant opportunities for securing my dream job as a broadcast journalist, I accepted a position at a publishing house near Faneuil Hall as an advertising sales associate.

By 1988, I was comfortable in my East Coast life. I'd become a fixture on Boston's Green Line, taking the train from Allston to my six a.m. aerobics class at Kenmore Square, then heading to my final stop at Government Center. There, I'd grab my daily coffee and a slice of zucchini bread as I walked through the North End's Little Italy to my office job. I enjoyed my work in advertising sales at the magazine and was well suited to my tasks, which included laying out pages that allowed me to draw from my experience with Mom at our kitchen table. Although it wasn't what I dreamed of doing, I admired my female boss and gained invaluable East Coast work experience.

On the weekends, my roommates and I took advantage of New England's quaint attractions, traveling to the Cape, Nantucket, or Newport. We'd soak in the seasonal change, road-tripping to Vermont to bask in the autumn foliage and eat warm apple-cinnamon donuts, aware of the approaching cold winds. I learned the true definition of "cocktail hour" as I sipped a sea breeze in a crowded bar on Charles Street, managing small, uninspiring talk with young men focused on their financial careers.

I loved being surrounded by American history and adored the church bells, endless steeples, and ubiquitous plaques noting famous moments in our country's past. I was enamored with it all. I found it charming and polished in contrast to my past rural life. I survived on bags of cheesy popcorn between my minimal paychecks and shared a queen bed with my best friend to manage my tight budget. I was having my own small adventure, but it was nothing compared to what was happening at home.

Mom was ecstatic when she called me one evening just before I was heading to bed.

"Maria, I have really big news!"

"What happened?!"

"Robert Parker says your father is one of the world's best winemakers!"

"What?"

"Yes. He's listed as one of the top winemakers in the world, in the same list as DRC, which sells for more than $500 a bottle."

Apparently the wine accolades hadn't stopped. Only fifteen wine personalities were on Robert Parker's list, and Pop was the only one representing Oregon. The impressive roster included Marcel Guigal, François Faiveley, Corinne Mentzelopoulos from Chateau Margaux, Patrick Leon from Chateau Mouton Rothschild, Lalou Bize-Leroy, and Aubert de Villaine of Domaine de la Romanee-Conti. These legends had built their reputations by producing some of the world's most prestigious wines. And my Pop was among them.

"That's just crazy, Mom."

"It's wonderful. The phone won't stop ringing!"

I was stunned by the news. How was this possible? After working on our wines for nearly fourteen vintages, he was being recognized among some of the greatest European domaines. These were established producers, many who had been operating their family businesses for centuries. It was extraordinary. I reflected on what it meant for the industry and our small winery. Going to bed that night, I missed Scholls and imagined the excitement that must be whirling through our quiet valley.

The *Wine Advocate* followed a year later with another article declaring Ponzi as "Oregon's top producer, continuing to make Oregon's most complex wines." Parker again compared Ponzi Pinot Noir to the great Burgundies of France. It was difficult for me not to take notice.

Maybe something was finally happening.

In Boston, I couldn't deny I was enjoying personal success. My performance was rewarded with an Hermès scarf and later a Rolex watch, as I'd become the company's top salesperson. Within months I was promoted from selling classifieds to selling large display ads. I enjoyed the cold calls, negotiating agreements, laying out the pages, and managing my clients. It was a good entry-level position, but over time I found my enthusiasm waning. I remained loyal, earning large raises, but after

three years I was restless. In 1990, I was offered another promotion, taking on the responsibilities of the company's southeast regional sales. The management role meant a significant
pay increase and a move to Atlanta. Honored by the offer and
sorely tempted by the compensation, I called Pop for advice.

"So, I've been offered another promotion, but this is a big
one. It would mean moving to Georgia."

"Sounds exciting! What would you be doing?"

"Managing the regional sales there. It's a lot of money."

"Great! What are you thinking?"

"I love the idea of earning more money, but I'm not sure I
want to stay in sales. What's happening at the winery?"

"Well, it's definitely changing around here. More wineries
have moved in, bringing with them experienced winemakers
and good financing. They're arriving with degrees in viticulture and enology. The wine quality is definitely improving."

"Uh-huh." I followed along, imagining myself back in
Oregon.

"The wines are becoming more consistent, and as a result
we're getting a lot of good press, keeping your mother busy
with all the public relations work."

"Hmm." I imagined Mom doing this work alone.

"And there's a lot happening with the brewery too. It's definitely busy!"

Despite what he said, I couldn't believe it. This was sleepy
Oregon, after all. But for the first time, I was intrigued. I was
curious about the newcomers to the valley and suddenly felt
territorial. I realized I missed my parents and the bustling
family activities. I felt a slight tug, especially when Pop mentioned the public relations work. This was one part of the operation I had enjoyed.

"Yeah? Do you think there would be a place for me?" I was
afraid to broach the topic, but had to ask. "I don't want to come

back and just be Dick and Nancy's daughter, you know? I need
to be useful. I've really enjoyed my independence here."

"I understand. Well, you'd have to talk with your mother.
But do what you want to do. The winery will always be here."

I called Mom a couple days later, still tossing the idea
around in my head.

"Well, yes, there's a lot going on here for sure," she said
when I asked about the situation.

"I just don't want this to be a handout, Mom. I need to per-
sonally contribute. I need to be my own person."

"Well, I could certainly use the help," she replied, not
responding directly to my concern.

I spent the next week contemplating my options. I had an
opportunity to make twice my current salary, live in a new city,
meet new people, develop a career, and remain independent.
These were all positives—all things I had dreamed of doing as
a child. But the actual job of selling ads had lost its appeal,
leaving me unfulfilled and empty most days. I needed to be
challenged, and I wanted to find greater purpose. As a child
my main objective was to get off the farm and away from my
crazy family life. Now after reaching that goal, I found I was
relatively unsatisfied with it.

After another week of pondering the pros and cons, I
turned down the promotion. I made the difficult decision to
leave the freedom Boston provided. I was unsure of my destiny,
slightly reluctant to return to Oregon and begin work again
with my family. I wasn't sure what that looked like or exactly
how I would fit in.

On the other hand, I'd grown tired of the crowds, the
grumpy Bostonians, sticky summers, and brutally cold winters.
I'd begun to miss the comfort of home and the West Coast lifestyle. But, mainly, I yearned for something more. I felt perhaps
the "grown-up" winery could provide that for me. The idea of

continuing to grow the business and work for myself, and the family, was intriguing.

The decision surprised me. I was leaving my conventional life—what I had always wanted. But what I realized was that I was missing the chaos, the long discussions, and the collaboration my family represented. There was a sense of emptiness after years of distance from my parents' ingenuity, tenacity, and vibrancy. In general, I missed being included in their adventures.

Although I had been earning a solid income for a young professional, I'd lived modestly and managed to save most of my earnings. I had no interest in buying a house or investing. Instead I felt this transition period was the time to splurge. I purchased an Around the World airline ticket. This was a book of vouchers allowing one to travel in a single direction around the world, stopping in as many places as desired. It had been a dream of mine to travel the globe. It seemed like the ideal time to do it before heading home. I knew it was possible I might never have the opportunity again. Unfortunately, most of my good friends were still building their careers, and I was concerned about traveling solo, so I called Luisa.

Since she graduated from high school, my younger sister had been moving from college to college, trying to find her ideal learning environment. From Pomona, to Occidental, to the University of Oregon, she moved often, changing her major from English literature to biology to chemistry. It seemed like a good time for her to take a break. When she explained she had no money, I offered to cover her ticket. After weeks of pondering, she finally decided to join me, and we quickly put the trip together.

Our first stop was Borneo. Through the Earthwatch Institute, Luisa and I were able to do volunteer work with Dr. Biruté Galdikas and her orangutans. We spent four grueling weeks in the wet, leech-infested rain forest tracking the gentle apes from the ground as the strong, graceful athletes glided across the canopy with their great arms grasping tree limbs. We survived three weeks on canned tuna, steamed rice, and an occasional hard-boiled egg. We spent our days pulling leeches from our boots as we made our way through the swampy forest floor and swatting hungry mosquitoes as we sat in hammocks waiting for the majestic animals to carefully construct their beds each night atop massive mangrove trees.

Our twelve-month backpacking adventure took us through Indonesia, Thailand, Hong Kong, New Zealand, Australia, China, Japan, India, Nepal, Sweden, Germany, Italy, and France. Along the way, we met hundreds of interesting people, and the free time allowed us to reflect on our futures. Luisa and I spent hours considering her interests, and eventually the possibility of her becoming a winemaker came up.

Luisa was comfortable being uncomfortable; she was fearless and sought out the unknown. While I struggled with math or science-related subjects, she sailed through the advanced courses and sincerely enjoyed them. She was a natural at biology and couldn't wait to dissect creatures or view cadavers. In contrast, I deliberately chose a major that enabled me to avoid numbers, graphs, and body parts.

Our opposite personalities were revealed multiple times during our global adventure, starting the morning of our departure. All my belongings had been neatly organized and secured within plastic baggies inside my backpack three days prior to the day of departure. I rang the bell at her Portland apartment. There was no answer. I rang again and another three times before picking up two rocks and throwing them at her window. The door finally opened, and she stood there in an oversized T-shirt.

"Are you kidding me?" I shouted in disbelief.

"Sorry. I guess my alarm didn't go off." She rubbed her eyes.

"Unbelievable, Luisa," I grumbled. "We have to get to the airport!" I helped pack her year-supply of disposable contact lenses and too many paperback books. We rushed to the airport within seconds of the flight closing. The rest of the trip followed in similar fashion.

Following an extended stay in Europe on account of a cute guy she'd met along the tour, Luisa completed her degree at Portland State University. She ended up petitioning the school for her unusual degree, a bachelor of science in English literature. Simultaneously, my parents worked diligently to pull strings in France, focused on getting her enrolled at the CFPPA, Les Centre de Formation Professionnelle et de Promotion Agricole, the prestigious wine school in Beaune. My parents were well aware this would be the best opportunity for Luisa to learn firsthand from the masters of Burgundy.

After weeks of several expensive long-distance calls between my parents and the French producers, Luisa was accepted. This would make her the first American woman to attend this school in the heart of one of France's most notable wine regions. My parents arranged for her to live in Chambolle-Musigny under the warm hospitality of the Roumier family of Domaine Georges Roumier. The family was gracious and generous as my sister slowly developed an appreciation for the French culture, the country's people, and the vineyards that surrounded her.

The move to Beaune was life changing for her. Studying viticulture and enology in French, among other subjects, without any knowledge of the language was challenging. Being the only woman in an otherwise male-dominated classroom made it even more intimidating. Nevertheless, Luisa's character emerged: tough, intelligent, and blissfully competent. She proved her worth to the neighboring domaines and once harvest arrived was able to work in the great cellars. Despite the obstacles, she graduated with a degree in viticulture and enology in 1993. With her accomplishment, Luisa opened doors for other American winemakers to follow. She told me those years were some of her most valuable as she had the tremendous fortune to taste some of the world's greatest and rarest regional wines and to train among the true masters of Pinot Noir and Chardonnay.

BACK HOME

After moving back to Oregon in 1991, I found myself a modest apartment in the West Hills of Portland. It was perfectly situated between the rather sleepy city and quiet country. I was able to commute to the winery in the morning and easily return home in the evenings.

Luisa was still in Beaune. She'd occasionally call me with news of her international life, telling me about her continued attempts to gain respect from her French male colleagues. Drinking beautiful wine didn't come without its difficulties. She struggled to learn the language, understand the challenging classes, and fit in with a proper French lifestyle.

A few years prior, Michel and his first wife moved into a home in southeast Portland. He graduated from the University of Oregon in 1985 with a music degree and went to work at the winery. When my parents opened the brewery, Michel helped to support that operation as well. He was comfortable with the new technology, developing and navigating accounting and inventory systems. These tools were becoming critical components of our growing businesses, and he showed an aptitude for this critical part of the operation.

I was ready to jump in. Mom, Pop, and Michel had created a small office space above the winery garage, in the attic we used to play in as kids. Pop had installed a skylight to bring more light into the otherwise dark space, but the ceilings were still low. I made myself at home in the broom closet at the top of the stairs. The sounds and smells of the working winery below rose into the tight space, grounding me to our product. Childhood memories would often mix with my professional tasks in the small room.

It was in this closet that I started my career creating marketing campaigns and continuing to develop a network of national distributors. My parents had established a relatively good collection of wholesalers over the previous years, although I discovered many of them were small operators. It had been twenty years since our founding, and people remained hesitant to present Oregon wines on their wine lists or shelves. California reigned as the domestic wine of choice, and the Pinot Noir varietal was still relatively unknown.

I realized my mission would be to continue to spread the gospel of this rare grape. Although I lacked substantial wine knowledge, I was fueled by my family's passion and their devotion to the varietal. Each morning, driving out to the country, I would brainstorm how to garner attention for the wine, knowing it was vitally important to have the media taste the wines. We needed never-ending strong scores and constant exposure.

My enhanced sales skills were revealed when I was presented with the opportunity to convince someone to choose a Pinot Noir over another varietal. I enjoyed the challenge of transitioning a consumer with a love for heavy-bodied Cabernet to a refined Pinot Noir. No longer timid, I found it amusing and enjoyed the game. Dialogue I'd overheard my parents use so many years before I found myself repeating, but now crafting my own message. Best of all, I had developed a palate for wine and now actually enjoyed it.

Over the following months, my responsibilities included communicating with distributors over wine allocations, new vintage releases, and pricing, scheduling and visiting the trade, discussing the wines, and hosting vineyard tours. My role was to educate people about our wines and our story. I was comfortable writing press releases, creating marketing pieces, and growing our fan base. All these tasks came naturally to me.

Within a year, we were bustling. The brewery had become particularly demanding. Hoping to expand our sales, we had moved beyond keg distribution to bottle production. The pressures of daily brewing, pub management, and launching and maintaining the growing bottle sales were great. Locals flocked to the pub, packing the place in the evenings and on weekends. There were only three brewpubs in Portland—and even fewer in other major cities across the country. When Mom and I weren't fussing over the fresh flowers, menu fonts, and paper stock or hiring new bartenders or sewing curtains for the pub windows, we were working on another package design for a new brew Pop and Karl decided to make. Things moved at an intense pace at the brewery, especially in contrast to the winery. A new beer was produced almost every three months, and each one required a name, a label, a six-pack and case design, and marketing collateral. It was nonstop.

Meanwhile, back in the wine world, the Willamette Valley was now home to nearly seventy wineries. The number had more than doubled since my move to Boston. I was shocked at the developments in the state over just the few years I'd been away. One afternoon, I ran an errand for the Washington County Wineries Association, headed for Montinore Estate on the edge of Forest Grove. I felt my stomach drop as I turned onto the large property. The grand gated entrance and landscaped driveway to the winery opened to lush vineyard rows that stretched for acres on either side. It felt like Napa. In a state of shock, I slowly drove along the wide drive to the stone facility.

What is happening around here? Where am I right now?

The sense of disbelief continued. A few days later, I was driving to Dundee for another errand. Along Highway 99, a highway I had driven many times before as a little girl sitting in Pop's yellow banana truck, I looked up at the hills past Sokol Blosser to the new Domaine Drouhin winery. I heard a rumor it had been established four years ago, about the same time I moved to Boston, but I hadn't seen it until now. The sleek building was stunning, positioned purposefully down along the natural curve of the land in an elegant fashion. The gravity-flow facility was the first of its kind in our valley. When Pop said it was made for the legendary French producer Joseph Drouhin of Burgundy, I wasn't surprised. It made some of the Oregon wine pioneers who were still crafting wines out of their basements and garages envious.

I wondered how such a grand place could have been built here in rural Dundee. I was even more impressed when Pop reminded me of the Drouhins' European heritage and the generations of winemaking tradition and the rich Burgundian history they brought to our valley of homegrown wine. I couldn't help but wonder what would have happened if Mom and Pop had just faked a French accent when they asked for that first bank loan twenty years ago. I learned the domaine's daughter, Véronique Drouhin, was the head winemaker and realized this was an unusual role for a French woman. I imagined the facility on the hill as her palace, and she was our French Wine Queen. Despite my undeniable envy, we were proud of the domaine and knew the positive impact this outside investment would have on the region.

THE GREAT
WHITE

We had been selling Pinot Gris for nearly ten years and at half the price of our Pinot Noir. Many of the "Pinot Obsessed" followed our lead, realizing the potential it had for opening doors in the marketplace. The wine was a natural for the valley. Regardless of vintage, it seemed to retain balanced acidity and good fruit character. It had enjoyed slow popularity over the years, most especially in the southeast, where it was warm most of the year and a chilled glass of white wine was always welcome. For those who believed in the beauty of this white grape, it became an important part of their portfolio.

Walking through our humble winery one July morning in 1991, I noticed Pop in the lab. This tiny room originally referred to as the tool shop was long and multipurposed and had one narrow wooden counter. When I was a child, this was where my father used to store all his woodworking equipment, along with hammers, nails, screws, saws, and his coveted welding machine. But over the years, it had morphed into a kind of limited lab, housing his hydrometer, refractometer, some pH testing equipment, test tubes, plastic cylinders, and the like. The space, although minimally equipped, served its purpose and was conveniently situated beneath the attic office. I stopped in before heading up the stairs.

"Hey, Pop. How's it going?"

"Unfortunately, we have a bit of bad news. It seems we have an issue with our Pinot Gris this year."

"In what way?" I knew the value of the wine to our business. It had become essential for cash flow.

"Well, you know all those farmers we convinced to plant Pinot Gris all those years ago?"

"Yeah." I remembered the hundreds of calls Pop had made nearly ten years ago to neighboring landowners asking if they would be interested in planting wine grapes. He had driven around looking for ideal hillsides, then searched county records to find the property owners and reached out. Most inquiries went nowhere, but occasionally, someone would return the call. If he got someone to listen, Pop explained if the farmer invested in the cuttings, we would plant, maintain, harvest, and pay for the fruit. All they had to do was commit some of their land to grapevines and wait for the paycheck. It seemed like a great deal for those with idle land, especially when they learned wine grapes yielded a gain much larger than cherries or Christmas trees.

Since we had limited means and were unable to purchase land ourselves and while most of the prime sites were under current ownership, this practice worked well. If the farmer honored the deal, we'd be able to increase our Pinot Gris production, which had become increasingly important to us. Any profit from Pinot Gris went right back into the costs required to elevate the Pinot Noir quality and keep our business running.

"Apparently there's a new guy in the valley, Ed King, who has come down from Seattle to get in the wine business. He's interested in Pinot Gris," Pop said.

"That's strange. Why is he so interested in Pinot Gris?" Most everyone else moving to the valley was interested in Pinot Noir.

"Not sure, but I assume he sees promise in the varietal. Problem is, there's not much available, but he wants to get started right away."

"I don't get it."

"Well, sounds like he's looked up most of our growers and has reached out to them, offering more money than we can, and in some cases he's able to pay cash on delivery."

"Whoa. Really?"

"We just can't compete." I could tell he was concerned; his eyes were not their usual sparkling blue. I paused before asking the most obvious question.

"But, Pop, don't you have contracts with these guys?"

"Ha." He grinned and looked down at the floor, then shrugged his shoulders. "You know, I never thought I'd need a contract. A handshake has always been enough." Then he took a deep breath and admitted, "I guess times are changing."

I was completely blown away. I couldn't imagine anyone selling their grapes to someone else besides my father. We were the ones who had encouraged the plantings in the first place. Most of these farmers didn't know the first thing about grape growing. We established the sites, and now it felt like they were abandoning us. My heart hurt for Pop. He was so trusting.

"What are we going to do?"

"Not much we can do. We'll just have a whole lot less Pinot Gris this year. We'll have to make it through somehow."

Pop's disappointed voice conveyed the impact this would have on the year's harvest and our income. As disheartening as it was, it also presented us with a great lesson. We had to take our business more seriously and insist on formal contracts. With outsiders coming into the valley, we realized we needed to change our approach.

In the end, we produced fewer cases of Pinot Gris than past vintages and raised our price to compensate. Pop got aggressive well before the following harvest and offered the better sites more per acre. He also insisted those growers sign a five-year agreement. The situation emphasized the most sensible long-term solution to maintaining our production levels was to establish our own vineyards. It was a painful but important lesson.

King Estate increased its plantings of Pinot Gris over the years and went on to become one of the largest and most successful wine producers in the state, with this varietal at its core. There was never any animosity against the King family or King Estate by our family for what happened in the early years. On the contrary, our family always supported their advancement of Pinot Gris. We were proud to see its growth and increased popularity as a result of the winery's increased volumes and terrific marketing campaigns. It gave all of us tremendous exposure. It was something we would have never been able to do.

AURORA

We began our hunt. We knew we had to secure more land if we wanted to maintain the business. It was obvious we were too dependent on contracted fruit. There was a large vineyard, nearly sixty-five acres, that had been established on a gentle slope of the western hills in Scholls. It was owned by a German family who had been making wine in the basement of their large home for years. The property had recently fallen into bankruptcy. With the modest savings my parents had accumulated from recent beer sales, they decided to bid on it. It shared the same soil, elevation, and exposure as our prized Madrona and Abetina Vineyards near Hillsboro, making it a promising site.

The large house on the estate had expansive views to the valley below and back to Portland. It would be a dream home for my parents. Mom and Pop were ready to move away from the current winery activities and now relatively busy tasting room.

The day of the bank auction arrived, and we were surprised to discover we weren't the only interested party. Some woman had deeper pockets, and we lost it. Mom and Pop had decided to take out a few rows at the Madrona Vineyard site to build a new home when they received a voice mail message almost a month later. The original bidder decided it was too large a project and asked if we were still interested. Michel, Pop, and I all went to court to rebid on it and were thrilled to learn there was no other competition. It was ours. This purchase, as Michel so succinctly put it, set us up for the future. He was right. We chose to name the new property Aurora, the Italian word for "sunrise," in recognition of the breathtaking sun that presented itself so dramatically each morning behind majestic Mount Hood.

Unfortunately, although the vineyard was well established, the vines had been poorly maintained in recent years. Pop decided the entire piece needed to be torn out and replanted. This was a huge and very expensive undertaking, but it also provided us with a unique opportunity. We were able to put into practice several of the new viticultural discoveries made over the past twenty years. This meant working with updated clones of Pinot Noir and Chardonnay, rootstock trials, tighter vine spacing, drip irrigation, and new varietals! With resources still tight, it took nearly ten years to complete the project. It has since become one of our most significant vineyards.

MY PLACE

By 1992, I had found my footing at the winery. I enjoyed communicating with the distributors, hosting tours, and setting up the tasting room for guests. I was confident about building marketing campaigns around new wine releases and wine events. And although I remained intimidated by the wine press, I reached out and sent samples and was diligent about the follow-up work, always trying to build relationships and create opportunities. The pace was fast, so multitasking became second nature to me, as I moved from project to project, constantly pushing myself to be resourceful and efficient with my time. Everything was a never-ending challenge. I never had enough time in my day. I was more than fulfilled.

I joined the family business with the understanding that I wanted to contribute and have an impact. I wasn't interested in simply following in my mother's footsteps. But I soon realized I shared her same drive for working hard and collaborating with others. There were more faces in our community than in my youth, but the energy, enthusiasm, and devotion remained. I was caught up in it all. Unlike my childhood days, I wanted to be here.

As usual, Mom encouraged me to get involved with leadership, so I sought out the Oregon Wine Advisory Board. Because it was the most important organization for the industry at the time, I felt it would help me understand what was happening across the state beyond the Willamette Valley. I was appointed to the board by the governor of Oregon in 1992. After a couple years of service, I was asked to serve as the organization's marketing chair. It was a huge honor, especially since I was nearly half the age of the other board members. Serving on behalf of the industry, making decisions on how we would spend our industry's tax dollars, and helping to create its marketing campaigns was enormously exciting.

I was tasked with several marketing opportunities. One in particular was to design the "Discover Oregon" brochure. This touring guide was a continuation of what Mom and the wine women created back in the 1970s. Those promotional pieces started out as single-panel handouts, then evolved into bifolds, then trifolds as the number of wineries grew. At one point, the women created a multipage brochure that required staples to keep it together. Leafing through that piece felt significant then, but now the board was discussing how to create a listing for over a hundred wineries! I was thrilled with the challenge, wanting to make it the best directory ever.

In my role as the Wine Board's marketing chair, I quickly realized the challenges of the volunteer position. I frequently found myself centered between passionate conversations among members from across the entire state. I was often uncomfortable and left the Salem meetings feeling pushed to my limit after hours of trying to remain diplomatic. I realized it took a tremendous amount of tenacity and levelheadedness to appropriately lead. For a young leader, it was a valuable period of growth and perspective. I discovered the growth of our community and realized the importance it now had in the state. Above all, it was apparent how many new personalities were involved and that politics and opinions came along with the development.

The early 1990s was a time of spirited discussion surrounding the subject of alcohol and drugs. The excessive and abusive use of these products was recognized as an increasing problem at both the national and local level. Organizations like MADD (Mothers Against Drunk Driving) and DARE (Drug Abuse Resistance Education) were making headlines. Driving past Groner Elementary on my way to Aurora, I often cringed seeing one of the marked DARE police cars parked in the lot. I imagined young children being lectured on only the negative effects of alcohol, without any balanced approach toward educating them on its benefits.

The antialcohol movement had been a pain in my side since I was a child. I never understood how alcohol could be considered as harmful as pistols or cigarettes. I was also shocked at the lack of balanced information surrounding wine. It seemed I was not alone in my frustration. In 1992, I joined a progressive group of women who had formed an organization called Women for WineSense (WWS). While MADD and DARE opposed drinking alcohol, the mission of WWS was to educate the public on moderate drinking and its health benefits. I was one of the youngest in the group and felt proud to be among dynamic women.

The group was originally formed in Napa Valley by female winery owners, many of them mothers themselves. This circle of women knew that moderate wine drinking was harmless to pregnant women, though the authorities dictated otherwise. We recognized that thousands of pregnant European and

Asian women had birthed healthy children despite their occasional enjoyment of a glass of wine. They had been doing it for centuries. We knew pure wines had positive effects on the heart when enjoyed in reasonable fashion. We understood wine contained HDL cholesterol, which reduced bad LDL cholesterol. In 1991, Morley Safer of the hit TV show *60 Minutes* aired a piece called "The French Paradox" in which he explained how drinking red wine in moderation could reduce heart disease. We knew all this to be true, but having others understand it seemed impossible.

Later that year, I was elected president of the Oregon chapter and enjoyed working with Helen Dusschee, Nancy McDaniel, and my late friend Lori Wisbeck in bringing education to the topic of drinking moderately. This leadership position had a huge impact on me, establishing my identity in the wine community aside from being Dick and Nancy's daughter.

GIVING BACK

While I was diligent about getting on industry boards and stretching my wings, Mom was doing the same—but as usual in a more powerful way. My parents had become friends with two local doctors, Larry Hornick and Jim Ratcliff, both from Hillsboro Tuality Healthcare. Both men had an affection for local Pinot Noir, and as they became more acquainted, they began to discuss the reliance the wine industry had on vineyard workers—many who lacked medical care. As small businesses, wineries couldn't afford this benefit, and many of the workers were ineligible due to their seasonal employment. Additionally, many were intimidated by traditional healthcare.

By this time, local winegrowers had positioned themselves as stewards of the land, adopting sustainable or organic farming techniques. This meant long hours of repetitious physical work throughout the year. Many wineries in the valley had become dependent on migrant and local farm workers to produce quality fruit for their wines. This year-round labor took its toll on the crews, yet there was no access to basic healthcare for them. For many the cost for care was out of reach, or they were too intimidated to seek help from a clinic. Yet without these skilled people in the vineyards, our quality wines could not be produced. My parents saw the irony. It seemed our responsibility as employers to provide support.

Mom considered the example of the Hospices de Beaune in Burgundy, where Pinot Noir cuvées had been produced by the local domaines for centuries with the specific purpose of raising funds for the regional hospital. She felt a similar event could be established in the Willamette Valley. The doctors wanted to help.

¡Salud! was born in 1992. Mom, Hornick, Ratcliff, a handful of wineries, local business owners, and Tuality Healthcare Board members formed to create The Vintners Circle. The original circle represented eighteen wineries that crafted a barrel each of Pinot Noir to be auctioned off at a black-tie affair. All proceeds from the event would fund a mobile health van to bring medical services directly to the workers in the vineyard. It was a brilliant, innovative plan quickly embraced by our community. The inaugural event was staged in November atop one of Portland's most prominent restaurants, Atwaters. On the heels of harvest, winemakers switched out their rubber boots and fleeces for tuxedos, high heels, and gowns.

As the grand event neared, Mom asked me to attend. I anxiously sat at one of the tables among some of Portland's most prominent wine buyers. I'd never seen my mother so anxious. Larry was nervous too. Nobody knew how it would be perceived or the level of support they could expect. The first event raised $127,831 and went on to be one of the most prestigious wine events in the state.

The affair continues today and has had a dramatic effect on our local farming community and their families. Of all her contributions, Mom often remarked about how this is one of her proudest accomplishments.

TOGETHER
AGAIN

It was 1993 and the winery was on relatively stable ground. The string of past vintages had been healthy, and with our small but sturdy network of distributors, we were selling our supply of wines comfortably throughout the year. The main wine critics continued to enjoy our wines for the most part, although we still received more accolades from outside the state than within it. As disappointing as that was, we realized that this approval was vital to the overall success of the entire state. Word spread across the world that our region was legitimate and deserved attention.

We enhanced the small tasting room by decorating the walls with framed reviews and articles about Pop. No longer were we surprised when visitors stopped by with the latest issue of the *Wine Advocate* crammed in their back pockets, seeking only wines with 90+ scores. Frank Prial from the *New York Times* continued to rave about our Pinot Noir, and in one important review he noted how our twenty-five-dollar bottle was selected out of a blind tasting of Burgundies, including a bottle of Domaine de Romanee-Conti La Tache priced at four hundred and fifty dollars. This began several discussions among other prominent wine writers, including those from the *Wine Spectator.*

Luisa returned to the winery just in time for the 1993 harvest. It was a tough reentry for her. After a string of warm vintages, this one hit us with much cooler temperatures and a lot of rain during the growing period. Fortunately, Pop resumed his natural role of educator and listener and graciously allowed Luisa to step into the winemaking role. The transition was only seamless due to his generous nature and fearless approach to new ideas, paired with his genuine love for the journey. Even after his success and years of experience, he was still willing to learn and discuss all options with his daughter. Together they moved through the winery, considering techniques she witnessed in France and comparing them against what Pop had been doing for years. Neither one took sides; they were just listening to the other one's ideas. I couldn't help but feel a tinge of jealously as I watched them working side by side. I knew I would never share their mutual understanding and appreciation of the biology, chemistry, and natural processes that went into the winemaking process. So, rather than stay in the dark cellar with them, I climbed the narrow stairs up to the attic office to resume my desk work.

The tight space was hot in the summer and cold in the winter due to the lack of insulation and HVAC system. We got accustomed to finding mice in our desk drawers and working with box elder bugs that would climb across our computer keyboards and onto the screens. I'd often get into my car at the end of the day, feel one in my hair or on my shoulder, and have to pull off the road to flick it off. It was a daily reminder that I hadn't left the farm.

Michel and I finally decided to make some improvements to our work space. We installed low-pile carpet, a few walls, and a couple doors that allowed for some privacy. Michel brought the office into the digital age with desktop computers and an inventory and accounting system that significantly improved the operation. We were fortunate to have his expertise as our little winery began to expand to nearly fifteen thousand cases.

At this level we were able to hire outside help, starting with our loyal office manager, Jackie Stansgar, who worked alongside Michel and me for many years. We realized the value of the tasting room and began hiring part-time help to oversee the retail operation that became vital to our cash flow demands while continuing to expose people to our wines. Our vineyard crew was also beginning to grow, since we now farmed over forty acres, and everything was still being done by hand.

By 1993, all three of us had returned to work at the family winery. Each of us had found our area of focus: Luisa in winemaking, Michel in operations, and me overseeing sales and marketing. Although it's often assumed that we returned to win parental approval, the reality is I don't think any of us expected to come back. Moreover, Mom and Pop had never pressured us or assumed any of us would return. I do, however, feel we shared a common and strong connection to the business, land, and seasons, and we had a drive to continue developing what we had begun so long ago.

Now reunited, we were moving forward as a family again, operating both thriving businesses. Our days were full. If I wasn't making improvements to the tasting room, I was finishing a flyer for a wine event or running to a press check for another six-pack or sending a fax to our New York wholesaler or announcing a new wine release or a new brew to the press. The work was never ending, but I loved it. I had found my place.

The tenacity, independence, and courtesies my mother taught me years ago mattered now as much as they did then. The thoughtfulness, attention to detail, and resourcefulness my father demonstrated to me as a child were just as critical as well. I woke up each day with a feeling of purpose and confidence. In contrast to pulling away from the business as a child, as an adult, I was now determined to dig deeper. I was all in.

The best part was the gift of continuing to work alongside my parents, who never stopped raising the bar, pushing forward, thinking outside the norm, and driving to make things better and create change. It was such a joy to collaborate among their wisdom, enthusiasm, infectious energy, and drive. More than twenty years later, I felt like we were on the next big adventure together.

DEVELOPMENT

Back in the fall of 1984, Brett Fogelstrom and I had met on the stairs of a Eugene apartment building near the University of Oregon campus. I was a sophomore with badly highlighted blonde hair, and he was a junior wearing shorts printed with sharks in sunglasses. I crushed over his broad, dimpled smile and free spirit. He was lean and appropriately immature. Although attracted, I wasn't ready to take him seriously. Instead, I remained intensely focused on my mission to complete school and become a working woman. After a couple months of dating, we both moved on.

Nearly ten years later, I had moved out of my West Hills apartment and into my first home in northwest Portland. The purchase came as a result of my Boston success and disciplined savings. It was then when I received a random call from the Eugene-born-and-bred guy. We hadn't spoken since parting from U of O. He'd found my name in the white pages of the local phone book, in the pre-Facebook era. Intrigued, I met him for a beer at a local McMenamins pub and five hours later felt my life had changed. It wasn't the drink that gave me a dreamy drunkenness; it was this handsome, easygoing guy with a master's degree in architecture. I couldn't shake the way he made me feel. It was as if he'd put a spell on me. Even my busy workload couldn't distract me. I couldn't wait to be with him. We spent as much time together as possible, traveling from his construction job and tattered shack in Eugene to my charming, newly renovated Victorian home in Portland.

Just a few months into our courtship, we decided to take a trip to visit his sister, who was temporarily living in Guatemala. Brett and I both shared a love for adventure and international travel. We spent a few days alone in Antigua and Tikal before hiking the rugged and steep terrain of Volcán Atitlán near Lake Atitlán. It was here, relaxing at the end of an uphill seven-hour trek of the volcano, sitting on an abandoned dock near the lake, that he proposed. I was scarfing Guatemalan chips while he attempted to declare his love for me. It was when he pulled out a warm and well-shaken bottle of Perrier-Jouët that things felt serious. The surprise had been hidden in the bottom of his camera case since we left Portland. It occurred to me he was currently unemployed. How could I refuse?

Elated, we traveled home with my quarter-carat diamond ring and the unexpected news. Brett announced our engagement to my parents while walking past a couple of dumpsters on the way to a dinner after the airport. Mom and Pop were equally excited for us. He was bright and full of energy, and we were in love. True to their character, that was all that mattered to my parents. The fact he didn't have a job didn't concern them. We planned each component of the wedding together and were married six months later. Aurora Vineyard was the selected venue for the summer affair. My parents had renovated the large abandoned home on the property and moved there in 1991. We felt there was no more appropriate setting to celebrate our new life together.

Being a private individual, Brett had hoped for maybe seventy-five guests, but being new to the family, he was short-sighted. Once we introduced the idea to Mom, she was thrilled to help host, and in traditional form, the guest list quickly increased to 250.

Aside from our wedding, 1995 was a momentous year for the family. We had made the big decision to sell BridgePort Brewery to a Mexican-born Texan, Carlos Alvarez of the Gambrinus Company. At the time, he owned the exclusive rights to the East Coast distribution of Corona Extra beer and was the founder of Shiner Bock in Texas. We made the tough decision knowing there was no way we could keep up with the pace of running both businesses. The craft brewing industry was at its peak, and we'd have to find investors if we wanted to stay competitive. Getting out of the beer business meant more time to thoughtfully grow the winery, which was where we all wanted to put our energy and effort.

At the same time, Pop was being romanced by a national wine marketing company out of Napa Valley. Wilson Daniels was a successful firm owned and operated at the time by Winston "Win" Wilson and Jack Daniels. Both men were devoted to representing many of the world's greatest wines, most importantly those from prominent Burgundy houses. They built their entire portfolio around the iconic brands of Domaine de la Romanee-Conti, Domaine Faiveley, Domaine Dujac, and Domaine Leflaive, along with the legendary Royal Tokaji of Hungary and Schramsberg Vineyards of Napa Valley.

With our total production at fifteen thousand cases, we were selling everything we produced. The challenge of selling our Pinot Noirs had seemingly been reduced, and we were learning the value of scarcity. It was surprising to observe when we were out of wine, people wanted it more. Moreover, when demand was high, I found we could increase prices. Because of this, my father felt no need for a middleman to promote the wines. But the attraction of joining this family of winemakers, many of whom my parents had admired for decades, was an enormous honor. After much deliberation, our family decided to work with Wilson Daniels. All at once, this meant Ponzi Vineyards would be represented by nearly twenty wine professionals across the nation on a regular basis. The firm would also take over the tedious responsibilities of compliance, licensing, and securing payments.

I felt a tremendous relief. This meant I would have more time to spend at the winery while experienced professionals worked with our wholesalers to present our wines across the country. We would no longer be in that uncomfortable position of having a distributor order more wine before paying for the previous shipment. We would no longer have to worry about collecting payments and negotiating deals. Wilson Daniels took over all the hard work, and as Jack Daniels once said to me, "We only expect you to continue to make beautiful wines. We will do the rest." And he was right.

It was a solid relationship that lasted twenty-five years and allowed us to grow our company to twice its size. We felt honored to be represented by some of the best wine professionals in the country and among some of the greatest wines in the world.

On the early evening of August 12, 1995, I peered over the Scholls valley, basking in the summer glow atop Aurora Vineyard. I was wearing my cream silk wedding gown and was about to wed my best friend. Brett had staged the ceremony with Mount Hood centered directly behind us as a stunning and very deliberate backdrop. The lush grapevines marched up the hillside to meet the level ground, where our guests gathered after passing through an old patch of hazelnut trees. I was overwhelmed with how the valley had become a part of me. I felt immensely grateful as I scanned the familiar view, appreciating the textured patterns of varied orchards, fields, pastures, and forests. I took it all in, feeling fortunate to have lived in such a beautiful part of the world. I felt even more grateful to have been able to return to it. The serenity of the countryside brought comfort. I was complete, and I was home.

The day was a day to reflect. I remembered how I yearned to leave this place, my family, and the winery. I remembered how desperately I wanted to just be normal and fit in. I thought back to the many days of embarrassment and shame I had for being part of such an eccentric and chaotic life. I had never fully appreciated the strong connection to the land and how we managed not only to live off it, but to build a responsible business from it. Just as my parents had envisioned, we had respected the earth while simultaneously making a life. Beyond that we responsibly helped to grow our state's economy and build an industry. I had been given such a gift, but it took me until now to realize it.

On this special day, I felt honored for the unusual and rich journey. My next chapter would begin with a partner who shared my parents' same love of adventure, enthusiasm for life, and a belief in setting new standards. I felt complete.

That evening we were gifted with a full moon.

PART TWO

GROWTH

Two summers later, I squealed when I learned my first birth was to a healthy baby girl. Lauren Berry was born on August 3, 1997, at five p.m.—quitting time. I felt that was so appropriate. Brett and I were blessed with a brilliant, independent child. When she was just six months old, I learned I was pregnant again. I cried with the unexpected news, overwhelmed and unsure I could simultaneously manage two babies and continue to work at my regular pace. Our beautiful son, Max, was born on November 19, 1998. He was a bundle of irresistible joy. We fell deeply in love with our little ones and moved from our Victorian home in northwest Portland back to rural Scholls.

It felt natural for us to raise our family in the familiar countryside. We purchased a fifteen-acre property with an old ranch house, barn, and shop. Brett began a decade-long renovation of the home and site, including the creation of a pond, while I tried to figure out how to be a mother. This was something I had never fully considered as a young person who was more focused on being a working professional than a wife and mother. I surprised myself with my uncompromising devotion for our children, and they quickly became the center of our worlds. Despite the exhausting attention our toddlers required, morning through night, I remained equally devoted to the winery. I was back at work a week after giving birth to each child, realizing the work wouldn't stop just because my private life had changed. Weeks-old Lauren nursed while I spoke on the phone to distributors, and I swaddled Max in a BabyBjörn while I set up for a holiday weekend just four days after his birth.

Luisa was no different. In fact, her two eldest children were both born during the busiest months of harvest. With each, she strapped them onto her chest as she drove the tractor and forklift, determined to keep the winemaking process moving. There were no breaks, except for the obligatory breastfeeding that forced us to sit down, breathe, and remember we were as essential to our children as to the operation. This was a value we both shared, the equal importance of family and business. Managing that balance was something we were both deeply conscious of over the following years. Fortunately, we leaned on each other for support, used the original family home as a shared daycare space, and took advantage of our parents' eagerness to help.

We created important milestones that continued to fuel our enthusiasm and passion for the family business. While having babies, we also developed a visitor center in Dundee. The years of feeling as if we were being missed by wine tourists heading down to Yamhill County, what was considered Oregon's wine country, needed to be addressed. Dundee presented the ideal location for us to set up shop halfway between Portland and McMinnville.

In 1998 wine country was limited to just a couple restaurants—only open for dinner or weekends and frequently closed during the winter. We saw an opportunity to create a regional wine bar and restaurant so travelers could truly experience the valley's wine and food. We accessed the brewery proceeds and Brett's talents as a designer and builder to get started. I reached out for tenants, but when we lost our local restaurateur, we decided to operate the main attraction ourselves.

As usual, Mom and Pop dug into the books, including their favorite: *Starting and Running a Restaurant for Dummies.* I reached out to my contacts in Portland and managed to snag a chef from one of the city's most prestigious restaurants, who brought along a team of young professionals with him. We opened The Dundee Bistro in 1999. The concept was ambitious—to showcase local foods—a decade ahead of the "farm to fork" concept. We learned and lost a lot in the early years, but the center quickly became the hub for wine travelers and local vintners alike.

MAKING
MOVES

Despite Luisa taking the reins back in 1993, my father continued to be hailed as one of the nation's top winemakers. In 1996, the *Wine Spectator*'s twentieth-anniversary issue recognized him as the only Oregonian in an exclusive list of international producers who had "innovated, perfected, promoted, and led the way for higher-quality wines—shaping an era." In the January 1997 issue of Forbes's *American Heritage*, Pop was listed as producing one of America's most important wines. Even later still, he continued to receive the accolades. In 2003, he was hailed by Harvey Steinman of the *Wine Spectator* as "one of the few American winemakers who had mastered New World Pinot Noir."

Although thrilled for Pop, Luisa felt the challenge of following in the footsteps of a famed parent, and we often discussed this reality and our shared desire to make our own marks on the operation. We were aware that being young women in an otherwise male-dominated industry wouldn't be easy. Fortunately, we didn't get hung up on the issue and looked past the attention our male colleagues received as the bright new stars of wine. Several of them had worked under Luisa, and she had helped them to launch their careers. But the lack of recognition didn't stop us; instead, it encouraged us to push forward.

By the late 1990s, the economy was strong, and Americans were spending big dollars on high-quality wines. The market was primed for us to take some risks, and with the encouragement of Wilson Daniels, we created our first single-vineyard Pinot Noir.

We knew in Burgundy, it was traditional for Gran and Premier Cru vineyards to be labeled under those names. Although it had been practiced in the United States and by others in the Willamette Valley, we had never felt the wine would be great enough on its own from a single site. Besides, we thought, who would recognize our little vineyards? We also felt the high prices would make us appear pretentious.

But with the 1998 vintage, we knew we had a candidate for such a label. The vintage was exceptional, and the Abetina Vineyard was unique because we planted multiple clones back in the 1970s. For years, we followed this vineyard, and regardless of vintage, it was consistently beautiful. In this vintage, it was a showstopper.

Two years later, we released our first single-vineyard wine, the 1998 Abetina Pinot Noir, for seventy-five dollars. The high price felt a bit gauche. It was a far cry from the first Pinot Noir we released back in 1974 for less than ten dollars. But with only two barrels from our most prized vineyard, we felt the price was justified, and the release was a tremendous success.

The continued media coverage helped the brand to grow in influence and wine sales. This period was a high point for the winery. There were more drinkers of fine wine in America than ever before, and the strong economy allowed more expensive wines to be bought and enjoyed. We saw more Oregon wines in the market commanding high prices. Then September 11, 2001, happened, and everything changed. People were suddenly uninspired to eat out and spend money on high-end wines, especially in New York City, the city where most of our Reserve wines were sold.

We began to discuss the possibility of producing a lower-end Pinot Noir that could deliver great flavor from 100 percent Willamette Valley fruit. The 2001 vintage made the idea possible. It was a bountiful harvest that produced fair-quality fruit from some of our young sites. Mom and Pop were hesitant about introducing a value Pinot Noir to the market under the Ponzi name, feeling it might negatively impact our brand and the prestige we worked so hard to build. But Michel, Luisa, and I felt it was a perfect time to reenergize the family winery while offering the market something delicious that would overdeliver in value.

At the family table, where we still met for our most important meetings, we spent hours debating the potential project. Eventually, the family unanimously decided to designate the Pinot Noir as Tavola, "table" in Italian, as a way of expressing its intended use as a casual everyday drinking wine. We released the 2001 vintage in the fall of 2003 at fifteen dollars a bottle. The objective was to use it as a marketing tool to build exposure for the brand, a nod to our similar approach to Pinot Gris so many decades earlier.

It was marvelously successful. *Food and Wine* magazine listed the first release as a top ten selection for Thanksgiving. The following year, the 2002 Tavola was a top selection in the

Wine Spectator, with a score of 91 points. I got the news over the phone from Luisa while I was working in New Orleans. I had to sit down and shake my head. *Oh no!* I thought. *It's too good!*

THE SILVER SCREEN

The next time I had to sit down after receiving an alarming call from Luisa was during a South Florida market visit in 2004. I was sipping a glass of cheap Chianti at the end of my workweek when my cell rang, and she gave me the news about a new film that had released. It was all about Pinot Noir. *Sideways* had debuted with Hollywood's take on Pinot Noir—more specifically, Santa Barbara's version of it. I was utterly stunned that another wine region had stolen the story about *our* grape.

I felt weak as I watched the film at home. My spine tingled as the actors described the subtle nuances and elegant flavors of the delicate grape. I couldn't believe what I was hearing, yet there it was, and millions of people across the nation witnessed it. The words were the same ones we had used, over and over again, to describe our grape, *our* wine. My heart felt heavy. This was *our* story, but it was being delivered on the silver screen by someone else.

The movie's impact was nearly instant. Within days of its release, Pinot Noir seemed to flood the marketplace. It was coming from everywhere and at all prices. On a following market visit to Texas, I walked into a wineshop that had cases stacked the ceiling and blocking the aisles. As I looked closer, I noticed the prices ranging from $7.99 to $11.99. *For Pinot Noir?* Naïvely, I thought, *How was this possible?*

I later learned most of what was instantly available was not 100 percent Pinot Noir. Producers were blending Pinot Noir with other varieties like Syrah and Merlot, making them more accessible for the masses—both on the palate and in the pocketbook.

I was disgusted with the disrespect for our beloved varietal and dismayed at how producers were going after the dollar without any regard for the grape. I was also concerned that this might change people's understanding and appreciation for authentic Willamette Valley Pinot Noir. The one silver lining was Pinot Noir had become mainstream. People were talking about it. That nasty word I'd heard so often as a child was now a household term.

FAME

We got word Pop was up for a big award in Napa Valley in 2005. Robert and Margrit Mondavi of the famed Robert Mondavi Winery had established Copia in Napa four years earlier. This eighty-thousand-square-foot facility was a nonprofit museum and educational center celebrating food, wine, and American culture. It was a unique concept at the time. As part of its event program, each year the center hosted a lavish industry awards night.

This year, Pop was up for vintner of the year. The other two nominees were California's Tony Soter of Etude and Joel Peterson from Ravenswood. We were thrilled about the nomination and made plans to attend.

It was a brilliant September day as Mom, Pop, Brett, and I drove along Highway 29. We crammed ourselves into a Ford Focus from Avis since my frugal father didn't feel it was necessary to upgrade for the short drive from San Francisco. Along the famous tourist route where travelers have flocked for decades hoping to experience Napa Valley romance, I peered out the car windows and noticed the changes in the area. Instead of being head pruned, the vines were trellised like our northern vineyards, positioned to grow upright. And although the clusters seemed enormous in contrast to our tight, small ones, there seemed to be fewer per plant. The rows weren't nearly as tidy as in the past, a sign of sustainable farming.

What I viewed from the car were techniques we'd been using in the Willamette Valley for years. In fact, we'd heard how several Napa vintners were pulling out Chardonnay and Cabernet and replacing them with Pinot Noir. Could it be that our unassuming valley was having an effect on this famous region? *Was Napa Valley following our quiet lead?*

We reached the grand building and approached the cold limestone lobby feeling like outsiders. My father was ushered into another room for an interview while the rest of us distracted ourselves by touring through the various exhibits. Out of the corner of my eye, I saw Andrea Immer Robinson, the famous author of several wine books and a rock star in the culinary world. I wondered who else we would see.

We passed several display cases featuring historical artifacts and wandered through long halls with framed literature from famous authors, poets, celebrity chefs, and winemakers. Everything was tied to the virtues of food and wine and the rich culture it bred. We roamed the building for about an hour before we were asked to join the crowd that had gathered in front of a large auditorium.

People were milling around outside its large doors, talking and laughing with one another. The opulent room was filled with beautiful people, luminaries from California's wine scene. As I gazed into the audience, I identified several wine celebrities, including Michael Mondavi, Garen and Shari Staglin, and Jess Jackson. I was immediately intimidated. *How do we size up?* Back in Oregon, a similar crowd would be wearing fleece vests and boots. This room was filled with leather, suede, and silk. I was distinctly aware that we were just simple folks

among some of the country's most famous names in wine. Pop
finally joined us, and we found our seats.

Andrea Immer Robinson opened the event, and the tributes
began. The accomplishments of the candidates were impressive
and extensive. One guy had planted hundreds of thousands of
certified organic acres, another had donated hundreds of thousands of dollars to a local children's organization, another had
built his career around helping Hispanic workers, and on it
went. I glanced at Pop, who remained calm and relaxed as we
listened to each introduction. In contrast, I was intimidated by
the inspiring stories and lofty crowd.

As the next round of clapping subsided, Robinson began to
talk about the makings of a "great winemaker." She explained
it's someone who has established himself as a leader in the
field, an innovator, someone who has taken great steps forward
and made significant changes. She told us Robert Parker dec-
orated him as "one of the best winemakers in the world" and
the *Wine Spectator* claimed he was the "founder of New World
Pinot Noir." And then, like a dream, familiar images began
to flash onto the enormous screen in front of us. It was Pop
planting our first vineyard, his hands in the dirt, his ambitious
eyes bright and clear. You could almost feel his energy pulsing
through the room.

That image was followed by both Mom and Pop working
next to the beat-up old tractor staking the vineyard and then
a shot of Michel, Luisa, me, and Bristol. Our family's past
was revealed in front of Napa Valley's luminaries. They were
listening to our story. They were learning about our lives up
in Oregon. In this room, packed with wine celebrities and
wealth, it sounded especially authentic and humble. My eyes
welled up, and my heart strained as Robinson opened the
envelope and announced my father was vintner of the year.
She called him the father of American Pinot Noir. I lost it.

Mom and I wiped tears from our faces as we laughed and hugged each other. Our honest reaction may have appeared a bit juvenile, but we couldn't contain ourselves.

Pop approached the stage, then turned to face the crowd with his warm smile and sparkling eyes. I expected him to recognize our family and the work we had accomplished in the Willamette Valley, but instead he did something so gracious, so unanticipated. He accepted the award on behalf of all the Oregon wine pioneers who shared the same dream and worked together to make their vision a successful reality. He said he would be taking the award back to Oregon to share with his colleagues and thanked them for the honor.

My father and the family's efforts had been recognized and accepted by a community considered to be the center of American wine. It was a pinnacle day for my parents, our family, and the winery, but also for Oregon's wine industry. We proudly returned to our quiet valley with renewed energy.

COLLINA DEL SOGNO

The winery was growing, which meant hiring more support. The tight attic could no longer house all of us, and the family home was no longer needed as a daycare, since all the kids now attended a Portland Montessori school. The vacant home became the obvious place to expand, so one day I took all my things up the stairs into the old TV room and created a private office for myself. We took down the wall that separated my original bedroom from Luisa's and created one large room.

I hired a marketing assistant to help with the promotional efforts, which included demands from the Dundee center. As usual, we were hustling. We had developed a wine club and used the empty space below my office, our original dining room, to host winery events. I felt we had to have all burners on, all the time. I was concerned if we slowed down, we might lose the momentum, and everything might tumble. I was committed to moving forward.

Luisa wanted the same, yet for each vintage, she struggled to work within the confines of the winery's limited space. She constantly complained about the lack of room and her need to focus on quality instead of logistics. There was no place for additional fermenters, and operating pallet jacks and forklifts within the space was nearly impossible. At harvest time, the roughly two thousand square feet was jam-packed with fermenters, tanks, barrels, and equipment. We were producing nearly twenty thousand cases. It was obvious to all of us if we didn't make a move soon that wine quality would suffer, not to mention our overall exhaustion from the unnecessary physical labor.

One afternoon, I got a knock on my office door. Michel walked in, and we had a critical conversation about growth. He expressed the need to take the winery to the next level, and although I was struggling to keep up with the daily demands, I knew he was right. All three of us now had children and mounting bills. Our situation was unsustainable. The only way for all of us to work at the winery would be to grow production.

It all made a lot of sense, but the idea scared me. This meant borrowing money and incurring debt. It was something we had never done, but I knew he was right. It was our responsibility. I felt it wasn't just what we needed to do for Ponzi, but that we also had an obligation to Oregon, to the wine pioneers. Luisa agreed.

Michel went to work, scouring the valley for an ideal site to build a gravity flow facility. His initial days were spent in Yamhill County, researching the Dundee Hills and Carlton. These areas had become recognized as home to some of the most notable wine producers in the valley. Because of this, it seemed like a logical place to relocate, assuming we wanted to remain in the spotlight. However, as Michel quickly learned, because the land there was marketed as "wine country," it was twice the cost as elsewhere. After further consideration, we realized establishing our winery there would require transporting grapes thirty minutes over the hill from our Washington County vineyards. My astute brother turned his search to our backyard, to the rolling hills of the Chehalem Mountains.

For generations, the Loughridges, a local nut-farming family, had owned several acres of hazelnuts and walnuts on Mountain Home Road just off Highway 219. Their trees were nearly a hundred years old, and the family was ready to sell some property. Michel realized the potential the sloping site had for building a multilevel winery. Further investigation revealed it was one of several forty-acre parcels along this stretch of road, just above the community of Scholls with a stunning view back to the valley. My brother reached out to the owner with an offer, and it was accepted. We agreed the most suitable name for the property would be Collina del Sogno, an Italian translation of "Hillside of Dreams."

This extraordinary site staged our future. We began clearing the land in the fall of 2005, and we planted twenty acres of vineyard in the spring of 2006. We named the vineyard Avellana, meaning "hazelnut" in Italian, in recognition of the original century-old orchard. We planted Dijon-cloned Chardonnay and Pinot Noir on the northwest-facing site. Luisa selected more than twenty different Pinot Noir clones, and our vineyard manager, Miguel Ortiz, planted them in a wildflower fashion along the rows. This was a relaunch of the innovative planting technique of the Abetina Vineyard.

With the planting underway, Pop resumed his role of architect and builder. He sat alone atop his home at Aurora in the large office surrounded by picture windows with views to the valley's crops below. It had been nearly forty years since he designed our family home while sitting at the small table in our shack at the end of Vandermost Road. Now, he sketched his dream winery. After decades of manipulating gravity, working without pumps, bucketing from fermenters to the press, and moving juice and finished wine using small vessels to eventually working with forklifts to ensure slow movement, he was at last able to create his ideal facility.

The winemaking would be processed using four separate levels, with gravity as the source. The plan would enable us to move grapes, juice, and wine gently down the hillside with efficiency and care, while allowing us to increase our volume. For the following two years, Pop's enthusiasm grew as he created the structure. He and Luisa spent hours discussing every detail of the facility. Made almost entirely from concrete and steel, the thirty-thousand-square-foot facility was built to last, with the ability for future growth. No longer would we concern ourselves with pouring additional slabs of concrete or welding another catwalk. By 2008, the building was ready for harvest.

FINAL MOVE

That summer was spent moving tanks, barrels, fermenters, hoses, forklifts, pallet jacks, the bottling line, and hundreds of other pieces of equipment from our garage winery to Collina del Sogno. Next door, from the original family home's lookout window, I watched the activity. Nearly forty years ago, I stood in the same place, panicking as I watched those first cars head down the road to our makeshift tasting room. Today, the perch allowed me a front-row seat to the bustling activity in front of the property.

There was tremendous excitement this day. The winery was busy, but upstairs in the home, it was quiet. As I peered over the grounds, I took a moment to reflect on everything that had happened over the past forty years. I thought back to the carefree days of running up and down to the woods and creek to pruning the vines with Mom and bottling with Pop. I thought back to hosting our first guests in our simple garage tasting room and our eager attempts to sell wine there. We learned so much here. Our adventure forced us to work hard, be persistent, be resourceful, think boldly, and remain curious. It taught us the importance and joy of collaboration, of respecting the land, and of creating new products for people to experience.

As the last load was strapped down and the flatbread truck pulled out of the driveway, my view shifted to our little vineyard. Its deep roots, now several feet below the earth, and its hearty old trunks, now covered with thick dark-green moss, confirmed decades of growth. It symbolized our family's strength and endurance. We had grown up together.

I acknowledged the stillness, but also the exciting anticipation of what was ahead. Through the spirit of adventure and working together we did it. That once-scrappy piece of land had taken us to where we stood today. I took in a deep breath and smiled, thoroughly grateful to have been a part of the adventure.

EPILOGUE

My parents passed full winery ownership to Luisa and me in January of 2018. We had been partial owners and sole operators since 2012, when the second phase of Collina del Sogno was completed. It was the same year Michel left the company to explore other business ventures in Italy. He assumed ownership of the Dundee complex in 2018. Currently, Luisa and I have successfully grown the operation to an annual production of nearly fifty thousand cases and sustainably farm more than 140 acres in the Chehalem Mountains. We have applied for a new AVA (American Viticultural Area) called the Laurelwood District in recognition of the pristine and rare soil from which we have made a life.

Luisa maintains the role of winemaker, and I serve as president, continuing to oversee marketing, sales, and hospitality. Our visionary parents, Dick and Nancy, reside at Aurora Vineyard, with views back to Collina del Sogno and Avellana Vineyard. They maintain their generous and active lifestyle of helping others, traveling internationally to the world's finest winegrowing regions, throwing gracious parties, staying involved with their community, and adventuring with their eight grandchildren while they continue to consider what's next.

At the time of writing, the Oregon wine industry is home to more than seven hundred wineries and contributes more than $5.6 billion to the state's economy. The industry's success continues to grow with the rapid development of many new vineyards and wineries being established in the region, with many investors coming from Burgundy, France. Each year, large wine companies from around the country and the world come to stake their claims in the Willamette Valley. I view this period with a mix of angst and pride, as I hope the wine community continues to uphold the authenticity and integrity the wine founders created. As I continue to travel the globe promoting our industry and wines, I have had the fantastic advantage and joy of witnessing the adoration and respect others have for our rare history.

FAMILY PHOTOS

*Stomping grapes with Michel and
Luisa in California in 1968.*

Our family arrival to the Willamette Valley in 1968.

The original garage became our winery for forty years.

All our new friends came out to plant the nursery row in 1969.

*My Italian Nonna expressed her love unconventionally,
holding my wrist instead of my hand. My grandparents
were strong supporters of the growing operation.*

Our family dog Bristol was always part of the working crew.

*We lived off our little farm for years while
growing the winery business.*

Summers meant wearing as little as possible.

*Learning to drive the tractor at age five
was an enormous achievement.*

*My mother tended our young vineyard while we
attended school and Pop taught classes.*

We proudly displayed recent awards in our original tasting room.

*Establishing the exterior winery wall meant
hosting another summer work party.*

Our family friends were instrumental in establishing the winery.

*My father was always taking risks, including
setting the beams for the winery extension.*

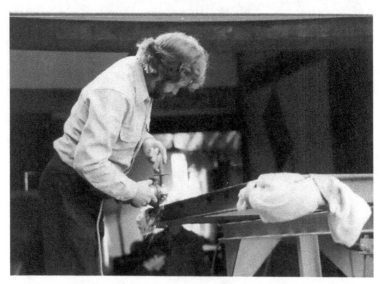

*Preparing for harvest meant finding Pop working
on perfecting some piece of equipment.*

Nothing made Pop happier than working through the process.

Gentle handling of the wine was critical to my
father. He treated it as if it was liquid gold.

*My mother has been my mentor—inspiring me with
her poise, wisdom, and determination.*

By 1993, all three of us had returned to work at the family winery.

As the Oregon Chapter President of Women for WineSense,
I adored working with other brilliant women in wine.

Punching down Pinot Noir. Despite our positions, it was a family value that we all helped with each harvest (2000).

Visiting The White House cellar was one of
my proudest moments (2007).

As passionate business partners, Luisa and I have been committed to growing the family operation (2019).

ACKNOWLEDGMENTS

A heartfelt thank-you to Larry Colton
and Tatiana de Figueiredo for their initial
encouragement, coaching and support.

Thank you to Rich Schmidt and the spectacular
Linfield Archives for preserving our wine
region's humble yet rich history.

Thank you to the early pioneers who shared their
personal stories and precious time with me.

Thank you to Luisa and Michel, my supportive
siblings and courageous business partners. I'm
so grateful we had this journey together and
am so proud of what we accomplished.

Thank you to my son, Max, for his careful
eye, intimidating vocabulary, constant
encouragement, and creative inspiration.

Thank you to my daughter, Lauren, my
toughest and best editor, who shared pragmatic
advice with plenty of much needed emotional
support and humor. You are my rock.

And of course, to Brett, my husband and
partner in life. Thank you for your devotion,
brutal honesty and tremendous inspiration.

ABOUT THE AUTHOR

 Anna Maria Ponzi is a second-generation vintner, co-owner, president, and director of sales and marketing for Ponzi Vineyards in Oregon's Willamette Valley. She has worked every aspect of the winery, from planting its original vines, to working on the bottling line, to making national and international sales calls. She has served the state's wine industry in myriad ways, including acting as an ambassador for Oregon wine growers internationally and building Oregon wine country into a travel destination.

Anna Maria earned her degree in journalism from the University of Oregon in 1987 and worked in Boston's publishing industry until returning to the rural family business in 1991. By the mid-90s, she was joined by her winemaking sister, and the two young women have trailblazed the growing tide of female vintners, formally taking over the family business in 2012. This ownership has distinguished Ponzi Vineyards as the nation's only winery solely owned and operated by second-generation sisters.

Ponzi Vineyards, celebrating its fiftieth anniversary in 2020, has experienced continued growth and success as producers of award-winning Oregon wine.

CPSIA information can be obtained
at www.ICGtesting.com
Printed in the USA
FSHW021556050620